AI – AUGMENTED INTELLIGENCE

Anthony van den Hondel

KDP

ISBN-13: 9789083512211

Cover design by: Dall-E 3

Printed in the United States of America

COVER

As to be expected, the cover-art was generated using AI. Here is the prompt used in Dall-E 3.

Generate a book cover in high resolution: "A futuristic and symbolic representation of augmented intelligence. Two human-like male figures stand facing each other like in a mirror, focusing on their heads and just and only their index fingers touching. The figure on the left, glowing and digital, is composed of intricate metallic and glass-like structures with subtle blue neon lighting, symbolizing AI. Its organic neural structure inside the head represents the infusion of human traits like emotions and ethics. The figure on the right, organic and human with lifelike skin textures and a red tones of color, features visible musculature and anatomical details. Subtle holographic data streams enter its head, where a glowing, lifelike human brain is visible, symbolizing the integration of digital intelligence and collaboration. Both figures are of equal size, with consistent anatomical proportions. Their hands are depicted with exceptional anatomical accuracy, matching the texture and tone of their torsos. The figures' index fingers touch gently in the center, creating a glowing spark of connection that symbolizes the harmonious exchange of capabilities. The lighting is soft yet dynamic, emphasizing the contrast between the metallic cool tones of the AI figure and the warm, natural tones of the human figure. The background is minimalistic, with soft gradients of blue and silver, evoking a futuristic, clean, and modern aesthetic."

"Some people call this artificial intelligence, but the reality is this technology will enhance us. So instead of artificial intelligence, I think we'll augment our intelligence."

GINNI ROMETTY

CONTENTS

PREFACE

Why Write Yet Another Book On AI?

As an engineer and entrepreneur with over 20 years of experience in expert systems and rule engines, I've witnessed firsthand how AI, particularly with the advent of large language models (LLMs), has become a daily fixture in business operations. This rapid evolution inspired me to contribute to the conversation with a fresh perspective.

I'm also an avid reader, tackling around 200 books a year, mostly in computer science, psychology, and productivity. Through a "second brain" system inspired by Tiago Forte's CODE methodology—Capture, Organize, Distill, and Express—I process what I learn and aim to share insights effectively. Writing a book is one of the best ways to accomplish that.

A quick Amazon search reveals over 60,000 books on AI. Yet, due to the field's rapid progress, most are outdated within a year. By 2025, it was time for another update—this time aimed at non-technical but curious readers.

Despite the daunting reality that the average book sells fewer than 300 print copies in its lifetime, I believe this book is worth your time. It's designed to provide an up-to-date, socially aware overview of AI, equipping readers to navigate one of the most transformative technologies of our time.

How Did This Book Come To Be?

In the evolving era of generative AI, Amazon has introduced a new AI policy for authors. This policy doesn't ban the use of AI but requires authors to disclose when AI is used to generate content. It distinguishes between AI-generated and AI-assisted content. Where 'AI-generated' refers to text created directly by an AI tool, even if heavily edited later, the AI-assisted content refers to content created by the author but enhanced using AI. This enhancement is done in tasks like editing, refining, error-checking, or idea generation.

To clarify, this book is **AI-assisted**, not AI-generated. It would feel strange to write a book about AI without involving AI in the creation process. Additionally, as a non-native English speaker, I rely on AI tools to check grammar, spelling, and word usage to ensure clarity and accuracy.

However, it's important to note that while large language models have advanced significantly, they are not yet capable of generating a complete, high-content book. Creating meaningful books still requires human insight, creativity, and expertise.

What Is The Structure Of This Book?

This book explores various aspects of living in a world and society shaped by AI, addressing both current influences and future possibilities. Each chapter is written to stand alone, allowing readers to engage with any section independently.

Nonfiction books are rarely read cover to cover, and I've structured this book with that in mind. You don't need to follow a specific order—feel free to pick and choose the chapters that interest you most and read them in any sequence you prefer. This flexible approach ensures you can dive into the topics that resonate with you without committing to the entire book at once.

A BRIEF HISTORY OF ARTIFICIAL INTELLIGENCE

What Is AI And Why Should You Care?

Artificial Intelligence (AI) is transforming the world in ways that previous generations, even those with the boldest imaginations, could scarcely have anticipated. What once seemed like science fiction—such as autonomous, driverless cars—has become a reality. The rapid pace of these advancements is astonishing and is made possible by the power of AI. But what exactly is AI? And why is it important for you to understand it?

Put simply, AI is a branch of computer science dedicated to creating machines that can mimic certain aspects of human intelligence. These machines can learn from experience, recognize patterns, make decisions, and even perform complex tasks. Today, we are surrounded by AI applications—from personal assistants like Siri and Alexa, to advanced algorithms helping doctors diagnose diseases, to AI artists capable of generating stunning pieces of art. The impact of AI is far-reaching, and understanding it is not only fascinating but also increasingly essential in a world where these technologies touch almost every aspect of our lives.

"Artificial intelligence is the science of making machines do things that would require intelligence if done by humans." —John McCarthy.

So, why should you learn about AI? For one, AI is not just a passing technological fad; it is here to stay, and its influence is only growing. To be an informed citizen, a skilled professional, or even a curious observer in today's society, a basic understanding of AI is invaluable. The decisions made today regarding the development and implementation of AI will have profound effects on our economy, our culture, and our very sense of what it means to be human. Learning about AI helps us understand its capabilities and limitations, so we can harness its power responsibly, ensuring that it serves us well without overstepping its bounds.

"Artificial intelligence, deep learning, machine learning — whatever you're doing if you don't understand it — learn it. Because otherwise, you're going to be a dinosaur within three years." – Mark Cuban

---

One of the biggest breakthroughs in AI came not when computers tried to think like humans, but when they stopped trying to. Early AI researchers believed that to create a truly intelligent machine, they needed to replicate human thought processes. They studied grandmasters to develop chess programs and built early expert systems in an attempt to copy human reasoning. But it became evident by the late 1980s that this approach was limiting. It was difficult for machines to mimic the complexity, intuition, and nuance of human thought, and AI progress had largely stalled.

The breakthrough in AI research came when engineers stopped trying to make computers think like humans.

The solution? Instead of trying to imitate the human brain, scientists began leveraging the sheer power of computation. Machines were tasked with solving problems in whatever way worked, regardless of whether that process mirrored human cognition. This shift towards pragmatism revolutionized AI research. Instead of painstakingly teaching a computer every rule and every possible scenario, scientists gave machines data —millions upon millions of data points—and let them figure it out. The result was the beginning of machine learning, and later, deep learning, where computers use large datasets to identify patterns and develop capabilities on their own.

Donald Michie was one of the first to pair computers with large sets of raw data, testing the concept in 1960 using the game of tic-tac-toe. Instead of programming a series of rules for the computer to follow, Michie provided it with numerous examples of game moves, allowing it to deduce basic principles on its own.

This pragmatic approach led to significant milestones. In 1997, IBM's Deep Blue defeated world chess champion Garry Kasparov, not by mimicking his thought processes, but by analysing millions of possible moves and choosing the best one. Later breakthroughs, such as Google's AlphaGo in 2015, used similar approaches to tackle even more complex games like Go—a game with far more possible moves than chess. These advances demonstrated the immense power of data-driven AI, moving the field beyond imitating human thought into realms of problem-solving that even humans could not comprehend in traditional ways.

Chess and Go are ultimately psychological games,
but for computers it's purely strategic.

As AI progresses, we must also consider the broader implications of its development. AI's potential to transform industries is both exciting and daunting. The promise of an AI-driven economy brings both opportunities and challenges. For instance, AI is already outperforming humans in certain domains like image recognition and complex decision-making, suggesting that it may replace or redefine many jobs that today require human skills. It is easy to think of AI as a futuristic novelty, but its applications have very real consequences for employment, privacy, and even how we view creativity and intelligence.

It is essential to recognize that the journey towards artificial intelligence has been punctuated by setbacks, triumphs, and paradigm shifts—and the future of AI is just as uncertain as it is promising. Today's AI systems, which can write essays, compose music, and diagnose diseases, are the result of decades of tireless research, fuelled by breakthroughs in computing power and data availability. However, these systems are still fundamentally different from human intelligence; they are brilliant pattern-recognition machines, but they lack common sense, intuition, and emotional understanding. As you learn more about AI, you will begin to appreciate not only what it can do but also the inherent limitations that come with it.

Learning about AI will also empower you to discern between myth and reality. AI has captured the public imagination for decades, often portrayed in movies and media as either an apocalyptic threat or a miracle cure for all of society's problems. The truth, as always, lies somewhere in between. AI has the potential to benefit humanity immensely—if we understand its capabilities, mitigate its risks, and use it ethically. Whether you are interested in its practical applications, its philosophical implications, or its impact on society, learning about AI offers you a front-row seat to one of the most exciting scientific advancements of our time.

"AI is going to change the world more than anything in the history of humanity. More than electricity." — Kai-Fu Lee.

To truly benefit from AI, society must navigate its challenges thoughtfully. Issues like privacy, bias, ethics, and accountability cannot be overlooked. Machines may now be able to learn non-routine skills, a feat once thought impossible, but it is still up to humans to ensure that these capabilities are wielded in ways that promote fairness and equality, rather than perpetuating or amplifying biases and inequalities. Understanding AI equips you to be part of these critical conversations and perhaps even help shape the rules and policies that govern its use.

So, understanding AI—what it is, where it came from, and why it matters—will make us better equipped to grasp its role in the world today, as well as its potential impact on our shared future. Whether you are a sceptic, a tech enthusiast, or simply someone curious about the world around you, there's value in learning about artificial intelligence. Because as AI continues to grow in capability and influence, understanding it may be the key to understanding the future itself.

How AI Is Already Part Of Your Daily Life

Artificial Intelligence has seamlessly woven itself into the fabric of our daily lives, often without us even realizing it. From the moment you wake up and check your phone to the time you fall asleep, AI is present in countless forms, making your routines more efficient, personalized, and convenient. While AI may seem like an abstract or futuristic concept, the truth is that many of us interact with AI-powered systems every day, sometimes without even knowing it. These interactions make mundane tasks easier, provide personalized recommendations, and even help keep us safe.

Ever wondered why certain websites top Google search results? Google's algorithm ranks a site based on how many other websites link to it and evaluates the value of those linking websites. For example, if your site is linked on high-value sites like CNN, it will rank higher. This intricate system of cross-evaluation involves analysing vast amounts of data.

Think about your morning routine. As soon as you reach for your smartphone, you are already engaging with AI. The facial recognition that unlocks your phone is powered by machine learning algorithms that have been trained to recognize the unique features of your face. When you open your email, spam filters powered by AI have already sifted through your inbox, sorting out potentially malicious messages and ensuring that you only see what matters most to you. These AI-powered tools work behind the scenes to make your digital interactions faster and safer.

If you ask a virtual assistant like Siri, Alexa, or Google Assistant for the weather forecast, traffic conditions, or a reminder to pick up groceries, you are using AI. These virtual assistants rely on natural language processing (NLP), a branch of AI that helps machines understand and respond to human language. NLP allows these assistants to interpret your spoken words, determine the intent behind your request, and provide a relevant response. It may seem simple, but this process involves complex algorithms that have been trained on vast amounts of data to accurately recognize speech and generate meaningful replies.

AI also plays a key role in how we consume information and entertainment. Streaming services like Netflix, Spotify, and YouTube use AI to analyse your viewing or listening habits and recommend content that you are likely to enjoy. These recommendations are generated by machine learning algorithms that track your preferences, compare them to those of millions of other users, and identify patterns to predict what you might like next. The same kind of personalization happens when you scroll through social media platforms like Facebook, Instagram, or TikTok. AI algorithms decide which posts, ads, and videos appear on your feed, based on your past interactions and interests, ensuring that the content you see is tailored to your preferences.

Even your daily commute is often influenced by AI. If you use navigation apps like Waze or Google Maps, you benefit from AI algorithms that analyse real-time traffic data to determine the fastest route to your destination. These algorithms take into account factors like traffic congestion, accidents, and road closures, providing you with up-to-date information to save you time and reduce frustration. Ride-sharing services like Uber and Lyft also rely on AI to match drivers with passengers, determine optimal pick-up and drop-off locations, and calculate fares. Without AI, the convenience and efficiency of these services would not be possible.

At the core of Uber's operations is the same "system of intelligence" technology that powers platforms like Facebook and Google. This advanced software identifies patterns and improves over time. Uber's system processes vast amounts of data generated during its rides to optimize services. In the pre-Uber taxi era, a ride generated only a few data points: the dispatcher's log, pickup and drop-off locations, and the fare. In contrast, Uber captures a wealth of information, including the request details, device used, GPS route, trip duration, fare breakdown, tipping habits, and driver ratings. With over ten billion trips completed per year, Uber leverages this data to uncover patterns, anticipate customer needs, and refine its offerings to deliver a more personalized and efficient service.

AI is also transforming the way we shop. E-commerce platforms like Amazon use AI to recommend products based on your browsing history, past purchases, and items that are trending among other customers. These personalized recommendations not only make it easier for you to find what you need but also introduce you to products you might not have considered otherwise. Additionally, AI-powered chatbots are becoming increasingly common in online shopping, providing instant customer service, answering questions, and even helping you complete a purchase—all without the need for human intervention.

Financial services are another area where AI is making a significant impact. If you use mobile banking apps, AI is likely helping to detect unusual activity on your account and protect you from fraud. Machine learning algorithms analyse your spending patterns and flag any transactions that deviate from your usual behaviour, alerting you to potential security threats. AI is also behind the personalized financial advice offered by some banking apps, which analyse your income, expenses, and savings goals to provide insights and recommendations for better managing your finances.

Healthcare is yet another domain where AI is becoming increasingly integrated into our lives. Wearable devices like smartwatches use AI to monitor your physical activity, heart rate, and sleep patterns, providing insights into your overall health and well-being. Some wearables can even detect irregular heart rhythms and alert you to seek medical attention if needed.

AI is also used in telemedicine apps that allow you to consult with healthcare professionals remotely, making medical advice more accessible and convenient.

Even something as simple as taking a photo on your smartphone involves AI. Modern smartphone cameras use AI to enhance image quality, adjust lighting, and even recognize scenes to optimize settings automatically. Features like portrait mode, which blurs the background to create a professional-looking photo, are made possible by AI algorithms that can identify and isolate the subject of the image. These advancements make it easier for anyone to take high-quality photos, regardless of their photography skills.

AI is also making strides in home automation. Smart home devices like thermostats, lights, and security cameras use AI to learn your preferences and adapt accordingly. For example, a smart thermostat can learn your schedule and adjust the temperature to suit your comfort while optimizing energy usage. Smart security cameras can distinguish between familiar faces and strangers, alerting you only when something unusual is detected. These AI-powered devices not only add convenience but also enhance the safety and efficiency of your home.

One of the most profound yet often unnoticed ways AI impacts our daily lives is through the infrastructure that powers our cities and communities. AI is used to manage power grids, optimize energy consumption, and even predict equipment failures before they happen, ensuring that essential services run smoothly. AI-driven systems help cities monitor air quality, manage waste collection, and control traffic lights to reduce congestion. These applications may not be as visible as a virtual assistant or a recommendation engine, but they play a crucial role in improving our quality of life.

As you can see, AI is already deeply embedded in our daily routines, often working quietly in the background to make our lives more convenient, efficient, and enjoyable. Understanding how AI is integrated into these everyday activities helps demystify the technology and reveals its practical value. It also highlights why it is so important to be informed about AI—its presence in our lives is only set to grow, and being aware of how it works empowers us to make better decisions about how we use it and how we shape its future development.

From Turing To Expert Systems

The story of AI begins long before computers became a common household item. It is a story shaped by visionary scientists, groundbreaking experiments, and an enduring dream of creating machines that could think. The early days of AI, starting from the mid-20th century, were characterized by bold ideas and significant challenges. It was a period when the foundations of AI were laid, fuelled by a combination of curiosity, optimism, and technological innovation.

The journey begins with the pioneering work of Alan Turing, often considered the father of modern computer science and artificial intelligence. In 1950, Turing introduced a provocative question: "Can machines think?" His paper, "Computing Machinery and Intelligence," proposed the famous Turing Test, a benchmark for determining whether a machine could exhibit human-like intelligence. The test involved a human evaluator engaging in a conversation with both a machine and another human. If the evaluator could not distinguish between the responses of the human and the machine, the machine could be considered intelligent. Turing's work laid the philosophical foundation for AI, challenging researchers to think deeply about the nature of intelligence and the potential for machines to replicate it.

In the 1950s, a group of researchers at Dartmouth College in New Hampshire organized a summer workshop that is often credited as the birth of AI as a formal field of study. Led by John McCarthy, Marvin Minsky, Nathaniel Rochester, and Claude

Shannon, the 1956 Dartmouth Conference brought together some of the brightest minds in computer science to explore the possibilities of creating "machines that can think." The term "artificial intelligence" was coined in preparation of this conference, marking the beginning of a new era in computing. The optimism was palpable, as participants believed that a breakthrough in machine intelligence was just around the corner. But unmet expectations lead to a downfall in interest, introducing winter like periods in AI development, more than once.

In 1956 researchers in Los Alamos created the first chess-playing computer, named MANIAC 1, weighing approximately 1,000 pounds. The scientist had to reduce the board to 36 squares, removed the bishops and still the program could not win from a human player.

During the 1960s, AI research gained momentum, and the focus was primarily on symbolic AI, also known as "good old-fashioned AI" (GOFAI). Researchers like McCarthy and Minsky worked on creating programs that could manipulate symbols and solve problems using a set of predefined rules. Early AI systems, such as the Logic Theorist developed by Allen Newell and Nobel Prize winning economist Herbert Simon, were designed to mimic human problem-solving processes. The Logic Theorist was capable of proving mathematical theorems, and it was hailed as one of the first successful AI programs. It demonstrated that machines could perform tasks that required logical (symbolic) reasoning, a key aspect of human intelligence.

Another notable development during this period was the creation of ELIZA, an early natural language processing program developed by Joseph Weizenbaum in 1966. ELIZA simulated a conversation between a user and a psychotherapist by using simple pattern-matching techniques. While ELIZA's responses were far from sophisticated, the program created an illusion of understanding, and many users were captivated by its ability to engage in seemingly meaningful conversations. ELIZA's success highlighted both the potential and limitations of early AI—it showed that machines could convincingly simulate human interaction, but it also underscored the fact that true understanding was still a distant goal. Furthermore, ELIZA shows us that there is a human tendency to anthropomorphize machines. We want it to be true, and therefore our wishful thinking takes over sometimes.

The horse Clever Hans from the late 19th century, amazed audiences across Europe with his supposed intelligence. He appeared to solve math problems, tell time, and recognize dates, tapping out answers with his hoof. However, psychologist Oskar Pfungst uncovered the truth: Hans was not reasoning but responding to subtle, unconscious cues from his questioners, like shifts in posture or facial expressions. This highlights how observer biases can skew results and contains a valuable lesson about the risks of attributing human-like abilities to animals or AI for that matter.

The 1970s and 1980s saw the rise of expert systems, a new approach to AI that aimed to capture human expertise in specific domains. Unlike earlier attempts to create general-purpose intelligence, expert systems were designed to solve specific problems by emulating the decision-making abilities of human experts. One of the first successful expert systems was DENDRAL, developed in the late 1960s by Edward Feigenbaum, Bruce Buchanan, and Joshua Lederberg. DENDRAL was used to analyse chemical compounds, and it proved that AI could be used to assist scientists in complex problem-solving tasks. The success of DENDRAL inspired the development of other expert systems, such as MYCIN, which was designed to assist doctors in diagnosing bacterial infections and recommending treatments.

Expert systems represented a significant shift in AI research, as they demonstrated practical applications for AI in real-world scenarios. These systems relied on knowledge bases—collections of facts and rules provided by human experts—and inference engines that used this knowledge to make decisions. By capturing the expertise of specialists in areas like medicine, engineering, and finance, expert systems showed that AI could augment human capabilities and provide valuable insights in specialized fields. This marked a departure from the earlier focus on replicating human thought processes and emphasized the importance of practical utility.

However, the early days of AI were not without setbacks. Despite the initial enthusiasm and significant progress, researchers soon encountered the limitations of the technology. Symbolic AI struggled to handle the complexities of the real world, as the predefined rules and logical structures could not easily accommodate ambiguity, uncertainty, or the vast amount of information needed to solve more sophisticated problems. As a result, funding for AI research began to dwindle, leading to a period known as the "AI winter." During this time, many projects were abandoned, and interest in AI waned as the challenges of achieving true machine intelligence became apparent.

Nonetheless, the groundwork laid during these early years was crucial for the future development of AI. The concepts introduced by pioneers like Turing, McCarthy, Minsky, and others provided the foundation upon which later advancements would be built. The limitations of symbolic AI and expert systems highlighted the need for new approaches, ultimately paving the way for the emergence of machine learning and neural networks in the decades that followed.

The early days of AI were marked by both optimism and disillusionment, by breakthroughs and setbacks. They were a testament to the enduring human desire to create intelligent machines and the challenges inherent in that pursuit. The lessons learned from these formative years continue to shape the field of AI today, reminding us that progress often requires not only vision and innovation but also the willingness to confront and overcome obstacles. As we move forward, it is important to remember the contributions of those who laid the foundation for AI, as their work continues to inspire new generations of researchers and innovators.

Milestones In AI Development

The development of AI has been marked by numerous major milestones, each representing a leap forward in the capabilities and understanding of intelligent machines. These milestones have not only shaped the field of AI but have also influenced our broader understanding of technology and its role in society. From early breakthroughs in computing to modern advances in machine learning, these key moments have paved the way for the AI-driven world we live in today.

One of the first major milestones in AI was the creation of the Perceptron in 1957 by Frank Rosenblatt, a psychologist at Cornell University. The Perceptron was an early attempt to simulate the way neurons work in the human brain, and it was one of the first artificial neural networks. The concept of a neural network—a system of interconnected nodes that could learn from data—was groundbreaking at the time and laid the foundation for later developments in machine learning and deep learning. Despite its limitations, the Perceptron demonstrated that machines could learn from experience, an idea that remains at the core of AI research.

Another significant milestone came in 1966 with the creation of ELIZA, an early natural language processing (NLP) program developed by Joseph Weizenbaum at MIT. ELIZA could simulate conversation by matching user inputs to pre-programmed responses, and it provided an early glimpse into the potential for human-computer interaction. While ELIZA's abilities were limited, it was one of the first programs to demonstrate that computers could engage in a form of dialogue with humans, sparking interest in the possibilities of conversational AI.

The 1970s saw the emergence of expert systems, which represented a shift in AI research towards practical applications. One of the most well-known expert systems was MYCIN, developed at Stanford University in the early 1970s. MYCIN was designed to help doctors diagnose bacterial infections and recommend treatments. Unlike earlier attempts to create general-purpose AI, expert systems focused on capturing the specialized knowledge of human experts in specific domains. The success of expert systems like MYCIN and DENDRAL demonstrated that AI could be used to solve real-world problems, and they found applications in fields such as medicine, finance, and engineering.

In the 1980s, AI research experienced a resurgence with the advent of machine learning techniques that allowed computers to learn from data rather than relying on explicitly programmed rules. This was the era when backpropagation, a key algorithm for training neural networks, was rediscovered and popularized by researchers like Geoffrey Hinton, David Rumelhart, and Ronald Williams. Backpropagation enabled neural networks to learn from their errors and adjust their internal weights to improve performance. This advancement marked a turning point in AI research, as it allowed for the development of more sophisticated and capable neural networks.

The next major milestone in AI development came in 1997, when IBM's Deep Blue defeated Garry Kasparov, the reigning world chess champion. Deep Blue was the first computer to defeat a world champion in a match under standard chess tournament time controls, and it represented a significant achievement in the field of AI. Deep Blue's victory was made possible by its ability to evaluate millions of chess positions per second and use advanced algorithms to determine the best moves. This event captured the world's attention and highlighted the potential for AI to outperform humans in specific tasks that required strategic thinking. But at the same time, it was the collaborative effort by IBM engineers to fine-tune Deep Blue's programming for Kasparov's style. This human involvement in designing Deep Blue's strategy should be acknowledged as Deep Blue was not an autonomous AI system but relied heavily on handcrafted heuristics and domain-specific optimizations by human experts. Deep Blue's strength lay in brute-force computation rather than outperforming in human-like strategic thinking.

In the early 2000s, AI research continued to advance, with breakthroughs in machine learning and natural language processing that led to the development of more sophisticated algorithms. One of the key milestones during this period was the creation of Google's PageRank algorithm. PageRank feels like AI technique used to rank web pages based on their relevance and importance, but it is more correctly to describe PageRank as a graph-based ranking algorithm. Nevertheless, this algorithm revolutionized the way people accessed information on the internet and demonstrated the power of algorithmic data analysis in organizing and analysing vast amounts of data.

The rise of deep learning in the 2010s marked another major milestone in AI development. Deep learning, a subset of machine learning that uses neural networks with multiple layers, allowed AI systems to achieve unprecedented levels of accuracy in tasks such as image recognition and natural language processing. In 2012, a team led by Geoffrey Hinton won the ImageNet competition, a large-scale visual recognition challenge, by using a deep neural network (a convolutional neural network or CNN) that dramatically outperformed all other entries. This achievement demonstrated the power of deep learning and set the stage for its widespread adoption in a variety of applications, from computer vision to speech recognition. As a result of the success investments and research into GPUs (graphics processing units) and hardware optimization for AI started to accelerate.

In 2016, another major milestone was reached when Google's DeepMind developed AlphaGo, an AI program capable of playing the ancient board game Go at a superhuman level. Go is a game of immense complexity, with more board configurations than there are atoms in the observable universe. Despite this complexity, AlphaGo defeated Lee Sedol, one of the world's top Go players, in a five-game match. AlphaGo's success was made possible by combining deep learning with reinforcement learning, a technique that allows AI systems to learn by interacting with their environment and receiving feedback. The victory of AlphaGo was seen as a breakthrough, as it demonstrated the ability of AI to master tasks that require intuition and creativity.

Go, an ancient Chinese board game, demands intelligence, skill, and creativity. Players alternate placing black and white stones on a 19x19 grid, aiming to capture their opponent's stones by surrounding them. Due to its need for complex pattern recognition and its virtually infinite possible game variations, teaching a computer to play Go was once thought impossible. However, in 2016, Demis Hassabis's AlphaGo defied expectations by defeating reigning Go champion Lee Sedol in a globally watched showdown, achieving a decisive 4-1 victory.

More recently, the development of large language models like GPT-3 and GPT-4 has marked a significant milestone in the field of natural language processing. GPT-3, developed by OpenAI in 2020, was one of the largest and most powerful language models of its time, boasting 175 billion parameters. It demonstrated the ability to generate coherent, contextually relevant text, answer questions, write essays, and even create computer code, showcasing a level of fluency that impressed researchers and the public alike.

In 2023, OpenAI introduced GPT-4 with an (undisclosed) estimated tenfold in parameters, further advancing the capabilities of large language models. GPT-4 features enhanced reasoning abilities, a broader knowledge base, and improved understanding of context, making it more adept at handling complex tasks and providing nuanced responses. It also integrates better multimodal capabilities, enabling it to process and generate both text and image-based content in some applications. GPT-4 has pushed the boundaries of what AI can achieve, reinforcing its potential to assist in creative, intellectual, and professional domains, and continuing to blur the line between human and machine capabilities.

The progress of AI has not only been marked by technical milestones but also by societal impacts. AI technologies have become integral to many aspects of our lives, from healthcare and finance to entertainment and transportation. The development of self-driving cars, AI-powered diagnostic tools, and personalized recommendation systems are all examples of how AI has moved from the laboratory to the real world, transforming industries and changing the way we live.

Each of these milestones represents significant progress in the ongoing journey to create machines capable of thinking and learning. The path of AI development has been anything but linear, often marked by moments of advancement followed by setbacks. It is a story of exploration, discovery, and innovation, with each breakthrough standing on the foundation laid by previous generations of researchers.

The AI Winters: Lessons From Setbacks

AI research has faced significant setbacks and periods of reduced funding and interest, commonly known as "AI winters." These periods of stagnation were influenced by external factors such as funding cycles, shifting academic priorities, and public perception. However, the primary causes were unmet expectations, technological limitations—such as insufficient data and computational power—and an increasing awareness of the immense complexity involved in creating truly intelligent machines.

The first AI winter occurred in the early 1970s, following a period of optimism and enthusiasm during the 1950s and 1960s. During the initial years of AI research, there was a widespread belief that the creation of human-like intelligence was just around the corner. Researchers and policymakers were optimistic that machines capable of human-level reasoning and problem-solving would soon be a reality. However, as the field progressed, it became clear that the challenges were far more complex than initially anticipated. The limitations of symbolic AI, which relied on predefined rules and logic, became evident. These systems struggled to handle real-world complexities, such as ambiguity, uncertainty, and incomplete information.

One of the key reasons for the first AI winter was the overreliance on symbolic AI, also known as "good old-fashioned AI" (GOFAI). Symbolic AI worked well for tasks that could be clearly defined by rules, such as solving mathematical theorems or playing simple games. However, it was unable to cope with more nuanced tasks, such as natural language understanding or visual perception. As a result, the field faced growing scepticism from both researchers and funding agencies. The inability to deliver on ambitious promises led to a decline in funding, and many AI projects were abandoned. The enthusiasm that had characterized the early days of AI was replaced by a sense of disillusionment.

The second AI winter occurred in the late 1980s and early

1990s, following the rise and subsequent decline of expert systems. During the 1970s and 1980s, expert systems were seen as a promising approach to AI. These systems were designed to emulate the decision-making abilities of human experts in specific domains, such as medicine, finance, and engineering. The success of expert systems like MYCIN and DENDRAL demonstrated that AI could be used to solve real-world problems, and they found widespread applications in various industries. However, expert systems had their own set of limitations. They were costly to develop and maintain, as they required extensive knowledge bases and constant updates to remain relevant. Additionally, expert systems lacked the ability to learn from experience, which made them rigid and unable to adapt to new situations.

As the limitations of expert systems became apparent, interest in AI began to wane once again. Many companies that had invested heavily in AI technology found that the costs outweighed the benefits, and they began to scale back their investments. The promise of AI as a transformative technology seemed to be fading, and funding for AI research dried up. This period of reduced interest and investment in AI became known as the second AI winter. Once again, the field faced scepticism and criticism, as the lofty promises of AI had not been realized.

"AI winters were not due to imagination traps, but due to lack of imaginations. Imaginations bring order out of chaos. Deep learning with deep imagination is the road map to AI springs." — Amit Ray

---

Despite the setbacks of these AI winters, they provided valuable lessons that ultimately contributed to the resurgence of AI in the 21st century. One of the key lessons learned was the importance of managing expectations. In the early days of AI, there was a tendency to overpromise and underdeliver, which led to disillusionment when the technology failed to meet expectations. The AI winters highlighted the need for a more measured approach to AI development, one that acknowledged the complexity of the challenges involved and set realistic goals.

Another important lesson was the recognition of the limitations of symbolic AI and the need for new approaches. The failures of symbolic AI and expert systems paved the way for the development of machine learning and neural networks, which represented a departure from the rule-based approaches of the past. Instead of trying to explicitly program machines to solve specific problems, researchers began to focus on creating algorithms that could learn from data. This shift in focus was instrumental in the development of modern AI techniques, such as deep learning, which have proven to be far more effective at handling complex, real-world tasks.

The AI winters also underscored the importance of data and computational power in the development of intelligent systems. One of the reasons that early AI approaches struggled was the lack of sufficient data and computing resources to support their ambitions. The resurgence of AI in the 2000s and 2010s was largely driven by the availability of vast amounts of data, as well as advancements in computing power that made it possible to train large-scale neural networks. The lessons of the past highlighted the need for a solid technological foundation to support AI research and development.

Perhaps most importantly, the AI winters taught researchers and policymakers the value of perseverance. Despite the setbacks and challenges, the dream of creating intelligent machines never truly disappeared. The lessons learned during the periods of stagnation were carried forward by a dedicated community of researchers who continued to explore new approaches and push the boundaries of what was possible. This perseverance eventually led to the breakthroughs that have defined modern AI, from the rise of deep learning to the development of advanced natural language processing models.

Today, as AI continues to advance and become an integral part of our lives, it is important to remember the lessons of the AI winters. The setbacks of the past serve as a reminder that progress in AI is not always linear, and that there will be challenges and obstacles along the way. However, they also demonstrate that setbacks can be opportunities for growth and innovation. The AI winters were not the end of AI research; rather, they were periods of reflection and recalibration that ultimately strengthened the field and set the stage for the remarkable progress we see today.

THE RISE OF AI MYTHS AND FEARS

Misconceptions About AI Capabilities

The rise of AI has sparked both awe and anxiety in the public consciousness, leading to a proliferation of myths and misconceptions about its true capabilities. AI is often depicted as an all-knowing, all-powerful technology poised to either revolutionize or destroy society. While these portrayals can make for thrilling headlines and science fiction plots, they frequently misrepresent the current state of AI, creating unrealistic expectations and unfounded fears. Understanding the limitations of AI is crucial to appreciating its true potential and mitigating the risks it may pose.

Human civilization has progressed significantly by leveraging inventions to minimize the need for human labour, leading to improvements in quality of life and advancements in human rights.

One of the most common misconceptions is that AI is already capable of human-level general intelligence. Many people mistakenly believe that today's AI systems can think, reason, and understand the world in the same way humans do. This misconception is fuelled by the portrayal of AI in movies and media, where machines are shown as having consciousness and emotions, or as being capable of making decisions independently, without any human intervention. In reality, AI today is far from achieving human-level general intelligence, known as Artificial General Intelligence (AGI). Current AI systems, such as those used for language translation, image recognition, or playing chess, are examples of narrow AI. They are designed to perform specific tasks and do so extremely well, but they lack the flexibility, adaptability, and depth of understanding that characterize human intelligence.

Another widespread myth is that AI can fully replace human jobs. While it is true that AI and automation are changing the nature of work, the fear that AI will lead to mass unemployment is often exaggerated. The reality is that AI is more likely to automate specific tasks within a job rather than replacing entire occupations. For instance, AI can help doctors by analysing medical images and flagging potential issues, but it cannot replace the nuanced decision-making and empathy required in patient care. Similarly, an AI-powered legal assistant can help review documents and identify relevant case law, but it cannot provide the strategic thinking and negotiation skills that a human lawyer brings to the table. The automation of tasks rather than complete jobs means that AI will likely augment human capabilities, allowing people to focus on more creative, complex, and interpersonal aspects of their work.

Some tasks handled by lawyers, paralegals, and legal secretaries are highly formulaic. Preparing real estate contracts, rental agreements, divorce settlements, or wills often involves starting with a standard legal template, adapting it slightly for the client, and filling in the necessary details. Online legal platforms like RocketLawyer, LegalZoom, and LawDepot

*streamline this process with algorithmic software
that automates the work, requiring only a few simple
questions from clients to complete the documents.*

There is also a common misconception that AI systems are inherently objective and unbiased. Many people assume that because AI relies on data and algorithms, it must be free from the biases that affect human decision-making. However, AI is only as good as the data it is trained on. If the data used to train an AI system is biased, the AI will learn and perpetuate those biases. For example, facial recognition systems have been found to be less accurate in identifying people with darker skin tones, largely because the datasets used to train these systems were not diverse enough. Similarly, AI used in hiring processes can inadvertently discriminate against certain groups if it is trained on historical data that reflects existing biases in hiring practices. The belief that AI is inherently fair, and objective is not only incorrect but also dangerous, as it can lead to the deployment of biased systems that perpetuate inequality.

Another myth is that AI is infallible and always provides accurate results. The reality is that AI systems, like all technologies, are prone to errors. These errors can result from a variety of factors, including poor-quality training data, limitations in the underlying algorithms, or unexpected changes in the environment in which the AI operates. For instance, self-driving cars have made significant progress, but they are still not perfect and can make mistakes that lead to accidents. Similarly, language models like GPT-4 can generate coherent and contextually relevant text, but they can also produce incorrect or nonsensical answers, especially when faced with complex or ambiguous queries. It is important to recognize that AI is not a flawless solution, and that human oversight is essential to ensure its reliability and safety.

In the 1980s, Michie attempted to build a chess-playing machine by loading it with raw data: millions of moves from grandmaster games. While the computer became an impressive player, it sometimes made perplexing decisions, such as sacrificing its queen without reason. This occurred because the machine had learned that grandmasters often sacrificed the queen in victorious strategies but failed to grasp the nuanced conditions required for the gambit to succeed. It was a case of understanding everything in theory but missing the practical context entirely.

The fear of autonomous AI systems, particularly autonomous weapons, has also contributed to misconceptions about AI capabilities. Many people worry that AI could lead to the development of killer robots that operate without human control, posing an existential threat to humanity. While it is true that advances in AI and robotics have led to the development of autonomous weapons, these systems are not yet fully independent and still require significant human oversight. The ethical concerns surrounding autonomous weapons are valid, and there is an ongoing debate about how to regulate their development and use. However, the idea that AI is on the verge of creating fully autonomous killing machines that could turn against humanity is more science fiction than reality. It is crucial to distinguish between the potential misuse of AI by humans and the idea of AI developing a will of its own.

Autonomous weapons, designed to independently identify and engage targets, have seen remarkable advancements in recent years. One example is "slaughterbots," miniature drones developed to autonomously locate and neutralize specific individuals. In 2016, the U.S. Air Force demonstrated

*a deployment of 103 such drones, describing them as
a unified system with a distributed brain, similar to a
natural swarm. Attempts to regulate these technologies
have proven difficult. In December 2021, United
Nations negotiations to ban lethal autonomous weapons
systems (LAWS) failed to achieve consensus. This lack of
agreement among nations has sparked concerns about
an unregulated arms race in AI-powered weaponry.*

Another misconception is that AI is inherently destined to become superintelligent and take over the world. This fear is often linked to the concept of an "intelligence explosion," where an AI system rapidly improves itself to the point of surpassing human intelligence and gaining uncontrollable power. While this scenario has been the subject of much speculation and debate, it is important to understand that we are still far from achieving AGI, let alone superintelligence. The development of AGI would require significant breakthroughs in understanding human cognition, learning, and reasoning, and there is currently no consensus among researchers on how or when such breakthroughs might occur. Moreover, the idea that superintelligent AI would necessarily pose a threat to humanity is not universally accepted, and many experts believe that with proper safeguards, AGI could be developed in a way that aligns with human values and interests.

*A 2009 survey of international experts at The Second
Conference on Artificial General Intelligence at the
University of Memphis revealed that most believe
machines as intelligent as humans will exist by 2075, with
superintelligence emerging within 30 years after that.*

Finally, there is a misconception that AI is a mysterious

and incomprehensible technology that only a select few can understand. This perception can lead to fear and resistance to AI adoption, as people may feel that they have no control over how AI is used or how it might impact their lives. In reality, while the technical details of AI can be complex, the basic principles are accessible to anyone willing to learn. AI systems are built on mathematical models and algorithms that process data to identify patterns and make predictions. By demystifying AI and promoting education and awareness, we can empower more people to understand how AI works, how it can be used, and how its risks can be managed.

In conclusion, the rise of AI has given birth to numerous myths and misconceptions about its capabilities. While AI is a powerful tool that has the potential to transform many aspects of our lives, it is not the all-knowing, all-powerful entity that it is often portrayed to be. Understanding the true capabilities and limitations of AI is essential for making informed decisions about its development and use. By dispelling these misconceptions, we can better appreciate the real potential of AI to augment human capabilities, improve our quality of life, and address some of the most pressing challenges facing society today, while also being mindful of its risks and limitations.

Popular Culture And Fear

The idea of artificial intelligence reaching a level of superintelligence—an event often referred to as the "Singularity"—has long captured the imagination of popular culture. The Singularity, a hypothetical point where machines surpass human intelligence, is both a source of fascination and fear. Popular culture has played a significant role in shaping public perception of AI, often portraying it as a looming existential threat or a miraculous leap forward for humanity. This dual narrative has led to widespread anxiety and misconceptions about AI's potential to become uncontrollable, leading to dystopian outcomes.

One of the most influential portrayals of AI and the Singularity in popular culture comes from science fiction literature and films. Stories like Isaac Asimov's "I, Robot," Arthur C. Clarke's "2001: A Space Odyssey," and more recently, movies like "The Terminator" and "The Matrix" have depicted a future where AI evolves beyond human control. In "The Terminator," for example, the AI system known as Skynet gains self-awareness and determines that humanity is a threat to its existence, ultimately launching a war against humans. Such narratives paint a picture of AI as an entity that, once it reaches a certain level of intelligence, will inevitably become hostile, leading to apocalyptic scenarios.

"Any sufficiently advanced technology is indistinguishable from magic." — Arthur C. Clarke

---

These depictions have had a profound impact on how people perceive AI. The idea that an AI could become self-aware and decide to eliminate humanity is a recurring theme in popular culture, and it has contributed to the fear of the Singularity. The concept of machines becoming self-aware and surpassing human control taps into deep-seated anxieties about losing autonomy and being rendered obsolete by our own creations. This fear is further amplified by the portrayal of AI as cold, calculating, and devoid of empathy—a stark contrast to the warmth and emotional depth that define human relationships.

The fear of the Singularity is not limited to fictional narratives; it has also been echoed by prominent figures in the real world. Visionaries like Elon Musk and Stephen Hawking have warned about the potential dangers of superintelligent AI. Musk has famously described AI as "summoning the demon," while Hawking cautioned that the development of full AI could "spell the end of the human race." These warnings, coming from respected figures in science and technology, have added a layer of legitimacy to the fears depicted in popular culture. The idea that AI could one day surpass human intelligence and potentially pose an existential threat has become a topic of serious debate among researchers, ethicists, and policymakers.

However, it is important to recognize that the portrayal of the Singularity in popular culture often oversimplifies the complexities of AI development. In reality, the path to creating Artificial General Intelligence (AGI) is fraught with challenges that are far from being solved. Current AI systems are highly specialized and lack the general intelligence, adaptability, and common sense that are essential for achieving AGI. The idea that AI could suddenly become superintelligent and pose a threat to humanity ignores the many technical, ethical, and philosophical hurdles that would need to be overcome. Moreover, the fear of AI as an independent, malevolent force overlooks the fact that AI is ultimately a tool created and controlled by humans. The risks associated with AI are more likely to stem from misuse or unintended consequences rather than from an AI developing a will of its own.

Another popular portrayal of the Singularity is the idea of humans merging with machines to enhance their abilities, as seen in movies like "Transcendence" and "Ghost in the Shell." In these stories, humans upload their consciousness into machines or augment their bodies with cybernetic enhancements, blurring the line between human and machine. This vision of the Singularity presents a more optimistic view of the future, where AI and humanity coexist and even merge to create a new form of life. While this narrative is less dystopian, it still raises important ethical questions about identity, consciousness, and what it means to be human. The idea of merging with machines challenges our understanding of selfhood and has led to debates about whether such a future would enhance or diminish our humanity.

*"The real problem is not whether machines think
but whether men do." — B.F. Skinner*

The portrayal of AI in popular culture also reflects broader societal anxieties about technological progress. Throughout history, major technological advancements have often been met with both excitement and fear. The Industrial Revolution, for example, was seen as both a pathway to progress and a threat to traditional ways of life. Similarly, the rise of AI and the prospect of the Singularity evoke both hope and fear—hope for a future where AI can solve some of humanity's greatest challenges, and fear that it could lead to unforeseen consequences that disrupt our way of life. Popular culture amplifies these anxieties, providing a lens through which we can explore our hopes and fears about the future.

The concept of the Singularity also raises philosophical questions about the nature of intelligence and the potential for machines to surpass human capabilities. If machines were to achieve superintelligence, what would that mean for humanity's place in the world? Would we become obsolete, or would we find new ways to coexist with our creations? These questions are at the heart of many popular culture narratives, and they reflect a deeper existential concern about the future of humanity. The fear of being replaced by machines is not just about losing jobs or control—it is about losing our sense of purpose and identity in a world where machines are more capable than we are.

*"The singularity isn't near—it's already here, in the way
we grapple with AI shaping our choices, our societies, and
ultimately, our humanity." Adapted from Kevin Kelly*

While popular culture has played a significant role in shaping public perception of AI and the Singularity, it is important to approach these portrayals with a critical eye. The fear of the Singularity is often based on speculative scenarios that are far removed from the current reality of AI development. By understanding the limitations of current AI technology and the challenges involved in achieving AGI, we can better appreciate the potential benefits of AI while also addressing its risks in a responsible manner. The Singularity, if it ever occurs, is likely to be a gradual process rather than a sudden event, and it will require careful planning, regulation, and ethical consideration to ensure that it benefits humanity as a whole.

In conclusion, the fear of the Singularity has been deeply influenced by popular culture, which has often portrayed AI as either a utopian dream or a dystopian nightmare. While these narratives provide a compelling exploration of the possibilities and risks associated with AI, they often oversimplify the complexities of AI development, and the challenges involved in creating superintelligent machines. By separating fact from fiction and engaging in informed discussions about the future of AI, we can better navigate the opportunities and challenges that lie ahead. The Singularity may be a distant and uncertain possibility, but the choices we make today will shape the role that AI plays in our future—whether as a tool that enhances our lives or a force that poses new risks.

Why People Are Afraid

The rise of AI has brought about a mix of excitement and apprehension, as people consider the profound changes that this technology could bring to society. While AI holds the promise of making life more efficient, convenient, and productive, it also brings with it fears and uncertainties. These fears largely centre around three key issues: job loss, privacy, and control. Each of these concerns reflects a broader anxiety about the potential impact of AI on our lives and our sense of security in an increasingly automated world.

"The development of full artificial intelligence could spell the end of the human race... It would take off on its own, and redesign itself at an ever-increasing rate." — Stephen Hawking

---

One of the most common fears surrounding AI is the potential for widespread job loss. Automation and AI have already begun to replace certain jobs, particularly those involving routine or repetitive tasks. Factory workers, cashiers, customer service representatives, and even drivers are seeing their roles increasingly automated by machines and AI systems that can perform these tasks more efficiently and at a lower cost. This has led to concerns that AI will lead to mass unemployment, leaving millions of people without the skills or opportunities needed to find new work. The fear of job loss is not just about the economic impact—it also strikes at the core of human identity, as work is often closely tied to an individual's sense of purpose and self-worth.

When machines and factories emerged in 19th-century Victorian England, Charles Dickens expressed concern about their impact on the country's working-class labourers.

However, the reality of AI's impact on employment is more complex. While AI is likely to automate some jobs, it will also create new opportunities and roles that did not previously exist. For instance, the rise of AI has led to increased demand for data scientists, machine learning engineers, and AI ethicists—jobs that were virtually unheard of a decade ago. Additionally, AI can be used to augment human capabilities rather than replace them, allowing workers to focus on more creative, strategic, or interpersonal aspects of their roles. Despite these potential benefits, the fear of job loss persists, particularly among workers who may not have the resources or skills to adapt to the changing job market. The challenge for society will be to ensure that the benefits of AI are distributed equitably and that workers are provided with the training and support they need to transition to new opportunities.

"Half of employers plan to reorient their business in response to AI, two-thirds plan to hire talent with specific AI skills, while 40% anticipate reducing their workforce where AI can automate tasks." — World Economic Forum Future of Jobs Report 2025.

Privacy is another major concern when it comes to AI. AI systems rely on vast amounts of data to function effectively, and much of this data comes from individuals. From social media activity and online shopping habits to facial recognition and location tracking, AI systems are constantly collecting and analysing data about our lives. This has led to growing fears about how personal information is being used, who has access to it, and whether it is being protected adequately. The use of AI in surveillance, for example, has raised concerns about the erosion of privacy and the potential for abuse by governments or corporations. Facial recognition technology, in particular, has been criticized for its potential to enable mass surveillance, track individuals without their consent, and infringe on civil liberties.

The fear of losing privacy is not unfounded. There have been numerous cases of data breaches, misuse of personal information, and lack of transparency in how data is collected and used. AI's ability to analyse and draw inferences from data also raises concerns about the potential for profiling and discrimination. For example, AI algorithms used in hiring processes may inadvertently discriminate against certain groups if they are trained on biased data, leading to unequal treatment. The fear of privacy loss is exacerbated by the fact that AI systems are often developed and controlled by large tech companies that may prioritize profit over individual rights. Addressing these concerns will require robust regulations, greater transparency, and a commitment to protecting individuals' rights to privacy in an increasingly data-driven world.

The third major fear associated with AI is the loss of control. As AI systems become more advanced and capable of making decisions autonomously, there is a growing concern that humans may lose control over the technology they have created. This fear is often linked to the concept of the Singularity—the hypothetical point at which AI surpasses human intelligence and becomes uncontrollable. While the Singularity remains a speculative concept, the fear of losing control over AI is grounded in real-world examples of AI systems behaving unpredictably or making decisions that are difficult for humans to understand. For instance, AI algorithms used in financial markets have been known to trigger flash crashes, causing significant economic disruptions without any clear explanation of why the crash occurred.

The fear of losing control is also tied to the increasing use of AI in critical decision-making processes. AI is being used to make decisions about who gets a loan, who is eligible for parole, and even who gets hired for a job. When these decisions are made by opaque algorithms, it can be difficult for individuals to understand how or why a particular outcome was reached. This lack of transparency can lead to a sense of powerlessness, as people feel that they have no recourse if they are treated unfairly by an AI system. The fear of losing control over AI is further amplified by the potential for malicious use of the technology. Autonomous weapons, for example, could be used to carry out attacks without human intervention, raising ethical questions about accountability and the potential for unintended consequences.

AI is revolutionizing defence but blurs traditional lines of control, introducing risks unprecedented in history. From autonomous cyber weapons to biased decision-making in combat, the potential for unintended consequences looms large. International cooperation and ethical frameworks are essential to guide responsible AI integration in security, ensuring diplomacy prevails over destruction.

Addressing the fear of losing control over AI will require a combination of technical, ethical, and regulatory solutions. Developing AI systems that are transparent, explainable, and aligned with human values is crucial to ensuring that people feel they have control over the technology. Additionally, establishing clear guidelines and regulations for the use of AI in critical decision-making processes can help build trust and mitigate the fear of losing control. The goal should be to create AI systems that are not only powerful and effective but also accountable and aligned with the interests of society as a whole.

In conclusion, the fears surrounding AI—job loss, privacy, and control—reflect broader anxieties about the impact of technology on our lives and our sense of security. While these fears are not without basis, it is important to recognize that they are not inevitable outcomes. AI has the potential to bring about significant benefits, from increased productivity and efficiency to new opportunities for innovation and creativity. By addressing the fears associated with AI through thoughtful regulation, ethical considerations, and a commitment to transparency and fairness, we can ensure that the technology is used in a way that enhances our lives rather than diminishes them. The challenge for society is to navigate the complexities of AI development and use in a way that maximizes its benefits while minimizing its risks, ensuring that the future of AI is one that is shaped by human values and priorities.

HOW DOES AI WORK AND LEARN?

AI In Simple Terms

Artificial Intelligence, or AI, is essentially about making machines smart. It involves creating systems that can learn, reason, and make decisions, similar to how humans do—but they don't have thoughts or emotions. AI is like giving a computer the ability to follow a recipe, but instead of just cooking, it can learn new recipes by observing patterns and examples. For instance, it can recognize a car in a picture after seeing enough images of cars.

AI is everywhere today. It is in the virtual assistants on our phones, the recommendations we get for movies, and even in cars that drive themselves. These systems use data—lots of it—to learn and improve over time. The goal of AI is not to replace human intelligence but to assist and enhance our capabilities, making our lives easier and more efficient. Whether it is predicting the weather or helping doctors diagnose diseases, AI is here to help us solve complex problems by processing information faster and more accurately than we can on our own.

"Artificial intelligence would be the ultimate version of Google. The ultimate search engine that would understand

everything on the web. It would understand exactly what you wanted, and it would give you the right thing." – Larry Page.

Different Types Of AI

Artificial Intelligence is not a one-size-fits-all concept; rather, it comes in different forms depending on its capabilities. AI can be broadly classified into three types: Narrow AI, General AI, and Superintelligence. Each of these represents a different level of complexity and capability in how machines can learn, reason, and interact with the world.

Narrow AI, also known as Weak AI, is the type of artificial intelligence that is most common today. Narrow AI is designed to perform a specific task, or a limited range of tasks, with a high degree of efficiency. It does not possess consciousness, self-awareness, or general intelligence; it simply excels at what it has been programmed to do. Examples of Narrow AI include virtual assistants like Siri and Alexa, recommendation algorithms used by Netflix or Spotify, and self-driving cars. These systems can analyse data, recognize patterns, and make decisions within their defined scope, but they cannot perform tasks outside of their specific programming. For example, a language translation AI cannot play chess unless it has also been specifically trained for that purpose.

General AI, sometimes referred to as Strong AI or Artificial General Intelligence (AGI), represents the next level of AI development. Unlike Narrow AI, General AI would be capable of understanding, learning, and applying knowledge across a wide range of tasks, much like a human being. AGI would be able to reason, solve problems, and make decisions in a manner similar to humans, using common sense and experiential learning. This kind of AI could seamlessly switch from writing an essay to solving a math problem, or from diagnosing an illness to holding a meaningful conversation. Despite significant progress in AI research, General AI remains largely theoretical at this point, as we have yet to create a machine with the cognitive versatility and adaptability of the human mind.

AI comes in three forms: Narrow AI performs specific tasks efficiently, like Siri or Netflix recommendations; General AI, still theoretical, aims to match human versatility; and Superintelligence, a speculative concept, could surpass human intellect, raising both opportunities and existential risks.

Superintelligence is a theoretical concept that takes AI even further, referring to an intelligence that far surpasses that of the best human minds in every field, including creativity, problem-solving, and emotional intelligence. Superintelligence could potentially outperform humans in all aspects, making decisions that are far beyond our understanding or control. This concept is often the subject of science fiction, and it brings up numerous ethical and existential concerns. For instance, thinkers like Nick Bostrom and Elon Musk have warned about the risks associated with creating a superintelligent AI that might not align with human values. The fear is that if such an entity were created without the necessary safeguards, it could lead to unintended consequences, possibly even posing an existential threat to humanity.

Understanding these different types of AI helps us appreciate both the current state of AI technology and the challenges and opportunities that lie ahead as we continue to develop more advanced forms of artificial intelligence.

AI, Machine Learning, And Deep Learning

Artificial Intelligence, Machine Learning, and Deep Learning are often used interchangeably, but they represent different concepts within the broader field of computing. Understanding their distinctions can help clarify how they relate to each other and the specific roles they play in developing intelligent systems.

AI is the broadest term of the three. It refers to the development of computer systems that can perform tasks typically requiring human intelligence. AI encompasses any technology that simulates human thinking, problem-solving, or decision-making abilities. It includes everything from rule-based systems that play chess to complex algorithms that interpret human language. Essentially, AI is the overarching discipline focused on making machines "smart." Any system that perceives its environment and takes actions to maximize its chances of success can be considered AI. This includes not only modern neural networks, but also simpler algorithms and systems designed decades ago.

Machine Learning (ML) is a subset of AI. It involves creating algorithms that allow machines to learn from and adapt to data without explicit programming for each individual task. Rather than being hardcoded with rules to solve a problem, machine learning models identify patterns and make decisions based on training data. This allows them to improve their performance over time as they are exposed to more information. For example, a machine learning algorithm can learn to distinguish images of wolfs from dogs by analysing thousands of labelled examples, although a well-documented example showed that training with data showing wolfs mainly with a snow covered background could lead to wrongly derived 'rules' where any dog with a snow filled background would be classified as a wolf. Training needs 'good' data.

Deep Learning is a specialized branch of machine learning that uses neural networks with many layers—often called deep neural networks—to analyse data. The term "deep" refers to the number of layers in these neural networks. Deep learning models are especially powerful when it comes to analysing large and complex datasets, making them useful for tasks like image and speech recognition. Inspired by the structure of the human brain, these neural networks consist of interconnected nodes (or "neurons") that process information in multiple stages, allowing them to recognize intricate patterns and relationships within the data. For instance, a deep learning model can learn to differentiate between different objects in an image, understand spoken language, or even generate new, original content, such as images or music. The ability of deep learning to solve complex problems with a high level of accuracy is what has led to many of the most impressive advancements in AI over recent years.

Artificial Intelligence is the goal, Machine Learning is the method, and Deep Learning is the powerhouse driving breakthroughs.

So, AI is the broad concept of creating machines that can simulate human intelligence. Machine Learning is a subset of AI that focuses on enabling machines to learn from data. Deep Learning is a further subset of machine learning that uses large, multi-layered neural networks to process massive datasets and learn complex patterns. Each plays a crucial role in advancing intelligent systems, and together, they represent the evolution of how we create machines capable of performing sophisticated tasks that were once the exclusive domain of humans.

Supervised vs. Unsupervised Learning

As mentioned, is machine learning (ML) a key part of artificial intelligence. ML involves enabling machines to learn from data without explicitly being programmed for every specific task. Within this category, there are different methods of learning, two of the most common being supervised learning and unsupervised learning. These two approaches represent distinct ways of teaching a machine to recognize patterns and make decisions based on data, and each serves different purposes depending on the kind of problem at hand.

Supervised learning is a type of machine learning where the algorithm is trained on a labelled dataset. In a labelled dataset, each data point comes with an associated output or target, essentially providing the answer key for the learning process. The goal of supervised learning is for the model to learn the mapping between the inputs and the correct outputs, which allows it to make accurate predictions on new, unseen data. For example, in a supervised learning scenario, a model might be trained to identify cats in images by analysing thousands of pictures labelled as either "cat" or "not cat." By finding relationships between features of the images and their labels, the model learns to classify new images correctly. Supervised learning is widely used in applications such as image classification, spam detection, medical diagnosis, and financial forecasting.

Unsupervised learning, on the other hand, deals with unlabelled data. The system is not provided with any explicit output labels, meaning the algorithm must find patterns or relationships in the data without prior guidance. The goal is to explore the structure of the data and identify meaningful groupings or hidden features. Clustering and association are two common techniques used in unsupervised learning. For instance, in customer segmentation, an unsupervised learning algorithm might analyse customer data and group customers based on similar behaviours or preferences without being told what defines each group. The patterns that emerge can help businesses understand their customers better and target their marketing efforts accordingly. Unsupervised learning is also used in anomaly detection, market basket analysis, and to reduce dimensionality in large datasets.

---

*Most human and animal learning occurs
through unsupervised learning.*

The key difference between the two approaches lies in the availability of labelled data. Supervised learning requires a labelled dataset to learn from, making it well-suited for problems where historical data is available, and precise predictions are needed. Unsupervised learning, by contrast, is useful when there is no labelled data, and the objective is to discover the hidden structure within the data. While supervised learning focuses on prediction, unsupervised learning focuses on uncovering patterns that might not be immediately apparent.

To illustrate this difference, consider a scenario where you have a collection of fruits. In supervised learning, you would provide labels for each fruit, such as "apple," "banana," or "orange," and train the model to recognize and classify new fruits based on these labels. In unsupervised learning, however, there are no labels. The algorithm would analyse the fruits and group them based on similarities, such as size, colour, or texture, without being told what type of fruit they are. The goal is to identify clusters of similar items and understand the underlying characteristics that define each group.

Both methods within machine learning have its own strengths and ideal use cases. Supervised learning excels in situations where labelled data is abundant, and precise, predictable outcomes are desired. Unsupervised learning shines when the goal is to explore data, discover hidden patterns, and gain insights without predefined labels. Understanding when to use each approach is crucial in developing effective AI solutions that can tackle a wide range of real-world challenges.

Neural Networks

Neural Networks are at the core of many of today's AI advancements, and they are a fundamental technology driving machine learning, especially deep learning. Inspired by the structure of the human brain, neural networks are designed to recognize patterns, make decisions, and adapt over time by learning from data. Understanding how these networks work can provide insights into why they are so effective at tasks such as image recognition, natural language processing, and playing complex games like chess or Go.

At their most basic level, neural networks consist of layers of interconnected nodes, also called neurons. Each neuron is a mathematical function that processes input data to generate an output. Neural networks typically have three types of layers: the input layer, hidden layers, and the output layer. The input layer receives the raw data, which can be anything from pixel values of an image to numerical features in a dataset. The output layer produces the final predictions or classifications, while the hidden layers in between perform intermediate computations that enable the network to learn and understand complex relationships.

The key feature of neural networks lies in how these layers are connected. Each connection between neurons has an associated weight, which determines the importance of the signal traveling between those neurons. Initially, these weights are assigned randomly. During the training process, the network adjusts these weights to minimize the difference between the predicted output and the actual output. This adjustment is made through a process called backpropagation, where errors are propagated back through the network to fine-tune the weights, ultimately improving the model's accuracy over time.

One of the strengths of neural networks is their ability to

learn from data through training. During training, the network is exposed to numerous examples, allowing it to detect patterns and relationships within the data. For instance, in image recognition, the network might learn to recognize edges, textures, and shapes in earlier layers, and then use deeper layers to identify more complex features like faces or specific objects. This hierarchical approach to learning—where each layer extracts increasingly abstract features—is what makes deep neural networks so powerful for tasks involving unstructured data like images, videos, or sound.

Neural networks, inspired by the structure of the brain, consist of layers of interconnected neurons. Take for example Optical Character Recognition (OCR). The process begins with a dataset of labelled images of letters. Each image, converted into numerical pixel values, is fed into the input layer of the network. The neurons process this information through weights (connection strengths) and biases (activation thresholds), passing it through multiple middle layers to identify patterns. The end result is the output layer of the network, say 26 neurons each corresponding to a unique letter of the alphabet. During training, the network predicts the letter and compares it to the correct label, calculating the error. Using backpropagation, it adjusts the weights and biases to improve accuracy. Over thousands of iterations, the network learns to recognize letters by breaking down complex shapes into simple patterns, such as edges and curves. Once trained, it can generalize to accurately classify new, unseen images.

Neural networks also have different architectures depending on the task at hand. For example, Convolutional Neural Networks (CNNs) are commonly used for image processing. CNNs use specialized layers called convolutional layers that scan the input in small regions, making them effective for capturing spatial relationships in images. On the other hand, Recurrent Neural Networks (RNNs) are well-suited for sequential data, such as text or time-series data, because they have connections that allow information to persist, essentially giving the network a form of memory.

Despite their capabilities, training neural networks can be computationally intensive, often requiring large amounts of data and significant processing power. This is where advancements in Graphics Processing Units (GPUs) and distributed computing have played a crucial role in enabling the practical use of deep learning. The training process can take hours, days, or even weeks, depending on the complexity of the problem and the size of the dataset. However, once trained, these models can make predictions very quickly, which makes them highly valuable for real-time applications.

In short, neural networks are a type of machine learning model inspired by the human brain, consisting of interconnected neurons organized into layers. By adjusting the weights of these connections through training, neural networks can learn to recognize patterns, make predictions, and solve complex problems. Their versatility and power have made them a cornerstone of modern AI, enabling breakthroughs in a wide range of fields, from healthcare to autonomous driving.

The Role Of Big Data In AI Learning

Big Data plays a critical role in the development and effectiveness of AI, especially when it comes to machine learning and deep learning. Big Data refers to extremely large and complex datasets that are generated at high volume, velocity, and variety. With the rapid growth of digital technologies and the internet, data is being generated by countless sources, including social media, IoT devices, sensors, transactions, and more. This immense volume of data serves as the fuel for training AI models, enabling them to learn, adapt, and improve over time.

Large Language Models (LLM) like ChatGPT are trained on massive datasets, including text from Wikipedia, Reddit, web pages, digitized books, and computer code, amounting to roughly 500 billion words. In comparison, a 10-year-old human has been exposed to about 100 million words.

AI, particularly machine learning models, relies on data to recognize patterns and make informed predictions. The more diverse and comprehensive the dataset, the better the model becomes at understanding subtle differences and generalizing its learning to new, unseen scenarios. Big Data provides the variety and quantity of information needed for AI systems to effectively discern patterns and anomalies. For instance, when training a neural network to recognize images, the availability of millions of diverse images helps ensure that the model is not only highly accurate but also robust against variations, such as differences in lighting, angle, or background.

One of the key strengths of Big Data in AI learning is its capacity to reduce bias and improve the generalizability of AI models. When models are trained on diverse datasets that encompass different demographics, situations, and conditions, they are less likely to be biased towards a specific subset of data. For example, in healthcare, AI models trained on a large, varied set of medical records can provide more accurate diagnoses across different patient populations, leading to better outcomes for all individuals, rather than favouring a particular demographic group.

Big Data also enables deep learning, a subset of machine learning that involves the use of neural networks with multiple layers. Deep learning models are particularly data-hungry; they require vast amounts of labelled data to achieve state-of-the-art performance. For instance, to create an AI system capable of understanding human speech, researchers use thousands of hours of recorded speech data from speakers with various accents, dialects, and languages. This helps the model to be more effective across a broad range of real-world scenarios. Just as a real-world example, Whisper from Open AI is trained on 680.000 hours of speech in 96 languages. Likewise, GPT-4 was trained on an estimated dataset of one petabyte.

The integration of Big Data in AI has also enabled models to evolve beyond just static learning. Real-time data streams allow AI systems to continuously learn and adapt, a concept known as online learning. With data being generated in real-time, AI models can be updated dynamically to accommodate changes in user behaviour or environmental conditions. This ability is especially valuable in applications like personalized recommendations, where AI systems must adapt to users' changing preferences quickly, or in financial markets, where models must react to fluctuations and emerging trends almost instantaneously.

In biology, the protein-folding prediction system AlphaFold has set a new benchmark by achieving accuracy far beyond previous scientific methods. By training on DNA data, it enabled biologists to validate theories at an unprecedented scale. Scientists leveraged extensive databases like the Protein Data Bank, containing over 170,000 experimentally determined 3D protein structures, and UniProt, which includes millions of protein sequences without known 3D structures. Combining these datasets, AlphaFold learned to identify properly folded proteins and generalized predictions for unsolved ones. After rigorous refinement, this training yielded groundbreaking results, advancing our understanding of diseases and drug interactions.

However, using Big Data for AI also presents several challenges. Data quality is a critical factor; having vast amounts of data is beneficial only if that data is clean, accurate, and representative of the problem domain. Poor-quality data can lead to models that are inaccurate or biased, thereby limiting their effectiveness. Furthermore, the infrastructure required to process and store Big Data can be substantial. Companies need high-performance computing resources and sophisticated data management systems to handle, preprocess, and feed these massive datasets into AI models. Privacy is another significant concern, as much of the data used to train AI models includes personal information. It is essential to ensure that data collection and usage comply with regulations like GDPR and that measures are taken to anonymize sensitive information.

"Forget artificial intelligence – in the brave new world of big data, it's artificial idiocy we should be looking out for." – Tom Chatfield.

Despite these challenges, the synergy between Big Data and AI has led to remarkable breakthroughs in various fields. In healthcare, Big Data has enabled the development of AI models that can predict disease outbreaks or assist in diagnosing rare conditions. In marketing, it allows AI to provide highly personalized recommendations by analysing customer behaviour at scale. Autonomous vehicles also benefit from Big Data, as they rely on enormous datasets of driving scenarios to navigate safely and make split-second decisions in real-world environments.

"The key to success with AI is not just having the right data, but also asking the right questions." – Ginni Rometty.

In conclusion, Big Data is indispensable to AI learning, providing the volume, variety, and velocity of information needed for effective model training and deployment. It enables AI to make more accurate predictions, adapt to new information, and perform complex tasks with high precision. As data generation continues to accelerate, the relationship between Big Data and AI will become even more crucial, driving further advancements, and unlocking new possibilities in technology and society.

The vast amount of data available today is staggering, with 90% of it generated in just the past five years.

EVERYDAY AI

How AI Often Goes Unnoticed

AI has woven itself so seamlessly into our everyday lives that, quite often, we do not even realize it is there. From the moment we wake up to the time we go to bed, AI is constantly at work behind the scenes, making our lives easier, more convenient, and more connected. Whether we are using a virtual assistant, streaming our favourite show, or even just browsing the internet, AI is present, subtly enhancing our experience.

One of the primary reasons AI often goes unnoticed is because it works in the background, handling tasks that we might take for granted. For instance, consider your smartphone's voice assistant, like Siri or Google Assistant, which can set reminders, play music, or answer questions. AI is what allows these virtual assistants to understand and respond to spoken language, converting natural speech into actionable commands. Similarly, the predictive text feature on messaging apps, which suggests the next word as you type, is driven by AI algorithms that learn your communication habits and adapt over time.

AI is also the force behind personalized recommendations on platforms like Netflix, YouTube, or Spotify. These services track your preferences and viewing habits, then use AI algorithms to suggest content that you are most likely to enjoy. This personalization helps make our interaction with media platforms feel intuitive and tailored, yet most of us seldom stop to think about the technology that makes it possible. The same goes for online shopping—AI curates product recommendations and tailors marketing efforts to each user, based on their search and purchasing history.

Many algorithms improve as you interact with them. Services like Netflix, Amazon, and Spotify seem to "understand" your preferences better over time because every interaction provides more data for their algorithms to analyse and learn from. For instance, Spotify might notice that you listen to a lot of jazz, but more specifically, you favour artists like Miles Davis. Instead of recommending generic jazz playlists, it could suggest similar artists like John Coltrane that probably align with your taste.

AI's role extends beyond entertainment and productivity tools. It is integrated into systems that keep us safe, like spam filters in our email accounts that identify and block unwanted messages. AI is also present in more invisible ways, such as in banking and finance, where machine learning models are used to detect fraudulent transactions in real time. By analysing vast amounts of transaction data and recognizing unusual patterns, these AI systems help protect users from identity theft and financial fraud—all without us even realizing the extent of its involvement.

Even seemingly mundane tasks are influenced by AI. When you use Google Maps to find the quickest route to your destination, AI processes real-time data on traffic conditions, road closures, and even construction work to ensure you get there as efficiently as possible. Self-driving technologies are also making their way into our transportation systems, employing AI to navigate roads, recognize obstacles, and keep passengers safe. Although fully autonomous vehicles are still a work in progress, the foundational AI technologies—such as advanced driver assistance systems that warn of potential collisions or help maintain safe distances—are already common in many modern cars.

The impact of AI is not limited to consumer-facing applications. It is also embedded within industries that touch our everyday lives, from healthcare to energy. In hospitals, AI helps doctors make better decisions by analysing medical images or predicting patient outcomes based on historical data. In the energy sector, AI contributes to the optimization of power distribution and smart grid management, improving efficiency and reducing waste. These applications make a significant difference, yet they operate in the background, largely unnoticed by the general public.

Imagine you have just ordered a book from Amazon. The process feels seamless—you click "Buy Now," and within hours, the package is at your doorstep. But behind the scenes, an intricate web of data and technology makes that speed and simplicity possible. On Amazon's end, the book you ordered is tied to a barcode, with details like its dimensions and exact location in the warehouse stored in a vast database. The moment your order is placed, a chain reaction begins: the system locates the item, dispatches a warehouse worker or robot to retrieve it, and sends it to be packaged. The package gets its own barcode, ensuring it can be tracked as it moves through the shipping process. A delivery service is assigned, shipping records are updated, and finally, you receive a confirmation message when the book arrives. This process involves a staggering amount of data—not just about the product and shipment but also the coordination between Amazon's database, warehouse systems, delivery services, and sometimes third-party merchants. For a single order, this data exchange spans multiple systems, each storing, processing, and transferring information in real time. To manage this complexity, Amazon relies on its own robust infrastructure, Amazon Web Services (AWS). AWS is not just Amazon's backbone; it is a cloud computing platform used by companies worldwide. By hosting data in the cloud, AWS allows businesses to store and access information from anywhere, eliminating the need for massive local servers.

AI's pervasive presence often remains unnoticed precisely because it is designed to blend in—to make our devices and services smarter, more responsive, and more efficient without demanding attention. The goal of AI is not to replace human interaction, but to augment our capabilities, providing us with tools that are intuitive and helpful. As AI continues to advance, it will only become more embedded in our lives, assisting us in ways that are often invisible yet incredibly impactful.

Chatbots And Voice Assistants

Chatbots and voice assistants have quickly become indispensable tools in our daily routines, simplifying tasks and providing assistance in ways that save us time and effort. They are not just cool gadgets or futuristic tech; these AI-powered systems are practical helpers, seamlessly integrating into our lives to provide information, reminders, and even companionship. From ordering groceries to setting an alarm, chatbots and voice assistants are making it easier for us to manage our day-to-day activities.

"Chatbots will be your new best friend." — *Christine Crandell*

Voice assistants like Siri, Google Assistant, and Amazon's Alexa are among the most recognizable examples of AI in action. These virtual assistants use natural language processing (NLP) to understand spoken language and carry out commands. Imagine starting your morning by asking your voice assistant about the weather, setting reminders for the day, and playing your favourite song—all without lifting a finger. It is this kind of convenience that makes voice assistants such a valuable addition to our daily routines. Beyond personal tasks, these assistants can control smart home devices, such as adjusting the thermostat, turning off lights, or even locking the door, thereby making our homes more efficient and secure.

Chatbots, on the other hand, are becoming increasingly common on websites and customer service platforms. These conversational agents provide immediate assistance, whether you are trying to track a package, troubleshoot an issue, or gather information about a product. Unlike traditional customer service, which often involves waiting on hold, chatbots are available 24/7, ensuring that you can get the help you need whenever you need it. Many businesses are leveraging chatbots to enhance customer experience, offering personalized support based on a user's previous interactions or purchase history. This not only improves customer satisfaction but also helps businesses operate more efficiently by automating repetitive queries and freeing up human representatives to deal with more complex issues.

Voice assistants and chatbots have also proven to be invaluable in accessibility and healthcare. For individuals with mobility impairments or visual disabilities, voice assistants can provide a sense of independence by allowing them to control their environment through spoken commands. In healthcare, voice assistants are being used to remind patients to take their medication, provide health tips, or even monitor symptoms that patients report verbally. Chatbots, too, are finding applications in healthcare, offering mental health support by engaging users in conversation, providing information on symptoms, or connecting patients with healthcare professionals.

"In a few years, artificial intelligence virtual assistants will be as common as the smartphone." — Dave Waters

---

One of the key advantages of chatbots and voice assistants is their ability to learn and adapt. The more you interact with these systems, the better they understand your preferences and anticipate your needs. For example, if you frequently ask your voice assistant to play music at a certain time of day, it can eventually prompt you with suggestions without you having to ask. This adaptability makes AI assistants highly personalized and efficient, turning them into indispensable helpers that grow more attuned to your habits over time.

Despite their convenience, it is important to note that these technologies also raise some concerns, particularly regarding privacy and data security. Voice assistants and chatbots collect vast amounts of data to function effectively and ensuring that this data is handled responsibly is crucial. Many companies are taking steps to improve transparency and give users more control over their data, but these concerns are worth keeping in mind when using these AI tools.

In conclusion, chatbots and voice assistants have become essential tools that simplify our daily lives by automating mundane tasks, offering quick access to information, and providing personalized assistance. Their ability to learn, adapt, and respond to natural language makes them incredibly powerful allies in navigating the complexity of our modern world. While challenges around privacy remain, the benefits they offer in terms of convenience and accessibility continue to make them an integral part of our everyday experience.

AI In Recommendation Systems

AI plays a significant role in shaping the way we consume content in our everyday lives, and one of the most impactful areas where this is evident is in recommendation systems. These systems have revolutionized the way we interact with platforms like Netflix, Spotify, Amazon, and YouTube, by offering us curated suggestions based on our tastes and preferences. AI recommendation systems work quietly behind the scenes, making sense of our behaviour to deliver personalized experiences that feel almost as if they "know" us.

"Personalization is the future of technology— and recommendation engines are the unsung heroes driving it forward." – Sundar Pichai

---

Platforms like Netflix use AI to recommend movies and TV shows based on what users have watched in the past. The idea is simple: the more you watch, the better Netflix becomes at predicting what you will enjoy next. But the underlying technology is anything but simple. Netflix uses sophisticated machine learning algorithms that analyse not only what content you watch but also how long you watch it, whether you binge entire seasons, and even the times of day you are most active. These algorithms then identify patterns and make recommendations based on similar user profiles, effectively narrowing down thousands of available titles to a handful that you are most likely to enjoy.

Similarly, Spotify utilizes AI to create custom playlists like Discover Weekly and Daily Mix that align with your music tastes. Spotify's recommendation engine uses a mix of collaborative filtering, NLP, and audio analysis to deliver a personalized listening experience. Collaborative filtering allows Spotify to identify users with similar musical preferences and recommend songs that others with comparable tastes have enjoyed. Additionally, NLP helps Spotify analyse blogs, articles, and reviews to understand more about artists, songs, and genres, while audio analysis examines the sound elements like tempo, key, and rhythm. These complex systems work together to ensure that every Monday, your Discover Weekly playlist feels almost magically aligned with your evolving music preferences.

Spotify's Discover Weekly playlist, powered by AI, has been streamed for over 2 billion hours since its launch in 2015.

One of the reasons these recommendation systems are so effective is because they are constantly learning and adapting. Every time you give a thumbs up or down, skip a track, or finish a series, the algorithms behind these platforms adjust and refine their understanding of your preferences. This adaptive learning process is what makes the recommendations feel increasingly accurate over time. YouTube, for example, learns not only from what you watch but also from how you engage with content —whether you like, comment, or share a video—to personalize your homepage and suggest videos that are likely to keep you watching.

YouTube's recommendation system drives over 70% of the total time users spend on the platform. This means the majority of videos people watch are not searched for but suggested by AI.

Beyond entertainment, AI recommendation systems are also used in e-commerce to suggest products you might be interested in purchasing. Amazon is a prime example, leveraging AI to recommend products based on your browsing history, what others have bought after viewing similar items, and even seasonal trends. This type of personalization has been shown to significantly boost sales, as users are more likely to purchase items that are relevant to their interests and needs.

However, while recommendation systems offer immense convenience and personalization, they also come with certain challenges. One concern is the creation of filter bubbles, where users are continually exposed to content that aligns with their existing tastes and viewpoints, potentially limiting exposure to diverse perspectives. For instance, if you consistently watch a particular genre of movies or listen to a specific type of music, the algorithms will keep recommending similar content, which could reduce the likelihood of discovering something entirely new or different. This can create an echo chamber effect, particularly on platforms like YouTube, where users may be fed more extreme or polarizing content based on their viewing habits.

Another issue is the amount of data collection required to make these recommendations effective. To provide accurate suggestions, platforms need to gather extensive data about user behaviour, which raises privacy concerns. Users are often unaware of the extent of data being collected or how it is being used. As these AI systems become more sophisticated, ensuring transparency, and giving users control over their data will be critical to maintaining trust.

Despite these challenges, the benefits of AI-powered recommendation systems are undeniable. They help us navigate the overwhelming amount of content available today, making our experiences more enjoyable and tailored to our individual preferences. Whether it is finding your next favourite TV series, discovering a new artist, or stumbling upon the perfect product, AI recommendation systems are quietly working to enhance our daily lives, ensuring that we spend less time searching and more time enjoying the things we love.

AI In Healthcare, Finance, And Entertainment

AI is transforming a wide range of industries, but its impact is particularly significant in healthcare, finance, and entertainment. These sectors have been at the forefront of integrating AI to improve efficiency, deliver personalized experiences, and solve complex challenges. From helping doctors diagnose diseases to predicting stock market trends and creating immersive entertainment, AI is reshaping how we experience and interact with these industries.

AI excels at identifying relevant patterns and analysing past cases. For example, a diagnostic system created by Tencent in partnership with a Guangzhou hospital uses over 300 million medical records to assess patients.

In healthcare, AI is revolutionizing the way medical professionals diagnose and treat illnesses. One of the key applications of AI in healthcare is in medical imaging. AI-powered systems, using machine learning and deep learning techniques, can analyse medical images such as X-rays, CT scans, and MRIs with remarkable accuracy. These systems are able to identify patterns that might be difficult for human doctors to detect, making it possible to diagnose conditions like cancer, heart disease, and neurological disorders at an earlier stage. Moreover, AI-driven predictive analytics is being used to assess a patient's risk of developing certain health conditions, enabling doctors to take preventive measures before problems become severe. Virtual health assistants, powered by NLP, are also becoming more common, providing users with instant information about symptoms, medication reminders, and even mental health support through conversational interfaces.

Researchers at the University of Toronto, using AI systems like AlphaFold to predict protein structures,

> *worked together to identify potential cancer treatment compounds. They pinpointed a promising candidate in just 30 days—a process that usually takes years.*

In the finance sector, AI is playing an increasingly crucial role in everything from fraud detection to personalized banking services. AI algorithms are used to analyse vast datasets in real time, identifying anomalies and potential fraudulent activities that might go unnoticed by human analysts. This is particularly vital given the rise of online transactions and digital banking, where security threats are constantly evolving. Additionally, AI is transforming investment management through robo-advisors, which offer automated, data-driven financial advice to individuals based on their financial goals and risk tolerance. These advisors use AI to make portfolio recommendations and adjustments, providing a more accessible and cost-effective solution for personal investing. Furthermore, AI-driven predictive analytics helps financial institutions evaluate credit risk, determine loan eligibility, and predict market trends, enabling more informed decision-making and reducing the risk of financial losses.

In the world of entertainment, AI has fundamentally changed how content is created, distributed, and consumed. As mentioned before, streaming services like Netflix and Spotify rely heavily on AI-powered recommendation systems to provide users with personalized content suggestions. These platforms use machine learning algorithms to analyse user behaviour, preferences, and viewing or listening habits, ensuring that users are presented with content they are likely to enjoy. AI is also being used in content creation, with generative AI tools that can produce music, scripts, and even visual art. For example, AI-generated music can help artists explore new creative directions, while AI-driven special effects in films are making it possible to create visually stunning experiences that were once unimaginable. In gaming, AI contributes to creating more dynamic and responsive non-player characters (NPCs), enhancing the realism and interactivity of video games. AI algorithms can analyse player behaviour and adapt the game environment, accordingly, offering a more personalized and immersive experience.

Despite these advancements, the integration of AI in these industries is not without its challenges. Privacy concerns are a significant issue, particularly in healthcare and finance, where sensitive personal data is involved. Ensuring that AI systems are transparent and ethical is crucial for maintaining public trust. In healthcare, while AI can assist in diagnosis, there are still concerns about over-reliance on AI without adequate human oversight, as well as potential biases in training data that could lead to unequal treatment outcomes. In finance, the use of AI in trading and investment has also raised concerns about the potential for market manipulation and the ethical implications of automated decision-making.

Overall, AI is dramatically transforming healthcare, finance, and entertainment by enhancing efficiency, accuracy, and personalization. As these technologies continue to evolve, they hold the promise of improving quality of life, making services more accessible, and providing richer, more immersive experiences. However, balancing innovation with ethical considerations and data privacy will be key to ensuring that the benefits of AI are fully realized in these industries.

PRODUCTIVITY GAIN OR JOB LOSS

How Automation Improves Efficiency

Automation is transforming industries by improving efficiency, reducing costs, and enhancing productivity. In the workplace, automation refers to the use of technologies like AI, robotics, and machine learning to perform tasks that were once handled by humans. By handling repetitive, labour-intensive, and mundane tasks, automation enables businesses to optimize their operations and allocate human resources to more strategic and creative activities.

In the early 19th century, 80% of U.S. workers were employed in agriculture. Today, that number has fallen to less than 2%, thanks to machines that handle key farming tasks like tending livestock and cultivating the land.

One of the most significant ways automation improves efficiency is through the streamlining of repetitive tasks. In many industries, employees spend hours performing tasks that require minimal decision-making but are essential to keep things running smoothly. For example, in manufacturing, robots have taken over assembly line tasks like welding, painting, and quality control, allowing products to be manufactured faster and with greater precision. This has significantly reduced production time and errors, leading to better quality products at lower costs. In offices, automation tools like Robotic Process Automation (RPA) are used to handle data entry, invoicing, and other routine processes. RPA is revolutionizing how organizations handle repetitive and manual tasks. Office workers spend countless hours on routine activities such as data entry and administrative processes, which often lack creativity or intuition and can lead to frustration and reduced productivity. By implementing RPA, companies can automate these mundane tasks, allowing employees to focus on more valuable activities like customer service, problem-solving, and strategic decision-making. Research by McKinsey suggests that a third of job activities in many professions could be fully automated, leading to significant efficiency gains. Adopting RPA not only boosts organizational efficiency but also enhances employee satisfaction, saving employees valuable time and minimizing human errors.

The human share of work task delivery in total firm output is expected to drop from 47% in 2025 to 33% in 2030. This is a reduction of about one third, mostly due to automation.
— World Economic Forum Future of Jobs Report 2025.

Automation also plays a crucial role in improving workflow management. AI-powered systems can monitor and analyse workflows in real time, identifying bottlenecks and suggesting optimizations. For instance, in supply chain management, automated systems can track shipments, predict delays, and reroute logistics to ensure timely delivery. AI algorithms are used to forecast demand, helping companies manage inventory efficiently and reduce waste. In customer service, chatbots provide immediate responses to customer inquiries, enhancing customer experience and freeing up human agents to deal with more complex issues that require empathy and nuanced understanding.

In knowledge-based industries like finance, healthcare, and law, automation improves efficiency by quickly processing vast amounts of information that would take humans much longer to analyse. In healthcare, for instance, AI-driven tools can sift through medical records, lab results, and other data to assist doctors in making faster and more accurate diagnoses. In finance, automation is used for algorithmic trading, analysing market data, and executing trades in milliseconds, something that would be impossible for human traders. By speeding up these processes, automation allows professionals to focus more on complex problem-solving and decision-making, rather than spending time on data collection and processing.

The Four S's of Automation Maturity by
Ghosh, Pallail, and Prasad:

Simple*: Begin by performing a thorough diagnostic of your IT and business infrastructure. Identify any gaps, inefficiencies, or areas for improvement. Focus on simplifying your applications and architecture to create functional, modular units that work seamlessly. The goal is to streamline your systems and ensure they are well-prepared for automation. This simplification lays the foundation for more robust and effective automation processes.*

Seamless*: Integration is key to successful automation. Ensure that your AI and automation technologies connect harmoniously with your core systems, enabling smooth operations. Equally important is fostering a company culture that supports and embraces these changes.*

Employees should feel energized and invested in the implementation of automation, seeing it as a tool that enhances their work rather than as a threat. Seamless integration means addressing both technical and cultural dimensions to create a unified and supportive environment.

***Scaled**: Once your automation systems are active, it is time to scale them thoughtfully. Test their agility, robustness, and sustainability under real-world conditions. Scaling should not happen all at once but through careful, incremental steps. Align the integration process with your business's strategy, culture, and goals to ensure long-term success. Additionally, focus on talent development. Just as your technology needs to evolve, your team must also adapt and grow. Provide training and resources to prepare your workforce to thrive in an increasingly automated environment.*

***Sustained**: Integration is not the end of the journey; sustaining your automation efforts is critical. Stay updated on industry developments and emerging trends to recognize new opportunities for growth and innovation. Observe how other businesses are adapting and integrating automation, and use these insights to refine your strategies. Equally important is fostering an open culture within your organization where employees feel comfortable sharing challenges and solutions related to automation. By thinking holistically and staying proactive, you can ensure your automation efforts remain effective and relevant over time.*

Moreover, automation fosters predictive maintenance in industries reliant on machinery, such as manufacturing and transportation. Through the use of IoT (Internet of Things) sensors and AI, machines can be monitored in real-time for signs of wear and tear. Predictive maintenance schedules repairs before a machine breaks down, reducing downtime and extending the lifespan of equipment. This proactive approach saves companies both time and money by avoiding unexpected disruptions in production.

In some U.S. towns, up to 30% of water is lost due to leaky pipes, but IoT sensors can detect these leaks instantly. These sensors are especially valuable in drought-prone regions like California, where their implementation in homes has shown a reduced water usage by 15% to 20%.

However, while automation undoubtedly enhances efficiency, it also presents challenges. One major concern is the impact on employment, as many fear that automation will lead to widespread job losses. While it is true that automation replaces certain tasks, it also creates opportunities for workers to engage in more value-added activities that require creativity, emotional intelligence, and complex decision-making. History shows that technological advances often lead to a shift in the types of jobs available rather than a complete elimination of employment opportunities. For instance, ATMs were initially feared as a threat to bank teller jobs, but they ultimately led to a shift where tellers took on advisory roles, enhancing the customer experience in banks.

A 2013 Oxford University study estimated that 47% of US jobs could be at risk from automation within 20 years. In contrast, the Organization for Economic Cooperation and Development (OECD) suggested only 9% of US jobs were at risk. A 2017 report by PriceWaterhouseCoopers (PWC) placed the figure at 38%, while McKinsey Global stated that roughly 50% of tasks worldwide are "already automatable." This wide range of estimates highlights why economists remain divided on the impact of automation.

Overall, automation is reshaping the workplace by improving efficiency, reducing errors, and allowing businesses to operate more effectively. By handling repetitive tasks and providing insights through data analysis, automation empowers workers to focus on innovation, creativity, and tasks that require a human touch, ultimately creating a more productive and dynamic work environment.

Jobs Most At Risk

As automation continues to advance, certain types of jobs are more vulnerable to being replaced by machines and artificial intelligence. These are typically jobs that involve repetitive tasks, predictable routines, and limited need for complex decision-making. The transformation brought by automation is expected to have a profound impact on the job market, with many jobs being automated out of existence while new types of work emerge.

Low-Skill and Routine Jobs are among those most at risk. This category includes roles in manufacturing, data entry, telemarketing, and warehouse operations. These jobs often involve simple, repetitive actions that can be performed more efficiently by machines. For instance, in manufacturing, robots have taken over assembly line jobs that require consistent precision and speed. Tasks such as packing goods in warehouses are increasingly being handled by automated systems like robotic arms and autonomous vehicles, which can work around the clock without fatigue. The use of Robotic Process Automation (RPA) has also significantly reduced the need for human workers in roles such as data entry and basic clerical tasks, as software bots are capable of processing and managing data far faster than people.

Economists suggest that technology is expanding opportunities at both ends of the skill spectrum, boosting low-skilled jobs like cleaners and high-skilled professions like engineers, while shrinking middle-class roles such as secretaries and salespeople. A theory proposed by three MIT economists explains this trend, arguing that "routine" tasks are easier to automate than "non-routine" work, which relies on creativity, judgment, interpersonal skills, or complex manual labour.

The service industry is also seeing significant impacts from automation. Jobs like cashiers, bank tellers, and customer service representatives are vulnerable due to the rise of self-service kiosks and chatbots. In retail, self-checkout systems have reduced the need for cashiers, while in banking, ATMs and mobile banking apps have diminished the demand for traditional bank tellers. Similarly, AI-powered chatbots are increasingly used to handle customer inquiries, reducing the reliance on human customer service agents. These technologies are able to provide instant responses to common questions and issues, allowing companies to cut costs while offering round-the-clock service.

Driving and Transportation Jobs are also among the most vulnerable to automation. The development of autonomous vehicles poses a threat to jobs such as truck drivers, taxi drivers, and delivery personnel. Companies like Tesla, Waymo, and Uber are investing heavily in self-driving technology, which has the potential to drastically reduce the need for human drivers. While fully autonomous driving is still being refined and faces regulatory hurdles, the trend toward automation in transportation is likely to continue, affecting millions of jobs in the coming decades.

Jobs in predictable physical environments are similarly at risk. For example, roles such as fast-food workers and cleaning staff are increasingly being targeted for automation. Robotic chefs are being developed to prepare simple dishes, and automated kiosks are allowing customers to place orders without interacting with a human employee. In the cleaning sector, robots like Roomba are already capable of performing basic cleaning tasks, and similar technologies are being adapted for larger-scale commercial cleaning.

Administrative and Clerical Jobs are not immune to automation either. Positions such as receptionists, bookkeepers, and payroll clerks are being replaced by AI-driven systems capable of managing appointments, processing payrolls, and maintaining records more efficiently than human workers. Advances in NLP (Natural Language Processing) have enabled virtual assistants to handle tasks like answering phone calls and scheduling meetings, which were once the domain of administrative assistants.

Even some roles in knowledge-based sectors are at risk due to automation. Jobs in accounting, legal research, and report generation are seeing increased automation through AI tools that can analyse large volumes of data and generate reports quickly. For example, AI-powered platforms are now capable of preparing tax filings, analysing legal documents, and drafting simple contracts, reducing the need for entry-level accountants and paralegals. The ability of AI to process and analyse data efficiently means that many tasks that were previously considered too complex for automation are now being performed by machines.

"AI is not going to replace managers, but managers who use AI will replace the managers who do not." – Rob Thomas.

However, it is important to note that while these jobs are at high risk of being automated, the future of work is not all bleak. Automation often leads to the creation of new types of jobs and opportunities. The roles most at risk are those that do not require creativity, critical thinking, emotional intelligence, or interpersonal skills—qualities that are uniquely human. As automation reshapes the workforce, there will be a greater emphasis on reskilling and upskilling workers to take on roles that involve managing technology, making strategic decisions, and applying human insight where machines fall short.

So as stated, the types of jobs most at risk due to automation are those that involve repetitive, predictable tasks that can be performed more quickly and cost-effectively by machines. While this shift presents challenges for workers in these roles, it also offers an opportunity for the workforce to evolve, adapt, and focus on areas where human skills and creativity remain irreplaceable.

Job Transformation vs. Job Elimination

The rapid advancement of AI and automation is significantly reshaping the world of work, raising fundamental questions about the future of employment. Will these technologies lead to widespread job elimination, leaving millions without work? Or will they transform existing jobs, creating new opportunities for people to work in ways that are more productive, creative, and fulfilling? The answer may lie somewhere in between, as AI has the potential to both eliminate certain types of jobs and transform others in profound ways. Understanding the dynamics of this transformation is crucial for workers, employers, and policymakers alike.

Have you ever visited a doctor who seemed more focused on typing into a computer than actually looking at you? Chances are, they were updating your electronic health record (EHR). While EHRs were originally designed to simplify clinicians' workflows, they have instead become a hurdle to effective doctor-patient communication. EHR is ripe for automation.

AI's impact on the workforce is not solely about taking away jobs. In many cases, AI is becoming an enabler, transforming roles, and making them more efficient by taking over repetitive, time-consuming tasks. For example (see also the next chapters), in industries like healthcare, AI can assist doctors by analysing medical images or providing diagnostic support, allowing medical professionals to focus on patient care and complex decision-making. In finance, AI algorithms can handle data processing and analysis, freeing financial analysts to concentrate on strategic planning and personalized client interactions.

This transformation means that many workers will need to adapt to new ways of working. Jobs are evolving, with an increasing emphasis on collaboration between humans and machines. Instead of replacing humans entirely, AI often augments human capabilities, helping workers make better decisions, be more productive, and focus on creative problem-solving. For instance, customer service roles are being enhanced by AI-powered chatbots that handle basic inquiries, allowing human representatives to address more nuanced and complex customer needs.

The Deloitte Shift Index reveals that 80% of people are dissatisfied with their jobs.

AI's transformative potential also lies in the creation of entirely new roles and industries. As technology evolves, it brings about new types of work that did not exist before—roles like AI trainers, data ethicists, and automation specialists. These new positions require different skill sets, such as data analysis, AI system maintenance, and ethical oversight. In this way, AI has the potential to create opportunities that lead to the emergence of new career paths, driving innovation across various industries.

It happened before. During the 19th century, the Industrial Revolution automated many jobs. A McKinsey study revealed that employment in the U.S. agricultural sector dropped from 60% to 5% between 1850 and 1970. While this initially caused unemployment, it also fostered new human-machine partnerships, as many farmers transitioned to work in the newly established mechanized factories.

However, it would be naive to ignore the threat of job elimination posed by AI and automation. The reality is that some jobs are at high risk of being fully automated, particularly those involving routine, repetitive tasks. Manufacturing, retail, and logistics are sectors that have already seen significant job losses due to automation. For example, self-checkout systems in retail and automated warehouses operated by robots are reducing the need for human labour in certain roles. Jobs that involve predictable physical work, such as assembly line work or data entry, are particularly vulnerable.

The potential for mass job elimination raises concerns about economic displacement and social inequality. Workers whose roles are automated may face significant challenges in finding new employment, especially if they lack the skills needed for the types of jobs that are being created. This has led to fears of a "bifurcated" labour market, where highly skilled workers thrive while those with outdated skills struggle to find their place in the new economy. Without proper support, this divide could widen, exacerbating existing inequalities and leading to social unrest.

"On average, workers can expect that two-fifths (39%) of their existing skill sets will be transformed or become outdated over the 2025-2030 period." — World Economic Forum Future of Jobs Report 2025.

The key to addressing the dual impact of AI on jobs lies in adaptation. To ensure that job transformation outweighs job elimination, there is a pressing need to invest in education, training, and reskilling. Governments, businesses, and educational institutions all have a role to play in providing opportunities for workers to learn new skills and transition into emerging fields. Lifelong learning and continuous skills development are becoming essential as the pace of technological change accelerates.

The World Economic Forum estimates that automation will create around 33 million new jobs a year.

Reskilling initiatives are already underway in various parts of the world. For example, several companies are investing in retraining their workforce to work alongside AI systems, teaching employees how to operate and maintain automated machinery or use AI tools effectively. Governments are also introducing programs aimed at helping displaced workers acquire skills in high-demand areas like programming, data science, and healthcare.

In addition to technical skills, there is an increasing emphasis on developing soft skills that are difficult for AI to replicate, such as creativity, emotional intelligence, and problem-solving abilities.

Jobs that require interpersonal skills and a deep understanding of human emotions—such as caregiving, counselling, and teaching—are less likely to be automated, making them more resilient to technological disruption. By focusing on these uniquely human capabilities, workers can improve their employability in an AI-driven economy.

"Generative AI could empower less specialized employees to perform a greater range of "expert" tasks … [and] create genuine shifts in the quantity or quality of output … if technology development is focused on enhancing rather than substituting for human capabilities." — World Economic Forum Future of Jobs Report 2025.

To navigate the challenges of job elimination, proactive policy measures will be critical. Social safety nets such as unemployment benefits, retraining grants, and, potentially, Universal Basic Income (UBI) will be essential to support workers affected by automation. UBI, in particular, has gained attention as a potential solution to provide financial stability to those whose jobs have been displaced by AI, allowing them to focus on retraining or exploring other opportunities.

Governments must also consider policies that encourage businesses to create jobs that are less susceptible to automation. This could involve offering incentives for companies that invest in human-centred roles or those that prioritize augmenting human work with AI rather than fully replacing it. Collaboration between public and private sectors will be essential to create a balanced approach that maximizes the benefits of AI while minimizing its disruptive impact on the workforce.

Ultimately, the impact of AI on jobs is not a simple matter of elimination versus transformation—it is about reimagining our relationship with work. As AI takes over many routine and mundane tasks, people may find themselves with more time to focus on work that is meaningful, creative, and fulfilling. This shift presents an opportunity to rethink the role of work in our lives, moving away from a narrow focus on productivity and economic output towards a broader understanding of well-being and personal growth.

In conclusion, AI and automation are driving a fundamental shift in the nature of work, with the potential for both job transformation and job elimination. While some jobs will undoubtedly be lost, many others will be transformed or newly created, leading to opportunities for those who are prepared to adapt. By investing in reskilling, supporting displaced workers, and embracing new ways of thinking about work, we can ensure that the future of employment is one where technology serves humanity, rather than the other way around.

Emerging AI-Driven Careers

The rise of AI is not just transforming existing jobs or leading to the automation of tasks; it is also creating entirely new career opportunities. As AI continues to advance, new roles are emerging across various industries, providing exciting opportunities for workers to be at the forefront of technological innovation. These AI-driven careers are reshaping the job market, demanding a different set of skills and offering promising pathways for those prepared to embrace change. Understanding these emerging careers is essential for individuals, businesses, and educators as they navigate the evolving employment landscape.

LinkedIn reports a 74% annual growth in machine learning-related roles.

One of the most obvious emerging career paths is that of AI

specialists and machine learning engineers. These professionals design, develop, and implement AI systems, creating algorithms that allow machines to learn from data and perform complex tasks. Machine learning engineers work to train models to recognize patterns, make predictions, and improve over time. As AI becomes more integrated into businesses, the demand for skilled engineers who can build and maintain these systems is skyrocketing.

The role of AI specialists is not limited to just building algorithms. They also need to understand the ethical implications of AI, ensuring that the systems they create are fair, transparent, and free of bias. This focus on responsible AI development means that those entering this field must possess a mix of technical skills, creativity, and a strong understanding of ethical considerations.

AI systems are powered by data, and the need to make sense of vast quantities of information has led to the rise of data scientists and AI data analysts. These professionals are responsible for collecting, cleaning, analysing, and interpreting data to extract valuable insights that can inform decision-making and optimize AI models. Data scientists use statistical methods, machine learning, and data visualization tools to understand patterns within data and provide actionable insights.

86% of employers expect AI to transform their business by 2030. — World Economic Forum Future of Jobs Report 2025.

As AI becomes more pervasive, data analysts are also playing a critical role in training AI models by labelling datasets and ensuring the quality of the data being fed into AI systems. This work is crucial, as the accuracy and reliability of AI outputs depend heavily on the quality of the input data. Data scientists and analysts, therefore, are at the heart of AI development, helping to ensure that AI technologies are built on robust, meaningful information.

With the increasing prevalence of AI-powered chatbots and virtual assistants, a new career path has emerged: AI trainers and conversational designers. AI trainers are responsible for teaching AI systems how to interact effectively with humans. They do this by providing examples of appropriate responses, correcting errors, and continuously updating the AI's knowledge base to improve its performance.

"Artificial Intelligence will drive not only innovation but also the future of work. Those who shape AI will shape the world." – Satya Nadella

Conversational designers, on the other hand, craft the user experience for AI-driven interfaces like chatbots and voice assistants. They combine knowledge of linguistics, psychology, and user experience design to create natural and engaging interactions between AI and users. As more companies turn to AI to improve customer service and engagement, the need for skilled conversational designers is growing.

As AI systems become more powerful and are increasingly deployed in critical areas such as healthcare, finance, and law enforcement, ethical considerations are becoming paramount. This has led to the rise of AI ethicists and policy advisors. These professionals are tasked with ensuring that AI technologies are used responsibly, without perpetuating biases or causing harm.

AI ethicists work closely with developers, policymakers, and other stakeholders to establish guidelines for ethical AI use, addressing issues such as data privacy, bias, and transparency. Policy advisors in this field help governments and organizations navigate the complex legal and regulatory landscape associated with AI. They play a critical role in shaping the policies that govern AI deployment, ensuring that technological progress aligns with societal values and norms.

AI is also driving the growth of robotics engineering, with robots increasingly being used in industries like manufacturing, healthcare, and logistics. Robotics engineers work on designing and developing robots that can work autonomously or in collaboration with humans. These engineers are at the cutting edge of innovation, combining AI with mechanical and electrical engineering to create machines capable of performing complex tasks.

Another emerging role is that of the AI integration specialist, who ensures that AI technologies are effectively integrated into existing systems and workflows. These specialists bridge the gap between AI developers and end-users, helping organizations implement AI solutions in ways that are seamless and beneficial. They must understand both the technical aspects of AI and the specific needs of the industries they serve, making their role essential for successful AI adoption.

The convergence of AI with other advanced technologies, such as virtual reality (VR) and augmented reality (AR), is creating new career opportunities as well. VR and AR specialists use AI to enhance immersive experiences, applying these technologies in fields like education, entertainment, healthcare, and training. AI helps create more realistic simulations and can adapt content in real-time based on user interactions, making these fields exciting areas for those interested in the intersection of creativity and technology.

"AI is not about replacing us, but making us better versions of ourselves." — *Rana el Kaliouby.*

AI is revolutionizing healthcare, leading to the creation of new roles such as AI healthcare specialists and clinical informaticists. AI healthcare specialists work on developing AI tools that assist doctors in diagnosing diseases, planning treatments, and managing patient care. They collaborate with healthcare providers to ensure that AI technologies are tailored to meet medical needs and improve patient outcomes.

Clinical informaticists work at the intersection of healthcare, data, and AI, focusing on managing health information and integrating AI into clinical practice. They ensure that data collected from patients is used effectively to enhance care delivery, improve diagnostics, and provide personalized treatment options. These roles highlight how AI is enabling more efficient and effective healthcare services, ultimately improving patient care.

As these AI-driven careers continue to emerge, it is essential for individuals to invest in upskilling to stay relevant in the changing job market. Skills in data science, machine learning, AI programming, and data ethics are becoming increasingly valuable. Many educational institutions and online platforms now offer courses and certifications in AI-related fields, making it more accessible for people to gain the skills needed to pursue these new opportunities.

In addition to technical skills, there is also a growing emphasis on soft skills such as creativity, adaptability, and communication. Many of these emerging AI-driven careers require individuals to work collaboratively across disciplines, communicate complex ideas to non-technical stakeholders, and think critically about the broader implications of AI technologies.

Creativity is playing an increasingly vital role in the workplace. A 2012 survey across five countries, conducted by research firm StrategyOne, revealed that 80% of respondents view creativity as crucial for economic growth. Similarly,

> *the World Economic Forum's 2025 "Future of Jobs" report ranked creativity as the fourth most valuable human skill, a significant leap from its position nine places lower in 2015.*

The rise of AI-driven careers is reshaping the employment landscape, offering new opportunities for growth, creativity, and impact. As AI continues to advance, it will open doors to new possibilities, creating roles that blend technology with human ingenuity. For individuals willing to adapt and upskill, the future holds exciting prospects in fields that are driving innovation and changing the way we live and work.

By understanding and preparing for these emerging careers, we can ensure that the benefits of AI are harnessed to create a more dynamic, inclusive, and prosperous future for everyone.

Preparing The Workforce For The Future

As automation reshapes industries and transforms the job market, the need for reskilling and preparing the workforce for the future has never been more critical. To ensure that workers are not left behind by technological advancements, it is essential to invest in education, training, and skill development that will equip them with the capabilities needed to thrive in an evolving economy.

> *"Employers [have] … a growing focus on continuous learning, upskilling and reskilling programmes." — World Economic Forum Future of Jobs Report 2025.*

Reskilling refers to training individuals in new skills that allow them to transition to different roles, particularly those less vulnerable to automation. As repetitive and routine tasks are increasingly taken over by machines, workers need to acquire skills that are uniquely human—such as critical thinking, problem-solving, creativity, and emotional intelligence. These skills are difficult to automate and are highly valuable in roles that require adaptability and human insight. For example, workers in manufacturing who may lose their jobs to automated machinery can be retrained in areas like machine maintenance, robotics, or quality control, where human intervention is still crucial.

When Shell decided to introduce intelligent, head-mounted displays for their miners, they prioritized explaining the practical benefits over highlighting the advanced technology behind them. Mining is inherently dangerous work, and real-time assistance can be lifesaving. To illustrate the value, Shell's leadership described how a miner could use the voice-controlled device to send an image of a technical issue and receive immediate guidance. This focus on safety and practicality resonated with workers, ensuring the new AI technology was welcomed without much need for persuasion.

Upskilling, on the other hand, focuses on enhancing existing skills to help workers adapt to changes within their current roles. For example, administrative assistants can learn how to use AI-powered productivity tools to improve their efficiency and take on more complex responsibilities that cannot be automated. The goal of upskilling is to help workers remain competitive in their current jobs by staying ahead of technological changes and being able to leverage new tools effectively.

Throughout history, working with tools has always improved our lives

---

To facilitate reskilling and upskilling efforts, governments, educational institutions, and businesses all have roles to play. Governments can invest in public education programs that provide training in high-demand skills, such as coding, data analysis, and project management. They can also offer incentives for companies that prioritize workforce development. Educational institutions, including universities and technical schools, can work closely with industries to develop programs that align with the changing demands of the job market, ensuring that graduates are prepared for the jobs of the future.

"AI has the potential to create new industries and new jobs, but it's important that we address the challenges it presents, including the potential for job displacement and the need for upskilling." – Angela Merkel

---

Businesses, too, have a responsibility to support their employees through this transition. Many companies are already implementing in-house training programs and partnering with online learning platforms to provide their workers with opportunities to acquire new skills. For example, Amazon launched a program called Amazon Upskilling 2025, aimed at providing training for employees to help them transition into higher-skilled roles within the company. Such initiatives are crucial for ensuring that workers have access to opportunities to learn and grow, even as their roles evolve.

"AI and big data top the list as the fastest-growing skills."
— World Economic Forum Future of Jobs Report 2025.

The shift toward automation also underscores the importance

of cultivating a mindset of lifelong learning. In an era of rapid technological change, workers can no longer rely on a static set of skills acquired at the beginning of their careers. Instead, they must be proactive in continuously updating their knowledge and seeking out opportunities for professional development. Online learning platforms like Coursera, Udemy, and edX offer flexible options for individuals to learn new skills at their own pace, allowing them to stay competitive in the job market.

Moreover, soft skills—such as communication, adaptability, empathy, and teamwork—will become increasingly important in the future workplace. These skills are essential for roles that involve managing people, providing customer service, or working in creative fields. While automation can handle routine tasks, it is human interaction, emotional intelligence, and the ability to understand complex social dynamics that will set workers apart. Training programs that focus on soft skills, in addition to technical competencies, will be vital for preparing a well-rounded workforce capable of thriving in a more automated world.

The automation of business process has three phases. The first involves identifying areas across your business applications where automation can be implemented. The second phase centres on creating, launching, and expanding these automation solutions. Lastly, the third phase focuses on measuring the realized value, and refining automation strategies based on the insights gathered.

Ultimately, preparing the workforce for the future is a collective effort that requires collaboration between governments, educational institutions, businesses, and individuals. By investing in reskilling and upskilling initiatives, we can help workers transition to new roles, ensure economic stability, and enable people to continue contributing meaningfully in a rapidly changing world. Automation will undoubtedly reshape the job market, but with the right strategies in place, we can harness its potential to create new opportunities and build a more resilient workforce.

Lifelong Learning

The rapid rise of AI is transforming industries and redefining the nature of work. As AI and automation become more pervasive, the skills required to succeed in the job market are constantly evolving. In this dynamic environment, lifelong learning is not just a luxury or an aspiration; it is an essential practice for individuals seeking to remain relevant and adaptable. The importance of lifelong learning in an AI-driven era cannot be overstated, as it provides the foundation for continuous growth, resilience, and success in the face of technological disruption.

AI and automation are accelerating the pace of technological change, creating new opportunities and challenges for workers. Jobs that were once secure are being transformed or eliminated, while entirely new roles are emerging. To navigate this evolving landscape, individuals must be willing to continuously update their skills. Lifelong learning is crucial for adapting to these changes, enabling workers to transition into new roles and stay ahead of industry shifts.

One of the key benefits of lifelong learning is that it helps individuals stay adaptable. In an AI-driven world, technological advances can render certain skills obsolete almost overnight. By embracing a mindset of lifelong learning, individuals are better prepared to acquire new competencies and pivot into emerging career opportunities. This adaptability is particularly important for workers in industries undergoing significant disruption, such as manufacturing, retail, and customer service, where automation is reshaping traditional roles.

AI may be highly efficient at performing repetitive tasks and analysing vast datasets, but there are still many areas where human skills are irreplaceable. The rise of AI has led to a renewed emphasis on uniquely human qualities such as creativity, emotional intelligence, critical thinking, and interpersonal skills. These skills are difficult for AI to replicate and are essential for roles that require empathy, nuanced decision-making, and strategic thinking.

How do you feel about automation? Start by writing down a list of the various aspects of your job. Next, highlight each task that drains your energy and feels like a chore. Now, imagine how you would feel if all these highlighted tasks were automated. By alleviating the least enjoyable parts of your work, automation becomes a much more appealing proposition.

Lifelong learning provides a pathway for individuals to develop and strengthen these complementary human skills. For example, while AI can assist in data analysis, it cannot replace the human capacity to think critically about the implications of that data or to make ethical decisions based on a nuanced understanding of context. By focusing on developing these distinctly human abilities, individuals can enhance their employability and contribute meaningfully to AI-driven workplaces.

As AI creates new job opportunities, it also leads to a growing skills gap in the workforce. Many of the emerging AI-driven careers require specialized knowledge in areas such as data science, machine learning, and AI programming. However, the rapid pace of technological change often means that traditional education systems struggle to keep up with industry needs. Lifelong learning plays a crucial role in bridging this gap by enabling workers to acquire new skills and qualifications outside of formal education.

"Skill gaps are categorically considered the biggest barrier to business transformation over the 2025-2030 period."
— World Economic Forum Future of Jobs Report 2025.

Online learning platforms, workshops, and professional development courses have become valuable resources for individuals looking to upskill or reskill in response to technological advancements. These flexible learning options make it possible for workers to gain the knowledge they need to enter new fields or adapt to changes in their current roles. By participating in lifelong learning, individuals can ensure they remain competitive in the job market and take advantage of the opportunities created by AI.

The importance of lifelong learning in an AI era extends beyond individual benefits; it also has significant implications for businesses and society as a whole. Organizations that encourage a culture of lifelong learning are better positioned to innovate and adapt to changing market conditions. By investing in employee development, companies can build a more resilient workforce that is capable of leveraging new technologies and driving continuous improvement.

Fostering a culture of curiosity and growth also helps to empower workers, giving them a sense of ownership over their career development. When employees are encouraged to explore new ideas, learn new skills, and take on new challenges, they are more likely to feel engaged and motivated. This not only benefits individual workers but also contributes to a more dynamic and innovative work environment.

Governments, educational institutions, and businesses all have a role to play in promoting lifelong learning. Policymakers can support lifelong learning by investing in accessible education and training programs, particularly for workers whose jobs are at risk of automation. This may include funding for vocational training, online learning platforms, or initiatives that encourage workers to pursue careers in high-demand fields such as healthcare, technology, and renewable energy.

Educational institutions also need to evolve to meet the demands of an AI-driven economy. This means developing curricula that emphasize not only technical skills but also the soft skills that are essential for success in a rapidly changing job market. Partnerships between educational institutions and industry can help ensure that training programs are aligned with current and future workforce needs.

Businesses, too, have an important role in fostering lifelong learning. Companies can invest in their employees by offering opportunities for professional development, providing access to online learning resources, and creating pathways for career advancement. By supporting lifelong learning, businesses can build a more agile and capable workforce that is prepared to thrive in an AI-driven world.

The era of AI presents both challenges and opportunities, and lifelong learning is the key to making the most of this new reality. By embracing lifelong learning, individuals can remain relevant, adapt to change, and take advantage of the exciting new careers that AI is making possible. At the same time, businesses and governments can create environments that support continuous growth and development, ensuring that society as a whole benefits from the transformative power of AI.

A study by the OECD, based on World Economic Forum research, predicts that emotional intelligence will rank among the top ten skills employers seek in new hires. Leading the list are complex problem-solving, critical thinking, and creativity—all inherently human abilities.

As seen, lifelong learning is essential in an AI-driven era. It empowers individuals to adapt to rapid technological change, develop complementary human skills, bridge the skills gap, and foster a culture of curiosity and growth. By investing in lifelong learning, we can build a future where technology enhances human potential, creating opportunities for meaningful work and continuous personal development.

TRANSFORMING INDUSTRIES

In the early 20th century, Henry Ford set out to make cars accessible to the masses. At the time, building a single car took a team of workers 12 hours—far too slow for large-scale production. Everything changed in 1913 when Ford introduced the assembly line. With this innovation, each worker focused on installing just one part before passing the car along to the next station. This approach reduced assembly time to just 2 hours and 30 minutes.

Robots On The Assembly Line

The manufacturing industry is undergoing a massive transformation, largely driven by the integration of AI and robotics. These technologies are reshaping how products are made, from the factory floor to the entire supply chain. With AI-powered robots taking over tasks on the assembly line, manufacturers are witnessing unprecedented levels of efficiency, productivity, and precision. This shift represents a fundamental change in how goods are produced, signalling the arrival of what many are calling the fourth Industrial revolution.

American economist Robert Gordon identifies four distinct industrial revolutions. The first began in late 18th-century Britain with the advent of steam engines and railroads, driving technological, social, and political transformation. The second, in the late 19th century, introduced electricity, combustion engines, and telephones. The third arrived in the 1960s with the invention of computers. Today, advancements in robotics and AI signal the dawn of a fourth industrial revolution.

AI-driven robots are increasingly present in factories, handling tasks that require speed, precision, and consistency. Unlike human workers, robots can operate 24/7, significantly increasing production capacity while minimizing the errors associated with fatigue or human oversight. For example, robots on automotive assembly lines weld car parts together with incredible accuracy and repeatability. They can also handle repetitive tasks like painting, part assembly, and quality inspection, all of which benefit from automation's capability to maintain uniform quality and efficiency.

In 2023, global average robot density reached 162 units per 10,000 employees, double the number measured seven years ago.

It is often misunderstood that robots "work for free." In truth, the cost of building, developing, and maintaining robots and AI is substantial, with the added challenge of potential obsolescence. A large industrial robot typically costs about $100,000 to acquire, and its maintenance over time can quintuple that expense. Consequently, human labour may remain the more economical option for certain use cases but where it is economical, robots will be used to replace human labour.

At Changying Precision Technology in Dongguan, a cell phone manufacturing company, 60 robots now perform tasks that once required 600 employees, reducing errors from 25% to 5% and more than doubling production output.

Collaborative robots, or cobots, represent another innovation transforming the assembly line. Unlike traditional robots, which typically operate in isolation due to safety concerns, cobots are designed to work alongside human workers. These machines are equipped with sophisticated sensors and AI algorithms that allow them to detect and respond to their environment. This collaborative approach enhances productivity by combining the strengths of robots—such as tireless repetition and accuracy—with the creativity, problem-solving ability, and flexibility of human workers. Cobots assist with heavy lifting, repetitive tasks, and hazardous duties, allowing human workers to focus on more strategic and creative aspects of manufacturing.

In factories worldwide almost five million large industrial robots are operational. This number has an annual growth rate of about 10%.

The use of AI in manufacturing is also transforming quality control processes. Traditional quality inspections often require manual labour, making them prone to inconsistencies and human error. AI-powered visual inspection systems, however, can detect even the most subtle defects with far greater accuracy. By using machine learning algorithms to analyse images of products, these systems can identify flaws in real-time, ensuring that defective items are removed from the production line before they make it to market. This not only improves product quality but also helps reduce waste, as issues are caught and corrected earlier in the process.

In 2000, global per capita GDP was over 30 times higher than in 1800—a testament to gradual yet transformative progress after the industrial revolutions 1, 2 and the start of 3. Likewise, the AI revolution may unfold as a process rather than a dramatic event, ultimately driving productivity, economic growth, and long-term prosperity for all.

Predictive maintenance is another key area where AI is making a substantial impact. In traditional manufacturing environments, machine breakdowns can lead to costly delays and downtime. AI-powered systems can predict when a piece of equipment is likely to fail by analysing data from sensors embedded in the machinery. This allows manufacturers to perform maintenance proactively before a breakdown occurs, minimizing disruptions to the production process. Predictive maintenance not only extends the lifespan of machinery but also helps companies save on repair costs and avoid unexpected downtime, thus improving overall operational efficiency.

Moreover, the implementation of AI in manufacturing is driving the rise of smart factories. In a smart factory, machines, systems, and humans are interconnected through the Internet of Things (IoT), enabling real-time data exchange and automated decision-making. This level of connectivity allows manufacturers to optimize their operations continuously, from inventory management to supply chain logistics. For instance, AI can predict supply chain disruptions, recommend alternative suppliers, and even adjust production schedules to minimize delays. By using AI to harness real-time data, manufacturers can create agile production systems capable of adapting quickly to changing market demands.

The paperclip problem, introduced by Nick Bostrom, introduces a hypothetical AI tasked with running a paperclip factory. As the AI becomes increasingly efficient, it eventually concludes that the optimal way to maximize paperclip production is to seize control from humanity and transform the entire world into paperclips. While deliberately exaggerated, this scenario underscores the potential dangers of AI becoming overly effective at pursuing the objectives it is programmed to achieve.

While AI and robotics are revolutionizing manufacturing, they are also changing the workforce dynamics within the industry. The demand for manual labour in repetitive assembly line jobs is decreasing, while there is a growing need for workers skilled in robotics, AI programming, and machine maintenance. As manufacturing processes become more automated, the role of human workers is shifting from performing routine tasks to overseeing and managing automated systems. This means that reskilling and upskilling are essential for ensuring that workers can transition into new roles and thrive in the evolving manufacturing landscape.

"I think what makes AI different from other technologies is that it's going to bring humans and machines closer together. AI is sometimes incorrectly framed as machines replacing humans. It's not about machines replacing humans but machines augmenting humans. Humans and machines have different relative strengths and weaknesses, and it's about the combination of these two that will allow human intents and business processes to scale 10x, 100x,

and beyond that in the coming years." – Robin Bordoli.

As AI and robotics are transforming manufacturing, production lines become more efficient, precise, and adaptable. Autonomous robots could handle repetitive tasks by which the factories of the future would need less manual labour. At the same time, opportunities will develop for workers to move into higher-skilled roles that focus on managing and optimizing advanced technologies. The rise of AI in manufacturing is not about replacing human labour; it is about creating a more efficient, resilient, and innovative production ecosystem.

The McKinsey Institute estimates that in wealthier nations, only 14% of jobs are 'highly automatable' and just 5% are 'entirely automatable.' While this does not justify fears of mass unemployment, it still means that by 2030, robots could render up to 700 million jobs redundant.

Autonomous Vehicles

The concept of autonomous vehicles, also known as self-driving cars, has captivated the imaginations of engineers, entrepreneurs, and the public for decades. At its core, the technology behind these vehicles is a sophisticated blend of AI, machine learning, sensor technology, and advanced computing systems. Each of these components works in tandem to enable vehicles to navigate complex environments, make real-time decisions, and move safely without human intervention.

The DARPA Grand Challenge, a prestigious self-driving car competition in the U.S., showcased the early challenges of autonomous vehicles. In 2004, the winner, Sandstorm—a modified Humvee—managed only

*seven miles before getting stuck on a rock. Fast forward
to today, and Google's self-driving cars, designed for
Lexus and Chrysler, have already logged over a million
miles on California roads without any major setbacks,
demonstrating remarkable progress in the field.*

One of the foundational elements of autonomous vehicles is the use of sensor technology. Autonomous vehicles rely on a combination of lidar, radar, cameras, and ultrasonic sensors to perceive their surroundings. Lidar (Light Detection and Ranging) uses laser beams to create a three-dimensional map of the environment, allowing the vehicle to detect obstacles, other vehicles, and pedestrians. Radar helps measure the speed and distance of objects, while cameras provide visual information that helps the vehicle interpret traffic signals, lane markings, and road signs. Ultrasonic sensors are used for close-range detection, such as when parking or manoeuvring in tight spaces.

The data collected from these sensors is processed using machine learning algorithms that allow the vehicle to make informed decisions in real time. These algorithms are trained on vast datasets of driving scenarios to help the vehicle recognize patterns and predict the actions of other road users. For instance, if a pedestrian suddenly steps into the road, the vehicle's machine learning system can predict the likely trajectory of the pedestrian and take evasive action.

Another critical component of autonomous vehicles is the decision-making system, often powered by deep learning and neural networks. These systems are designed to analyse the data from sensors, make sense of the environment, and determine the optimal path forward. The decision-making process involves both path planning and control systems that manage the vehicle's speed, steering, and braking. The ability to adapt to changing road conditions—such as sudden lane changes or adverse weather—is what makes autonomous vehicles so complex and challenging to perfect.

High-definition mapping and GPS technology also play a vital role in enabling autonomous vehicles to navigate. These maps provide detailed information about road networks, including lane configurations, speed limits, and traffic signals. Autonomous vehicles use this information in combination with real-time sensor data to localize themselves accurately on the road and make informed decisions about navigation.

Despite significant advancements, creating a fully autonomous vehicle that can handle all possible driving conditions remains a challenging task. Factors such as unpredictable human behaviour, weather variations, and unmapped roads are all variables that make the development of autonomous technology a formidable challenge. Nonetheless, continuous improvements in AI, sensor accuracy, and computational power are bringing us closer to a future where self-driving vehicles are a common sight on our roads.

While the technology behind autonomous vehicles is advancing rapidly, there are significant regulatory and safety challenges that need to be addressed before they can be widely adopted. One of the primary concerns is ensuring the safety of these vehicles in real-world conditions. Given that autonomous vehicles operate without human intervention, they must be able to handle unexpected situations and make split-second decisions that prioritize safety. This raises questions about how to certify and validate autonomous systems to ensure they meet stringent safety standards.

Every year, 1.2 million people lose their lives in road traffic crashes worldwide, with human error causing 90% of crashes.

Regulatory frameworks for autonomous vehicles are still in

their infancy, with many countries grappling with how to create laws that govern their use. One of the biggest challenges for regulators is defining the level of responsibility in the event of an accident involving an autonomous vehicle. Liability is a major concern: if an autonomous vehicle is involved in a collision, who is at fault? Is it the manufacturer, the software developer, or the owner of the vehicle? Answering these questions requires new legal definitions and frameworks that account for the unique nature of autonomous systems.

Public trust is another important factor in the widespread adoption of autonomous vehicles. People need to feel confident that these vehicles are safe and reliable. To build trust, manufacturers must conduct extensive testing, not only in controlled environments but also on public roads. Transparency in testing and sharing safety data with regulators and the public can help bridge the gap between technological capability and consumer confidence.

"AI will transform every industry, and it's critical that we all understand how it works and how to use it responsibly." – Andrew Ng

---

Moreover, there is a need to consider the ethical implications of autonomous decision-making. For instance, in a situation where an accident is unavoidable, how should an autonomous vehicle decide between two harmful outcomes? These ethical dilemmas require input from a diverse range of stakeholders, including ethicists, technologists, policymakers, and the general public, to ensure that autonomous systems operate in a manner consistent with societal values.

Another regulatory challenge involves infrastructure. To fully realize the potential of autonomous vehicles, road infrastructure may need to be adapted. This could include the development of smart roads that can communicate with vehicles, dedicated lanes for autonomous cars, or improved signage that can be easily interpreted by both human drivers and AI systems. Governments and city planners must work closely with the private sector to create infrastructure that supports the safe and efficient operation of autonomous vehicles.

Transportation And Delivery

The widespread adoption of autonomous vehicles has the potential to significantly transform transportation and delivery systems, affecting not only how people travel but also how goods are moved. One of the most promising impacts of autonomous vehicles is the potential to improve road safety. Human error is a major cause of traffic accidents, and autonomous vehicles, with their ability to constantly monitor the environment and react faster than human drivers, could dramatically reduce the number of accidents on the road.

Autonomous vehicles are also poised to bring about a major shift in public transportation. Autonomous shuttles and buses could provide on-demand transportation services, making it easier for people to travel within cities without the need for personal vehicles. This could lead to a reduction in traffic congestion and pollution, as fewer people may need to own cars, opting instead for convenient and affordable autonomous ride-sharing services. In addition, autonomous vehicles can optimize their driving patterns to reduce fuel consumption and emissions, contributing to a more sustainable transportation system.

The impact of autonomous vehicles on the delivery and logistics industry is equally profound. Autonomous trucks have the potential to revolutionize long-haul trucking, making it more efficient and cost-effective. By operating continuously without the need for rest breaks, autonomous trucks can significantly reduce delivery times and costs. This could have a ripple effect throughout the economy, as faster and cheaper shipping translates to reduced costs for businesses and consumers.

In urban areas, last-mile delivery could be transformed by autonomous vehicles and drones. Autonomous delivery robots are already being tested in several cities to deliver groceries, food, and other items directly to consumers. These small, self-driving units can navigate sidewalks and streets to bring goods right to a customer's doorstep, offering a glimpse into a future where deliveries are faster, cheaper, and more convenient than ever before. Drones, on the other hand, have the potential to bypass traffic altogether, providing rapid delivery for small packages and essential goods, especially in areas that are difficult to reach by road.

In Rwanda and Ghana, medical drones operated by Zipline have already delivered over 1 million doses of vaccines and critical medicines to remote areas.

The economic implications of autonomous vehicles are also significant. The reduction in labour costs for transportation and delivery services could lead to lower prices for consumers, while also reshaping the job market. While there are concerns about job displacement, new opportunities will emerge in fields related to autonomous vehicle maintenance, software development, and traffic management for these systems. The key to mitigating the negative impact on employment will be investing in reskilling programs that help workers transition to new roles in an AI-driven economy.

Autonomous vehicles also have the potential to change how cities are designed. With fewer people owning personal vehicles, the demand for parking spaces could decrease, freeing up valuable urban real estate for other uses, such as parks or housing. Traffic flow could also be improved, as autonomous vehicles communicate with each other to optimize routes and reduce congestion. This could lead to more efficient use of road space and a more pleasant urban environment.

If autonomous ride-sharing becomes widespread,
urban areas could reclaim the 30% of city
space currently dedicated to parking.

Overall, the rise of autonomous vehicles promises to reshape transportation and delivery in profound ways, improving safety, efficiency, and sustainability. However, realizing this potential will require addressing significant technological, regulatory, and societal challenges. By working together, governments, businesses, and communities can harness the benefits of autonomous technology to create a safer, more efficient, and connected world.

AI In Financial Services

The financial services industry is at the forefront of adopting AI to enhance risk management, improve decision-making, and offer personalized services to customers. With the ability to analyse massive datasets in real-time, AI is transforming the way financial institutions assess risks and make predictions, ultimately improving both efficiency and security. By integrating AI into risk management and predictive analysis, financial firms are becoming more resilient, agile, and better equipped to navigate a complex financial landscape.

Filing taxes is a task few enjoy, especially as regulations grow
increasingly complex. In the U.S. alone, tax laws are updated
nearly once per day, and collectively, Americans spend an

estimated 6 billion hours annually navigating the process—a workload comparable to three million full-time employees. AI is now transforming tax preparation and planning. For example, Deloitte has digitized the expertise of 250 tax specialists into a comprehensive AI-driven system that automates the review and extraction of information from business documents, reducing processing time by up to 50%.

One of the most significant applications of AI in financial services is risk management. Financial institutions have always faced a wide range of risks, including credit, market, operational, and regulatory risks. Traditional risk management processes often rely on historical data and human expertise, which can be time-consuming and prone to errors. AI, on the other hand, can analyse large volumes of structured and unstructured data in real-time, enabling financial institutions to identify potential risks more accurately and faster. For instance, AI-driven algorithms can detect patterns that indicate potential loan defaults or fraudulent transactions, allowing banks to mitigate these risks before they escalate.

AI-powered fraud detection systems are a prime example of how AI enhances risk management in financial services. By using machine learning algorithms and anomaly detection techniques, AI can monitor millions of transactions and identify unusual behaviour that may indicate fraudulent activity. Unlike traditional rule-based systems, which may struggle to adapt to new types of fraud, AI models can learn from new data and improve over time, making them more effective at detecting emerging threats. This ability to continuously adapt and evolve allows financial institutions to stay ahead of increasingly sophisticated cybercriminals and protect both their assets and customers.

Another key area where AI is transforming financial services is predictive analytics. Financial markets are inherently volatile, with prices influenced by a multitude of factors, from economic indicators to geopolitical events. AI's ability to analyse vast amounts of data from diverse sources—including market data, news reports, and social media sentiment—enables it to generate insights that can help financial institutions make more informed predictions. For example, AI-driven models can identify trends and forecast market movements, allowing investors to make strategic decisions that minimize risks and maximize returns. Predictive analytics also plays a crucial role in asset management, where AI can help portfolio managers optimize their investment strategies based on real-time insights.

Today, it is entirely possible to manage your banking for years without stepping into a physical branch. You can update your account details, make transfers online, and deposit or withdraw cash at an ATM. ATMs (Automated Teller Machines) now handle tasks that were once exclusively the job of human tellers. While bank tellers still exist, their numbers have significantly decreased thanks to ATMs and other automated services. As societies move toward cashless economies, with more transactions happening electronically and on digital platforms, the need for physical bank branches diminishes. Many banks are adapting by shifting entirely online. Virtual banks like Schwab.com and Robinhood.com operate without physical locations, relying instead on advanced algorithms and automated systems. This transition comes at a cost. With fewer branches, there are fewer jobs. In developed nations, up to 50% of all bank branches and their employees could disappear in the next decade.

In credit risk assessment, AI is providing a more nuanced approach to evaluating borrowers' creditworthiness.

Traditional credit scoring models often rely on a limited set of data points, such as income, employment history, and credit score, which may not provide a complete picture of an individual's financial health. AI, however, can analyse a broader range of data, including social media activity, spending patterns, and even smartphone usage, to assess a borrower's credit risk more accurately. This approach not only helps financial institutions make more informed lending decisions but also expands access to credit for individuals who may not have a traditional credit history but demonstrate responsible financial behaviour.

AI is also making significant strides in portfolio management through the use of robo-advisors. These AI-driven platforms provide automated investment advice and portfolio management services to clients, based on their financial goals, risk tolerance, and market conditions. By using advanced algorithms, robo-advisors can analyse market trends, optimize asset allocation, and make data-driven investment recommendations. This has democratized access to financial advisory services, making professional portfolio management available to a broader range of investors at a lower cost compared to traditional financial advisors.

Large investment banks are increasingly embracing automation, shifting their services online and replacing human financial analysts with algorithms. In 2015, JPMorgan employed over 9,000 software engineers and programmers out of a total workforce of 33,000—more than Facebook or X (formerly Twitter) at the time.

Moreover, AI is being used to enhance stress testing within financial institutions. Stress testing is a critical aspect of risk management, allowing banks to assess their resilience under adverse economic conditions. AI can improve the accuracy and efficiency of stress tests by simulating a wide range of scenarios and analysing their potential impact on a bank's balance sheet. By incorporating AI into stress testing, financial institutions can better prepare for unexpected events, such as economic downturns or market disruptions, and ensure they have adequate capital reserves to weather these challenges.

The use of natural language processing (NLP) is another area where AI is making an impact in financial services. NLP allows financial institutions to extract valuable insights from unstructured data, such as news articles, analyst reports, and regulatory documents. By analysing this information, AI can identify emerging risks, track regulatory changes, and provide financial analysts with the data they need to make informed decisions. NLP is also used to power virtual assistants and chatbots, which can provide customers with personalized financial advice and support, improving the overall customer experience.

Quill, developed by Narrative Science—a company co-founded by Northwestern University computer science professors Kristian Hammond and Larry Birnbaum—leverages AI to transform structured data into coherent, human-like narratives. By analysing data from various sources, Quill identifies key insights and generates written reports, enabling organizations to efficiently produce clear, actionable information without manual drafting. This automation allows employees to focus on interpreting and discussing findings rather than compiling them, enhancing productivity and decision-making. Quill's applications span multiple industries, including finance, journalism, and business intelligence, where rapid and accurate data interpretation is crucial. By automating the narrative generation process, Quill helps professionals to concentrate on higher-level analysis and strategic planning.

While the benefits of AI in financial services are clear, its adoption also presents challenges. One major concern is the lack of transparency in AI decision-making processes, often referred to as the "black box" problem. Financial institutions must ensure that their AI models are explainable and comply with regulatory requirements to maintain trust with customers and regulators. Additionally, there is the risk of data privacy and security breaches, given the sensitive nature of financial data. To address these challenges, financial firms must invest in robust data governance frameworks and ensure that AI systems are developed and deployed in an ethical and transparent manner.

Again, AI is reshaping an industry. Financial services can be reformed by enhancing risk management, improving predictive capabilities, and providing personalized services. From fraud detection and credit risk assessment to robo-advisors and stress testing, AI is enabling financial institutions to deliver better outcomes for their clients. However, to fully realize the potential of AI, it is crucial for financial firms to address challenges related to transparency, data privacy, and regulatory compliance. By doing so, they can harness the power of AI to build a more secure, resilient, and customer-centric financial ecosystem.

'The Economic Singularity'

The concept of the Economic Singularity refers to a future point in time when AI and automation lead to such profound changes in the economy that traditional employment structures become obsolete. It envisions a world where the majority of jobs as we know them today are performed by machines, raising significant questions about the role of humans in an economy dominated by autonomous systems. This shift could be as transformative as the Industrial Revolution, but on an even larger scale, fundamentally altering how people earn a living, contribute to society, and find meaning in their daily lives. To prepare for this radical transformation, we need to rethink everything from economic systems to education, social welfare, and even cultural norms.

"Automation is no longer just about doing things more efficiently—it's about redefining what work means in a world where machines might do almost everything." – Martin Ford

---

The Economic Singularity is driven by the rapid advancement of AI technologies and their increasing ability to perform not only repetitive manual tasks but also cognitive tasks that once required human intelligence. In previous technological shifts, such as the Industrial Revolution, new types of jobs emerged to replace those that were automated. But the capabilities of AI are becoming so broad that people feel threatened to be replaced. From diagnosing diseases and driving cars to writing news articles and providing legal advice, AI's reach is expanding, making the feeling that a large portion of today's workforce may become unemployable within a few decades plausible.

Of the world's workforce 59% needs training by 2030. 29% could be upskilled, 10% could be reskilled and redeployed but 11% is at risk. — World Economic Forum Future of Jobs Report 2025.

One of the most pressing challenges presented by the Economic Singularity is the potential for mass unemployment. Historically, technological advancements have led to the displacement of some jobs but also created new opportunities in emerging industries. However, as AI becomes capable of performing increasingly complex and creative tasks, the prospect of new job creation diminishes. The fear is that there may simply not be enough new roles to absorb the millions of displaced workers, leading to unprecedented levels of unemployment. This raises critical questions about the future of work, income distribution, and the structure of our economies.

Moreover, this shift could exacerbate inequality. Those who own AI technologies—typically large corporations and a small group of investors—stand to gain significant wealth, while displaced workers may struggle to find their place in an AI-driven economy. This potential concentration of wealth and power could lead to social unrest if not addressed through proactive policies. Preparing for the Economic Singularity requires finding ways to ensure that the benefits of AI are shared broadly across society, rather than creating a divide between those who control the technology and those who do not.

To address the challenges of widespread unemployment and income inequality, many experts have proposed the implementation of a Universal Basic Income (UBI). UBI is a system where every citizen receives a regular, unconditional sum of money from the government, regardless of their employment status. The idea is that by providing a financial safety net, people will be able to meet their basic needs even if they are unable to find traditional employment. UBI could also encourage entrepreneurship and creative pursuits, as people would have the freedom to explore new ideas without the fear of financial ruin.

In the 1970s, the Canadian government conducted the "Mincome" experiment in Manitoba, with Dauphin chosen as the main site. Residents received a guaranteed annual income, reduced by fifty cents for every dollar earned, ensuring work incentives remained intact. The program had positive effects: new mothers stayed home longer, teenage boys stayed in school longer, and the town saw lower rates of domestic violence, work-related injuries, and mental health issues. Contrary to concerns, significant labour force reduction did not occur.

However, UBI is not without its critics. Some argue that providing a guaranteed income could reduce people's motivation to work and contribute to society. Others raise concerns about the affordability of such a program, particularly in countries with large populations. To make UBI viable, it would require significant changes to taxation and government spending, potentially reallocating funds from existing welfare programs. Despite these challenges, many pilot programs have shown promising results, with participants reporting improved well-being, reduced stress, and greater freedom to pursue education or start their own businesses.

Another key strategy for preparing for the Economic Singularity is investing in reskilling and lifelong learning as mentioned before. As AI continues to evolve, the skills required in the job market will also change. To remain relevant, workers will need to continuously adapt and learn new skills. Governments, educational institutions, and private companies all have a role to play in providing access to training programs that help people transition into new roles that are hard to be automated.

In addition to technical skills, there will be an increased emphasis on soft skills such as creativity, emotional intelligence, and critical thinking—qualities that are difficult for AI to replicate. Jobs that involve human connection, such as healthcare, education, and creative industries, are more resilient to automation. By focusing on developing these uniquely human abilities, individuals can thrive in an AI-dominated world.

The Economic Singularity also challenges us to rethink the very nature of work and its role in our lives. For many, work is not just a means of earning a living but also a source of identity, purpose, and social connection. If traditional employment becomes less central to our lives, we will need to find new ways to derive meaning and fulfilment. This could involve a shift towards volunteering, community involvement, artistic endeavours, or other forms of self-expression that contribute to society in non-economic ways.

Some futurists argue that the Economic Singularity could ultimately lead to a more positive outcome—a world where people are freed from the drudgery of work and have more time to pursue their passions and interests. However, achieving this vision will require significant cultural and societal changes. We will need to redefine success, moving away from a focus on productivity and financial achievement towards a broader understanding of well-being and human flourishing.

To navigate the challenges of the Economic Singularity, proactive policy and governance will be essential. Governments will need to take an active role in managing the transition to an AI-driven economy, ensuring that the benefits of automation are widely shared and that vulnerable populations are protected. This could involve implementing progressive tax policies, providing incentives for companies to create socially beneficial technologies, and ensuring that ethical considerations are at the forefront of AI development.

International cooperation will also be crucial, as the effects of the Economic Singularity will be felt globally. Countries will need to work together to develop standards and regulations that promote the responsible use of AI and prevent a race to the bottom, where companies prioritize profit over social welfare. By collaborating on these issues, we can create a more equitable global economy that benefits everyone, rather than a select few.

It is also important to recognize that AI and automation are tools, and the impact they have on society will depend largely on how we choose to use them. Technological determinism— the idea that technology develops according to its own logic and dictates social outcomes—is not inevitable. Instead, we have the power to shape the future of technology to align with our values and aspirations. By prioritizing human well-being, inclusivity, and sustainability, we can harness the potential of AI to create a better world for all.

We need to shift the way we think about work, wealth, and human purpose. As AI and automation continue to advance, we must be proactive. This will require rethinking our economic systems, investing in education, and reskilling, and finding new ways to derive meaning and fulfilment outside of traditional employment. By tackling these challenges directly and harnessing the potential of AI, we can shape a future where technology enhances human well-being.

AI In Agriculture And Food Production

The integration of AI into agriculture and food production is revolutionizing the way we grow, harvest, and distribute food. By leveraging AI, farmers are making more informed decisions, optimizing resource usage, and ultimately boosting yields while reducing environmental impacts. As the global population continues to grow, the agricultural sector faces increased pressure to produce more food with fewer resources, and AI offers a transformative solution to meet these demands.

One of the most significant impacts of AI in agriculture is its ability to enhance precision farming. Precision farming involves using data and technology to manage crops and livestock with greater accuracy, ensuring that inputs like water, fertilizer, and pesticides are applied only where and when they are needed. AI-powered systems analyse data collected from sensors, drones, and satellites to monitor soil health, moisture levels, and crop growth in real-time. For instance, AI algorithms can process images captured by drones to identify areas in a field that require extra care, such as regions affected by pests or nutrient deficiencies. By enabling targeted interventions, precision farming helps farmers optimize the use of resources, improve crop yields, and reduce waste.

In Japan, 90 percent of crop-spraying is done by drones.

Predictive analytics is another area where AI is making a significant impact in agriculture. AI models can analyse historical data, such as weather patterns, soil conditions, and crop performance, to provide farmers with accurate predictions about future conditions. For example, AI can forecast the best times to plant, irrigate, or harvest crops based on expected weather changes, helping farmers avoid damage from adverse conditions such as droughts or heavy rainfall. Predictive analytics can also help farmers anticipate pest infestations or disease outbreaks, enabling them to take preventative measures before these issues become widespread. By giving farmers, the ability to plan more effectively, AI helps reduce uncertainty and improves overall productivity.

AI is also transforming farm equipment with the development of autonomous machines. Self-driving tractors and robotic harvesters are increasingly being used to perform labour-intensive tasks such as ploughing, planting, and harvesting. These machines are equipped with AI-powered sensors and cameras that allow them to navigate fields with precision and make real-time decisions based on their surroundings. For example, robotic harvesters can identify ripe fruits or vegetables and pick them without damaging the plant, reducing labour costs, and minimizing waste. This automation not only increases efficiency but also addresses labour shortages, which have been a growing concern in many agricultural regions.

In addition to crop farming, AI is playing a crucial role in livestock management. AI-powered systems are being used to monitor the health and well-being of animals, ensuring that they receive appropriate care. For instance, cameras and sensors can track the movement, eating habits, and physical condition of livestock, alerting farmers to any signs of illness or distress. AI models can also analyse data to predict when animals are most fertile, helping farmers optimize breeding schedules. By providing real-time insights into livestock health, AI allows farmers to maintain healthier herds, increase productivity, and reduce costs associated with veterinary care.

Supply chain optimization is another important aspect of AI's impact on agriculture and food production. AI-driven platforms can analyse data across the entire supply chain, from farm to table, to improve efficiency and reduce food waste. For example, AI can help predict demand for different crops, allowing farmers to adjust their production accordingly and reduce overproduction. AI can also assist in optimizing the logistics of food distribution, ensuring that perishable goods are transported and stored under optimal conditions to minimize spoilage. By enhancing supply chain visibility and efficiency, AI helps ensure that food reaches consumers in a timely and sustainable manner.

Moreover, AI is contributing to sustainable farming practices by helping farmers minimize their environmental footprint. AI-powered irrigation systems can monitor soil moisture levels and weather forecasts to deliver water only when it is needed, reducing water consumption. Similarly, AI can help farmers determine the exact amount of fertilizer or pesticide required for specific areas of a field, minimizing the risk of chemical runoff and soil degradation. By making farming more efficient and environmentally friendly, AI is helping to create a more sustainable agricultural sector that can meet the needs of future generations.

AI combined with genetic engineering is transforming agriculture with innovations like disease-resistant, high-yield crops and drought-defying plants.

The use of AI in agriculture does come with challenges, particularly for small-scale farmers who may lack the resources to adopt advanced technologies. High initial costs, limited access to data, and a lack of technical expertise can make it difficult for smaller farms to benefit from AI-driven innovations. To address these challenges, there is a need for greater investment in training programs, infrastructure, and affordable AI solutions that cater to the needs of small and medium-sized farms. Governments, tech companies, and agricultural organizations must work together to ensure that the benefits of AI are accessible to farmers of all scales.

The impact of AI on agriculture and food production is profound, offering solutions to some of the most pressing challenges facing the industry today. From precision farming and predictive analytics to autonomous machinery and supply chain optimization, AI is transforming how food is grown, harvested, and distributed. By making agriculture more efficient, productive, and sustainable, AI has the potential to ensure food security for a growing global population while reducing the environmental impact of farming. However, to fully realize the benefits of AI in agriculture, it is crucial to address the barriers to adoption and ensure that farmers of all scales have access to the tools and knowledge they need to thrive in the digital age.

PROMISES OF AI

Personalized Learning

AI is transforming many facets of modern life, including the way we learn and acquire new skills. In the realm of education, one of the most exciting advancements is the use of AI tutors to deliver personalized learning experiences. Unlike traditional classroom settings, where instruction is typically uniform and standardized, AI tutors can provide tailored lessons that adapt to each student's unique needs, learning pace, and preferences. This individualized approach has the potential to make learning more effective, engaging, and accessible for students of all ages.

> *"AI has the potential to revolutionize education,*
> *by personalizing learning and providing tailored*
> *feedback to students in real-time." – Bill Gates*

AI tutors are designed to mimic the role of a human tutor by assessing a student's strengths, weaknesses, and learning style. Through the use of machine learning algorithms, these systems are able to analyse vast amounts of data about a student's performance, including their test scores, response times, and even the types of mistakes they frequently make. By doing so, AI tutors can identify areas where a student may be struggling and adjust the difficulty or content of the lessons accordingly. This ability to continuously adapt ensures that each student receives instruction that is optimally suited to their needs, reducing frustration, and enhancing the learning experience.

One of the key benefits of AI-driven personalized learning is its capacity to provide real-time feedback. In a traditional classroom, students often have to wait for a teacher to grade their assignments before they know how well they understood a topic. With AI tutors, feedback is immediate, allowing students to correct their mistakes as they build a solid foundation of understanding before moving on to more advanced material. This immediacy not only helps students learn more effectively but also fosters a sense of independence and self-confidence, as they are able to take charge of their own learning journey.

Another advantage of AI tutors is their ability to enhance engagement. Many students find traditional, one-size-fits-all instruction to be monotonous and disengaging, particularly when they are either ahead of or behind the rest of the class. AI tutors address this issue by presenting material in a way that is both challenging and accessible, keeping students motivated and curious. Some AI learning platforms even incorporate gamification elements, such as rewards, leaderboards, and interactive activities, to make the learning process more enjoyable and to encourage students to push beyond their comfort zones.

AI tutors also play a significant role in bridging the gap in access to quality education. In many parts of the world, access to qualified teachers is limited, particularly in rural or underserved areas. AI tutors, which can be accessed through a computer or smartphone, provide a scalable solution to this problem. By making personalized learning available to anyone with an internet connection, AI has the potential to democratize education and ensure that all students, regardless of their location or socioeconomic background, have the opportunity to learn and succeed.

Moreover, AI-driven personalized learning offers benefits for teachers and educators as well. By offloading some of the more routine aspects of teaching, such as grading and tracking student progress, AI can free up teachers to focus on more meaningful activities, such as providing one-on-one support, facilitating group discussions, and inspiring students to think critically. Teachers can also use the insights provided by AI tutors to better understand their students' needs and adjust their instructional strategies accordingly. This collaborative approach, where AI and teachers work together, can create a more dynamic and effective learning environment.

Khan Academy, a non-profit educational platform founded in 2005 by Salman Khan, offers free online educational videos and resources to learners worldwide. By December 2022, the platform had approximately 137 million users, with over 30 million people visiting each month. Khan Academy provides more than 4,000 hours of educational video content and features over 13,000 short tutorials and instructional videos. In 2019, users spent 8.7 billion minutes engaging with the platform's content. Additionally, Khan Academy's resources are available in 43 different languages, making education accessible to a diverse global audience.

Despite its many benefits, it is important to acknowledge the challenges and limitations of AI-driven personalized learning. One of the primary concerns is the potential for data privacy issues, as AI tutors rely on collecting and analysing vast amounts of personal information about students. Ensuring that this data is handled responsibly and securely is crucial to maintaining trust in these technologies. Additionally, while AI tutors can provide valuable support, they are not a substitute for the human connection that is central to effective education.

Empathy, encouragement, and the ability to inspire are qualities that AI, at least in its current form, cannot fully replicate.

AI tutors represent a promising advancement in the field of education, offering the potential to deliver personalized learning experiences that adapt to the unique needs of each student. By providing real-time feedback, enhancing engagement, and expanding access to quality education, AI-driven personalized learning has the power to transform how we learn and teach. However, to fully realize the benefits of this technology, it is essential to address concerns around data privacy and to recognize the irreplaceable value of human educators in fostering a well-rounded and meaningful learning experience.

AI Diagnostics And Predictive Healthcare

AI is poised to revolutionize the field of healthcare, particularly in the areas of diagnostics and predictive healthcare. By leveraging vast amounts of medical data, AI can provide more accurate diagnoses, identify potential health risks before they become critical, and ultimately improve patient outcomes. This transformative technology is reshaping how healthcare professionals diagnose illnesses and make decisions, paving the way for a more proactive and personalized approach to medicine.

AI systems have uncovered surprising links between sleep patterns and various diseases, including specific sleep behaviours associated with Parkinson's disease. In related research, MIT professor Dina Katabi developed a system called Emerald, which uses Wi-Fi signal propagation to monitor patients' breathing and movement. Early findings show the system achieving up to 90% accuracy in detecting Parkinson's at its early stages—a significant breakthrough, as current methods often diagnose the disease only after 50% to 80% of brain damage has already occurred.

One of the most significant applications of AI in healthcare is in medical diagnostics. Traditionally, diagnosing a condition requires a combination of clinical experience, patient history, and often a series of tests. However, even the most experienced healthcare professionals are not immune to error. AI systems, particularly those powered by machine learning and deep learning algorithms, are capable of analysing medical images, lab results, and patient data with incredible precision. For example, AI models trained on radiology images can detect abnormalities, such as tumours, fractures, or signs of pneumonia, often with an accuracy that rivals or even surpasses that of human radiologists. This ability to rapidly and accurately interpret complex medical data is helping doctors make better-informed decisions, reducing the likelihood of misdiagnosis and improving patient care.

A healthy newborn went home three days after birth, but five days later, his mother brought him to the emergency room at Rady Children's Hospital in San Diego as he was suffering from worsening seizures. As his condition deteriorated, doctors performed rapid whole-genome sequencing on a blood sample. In just 20 seconds, AI analysed his medical record, and machine-learning algorithms pinpointed a rare genetic variant causing the seizures. Treatment with vitamin B6 and arginine supplements was administered, successfully counteracting the genetic issue.

As an example, every year, over two billion chest X-rays are performed worldwide. These scans are often challenging to interpret because issues like scarring or collapsed lung tissue can obscure other problems. However, AI's ability to process and analyse massive datasets offers a promising solution, with the potential to read X-rays with remarkable accuracy.

Recent advancements highlight this potential. A collaborative study between Warwick, King's College London, and NHS sites, developed an AI system capable of analysing X-rays with accuracy equal to or better than doctors for 35 out of 37 conditions. This AI software, trained on 2.8 million historical chest X-rays from 1.5 million patients, not only identifies abnormalities but also prioritizes urgent cases, making it an invaluable tool in addressing the growing radiology backlog.

The AI program scans X-rays immediately after they are taken, flags abnormalities, and assigns a probability to potential diagnoses. Its ability to focus on urgent conditions ensures faster response times for critical cases, such as strokes or severe lung conditions. Furthermore, the program reduces human bias by offering a second opinion and can filter out X-rays with no abnormalities—freeing radiologists to concentrate on more complex cases.

As much as 80% of tasks currently performed by human doctors could soon be handled by automated systems. However, this does not mean 80% of doctors will lose their jobs. Instead, routine tasks such as check-ups and tests will be automated, allowing doctors to focus on more complex and valuable aspects of their work.

Combining AI and human expertise enhances accuracy even further. While AI excels at precision and consistency, healthcare professionals bring the intuition and context needed for nuanced decision-making. Studies reveal that AI-augmented workflows help radiologists handle more cases efficiently and reduce burnout by automating repetitive tasks. For example, AI can measure lesions and anatomies over time, prioritize time-sensitive cases, and streamline administrative duties, allowing radiologists to focus on patient care.

Beyond radiology, AI's broader adoption in healthcare is transformative. Currently, 75% of AI applications in the field are imaging-related, underscoring its vital role in diagnostics.

The Face2Gene app aids professionals in diagnosing genetic disorders by analysing facial features. Leveraging advanced facial recognition technology, it identifies phenotypic markers associated with genetic conditions, enabling timely and accurate diagnoses. Currently, over 65% of clinical geneticists worldwide use Face2Gene in their practice. This broad adoption has greatly improved the app's diagnostic precision, as it continuously evolves by learning from the extensive data contributed by its global user community. Initially capable of accurately identifying about 300 genetic disorders, the app has significantly expanded its capabilities. Thanks to innovations, it can now distinguish nearly 1,000 conditions, representing a major leap in its diagnostic scope and effectiveness.

AI in radiology offers a dual benefit: improving patient outcomes and addressing systemic challenges like staff shortages. As healthcare systems adopt these technologies, AI will not replace medical professionals but will serve as an indispensable co-pilot, enhancing their capacity to save lives and improve care.

IBM developed Watson, a computer capable of competing in the trivia game "Jeopardy!" Playing "Jeopardy!" requires extensive general knowledge and an understanding of natural human speech. In a live televised match against the two greatest contestants in the game's history, Watson triumphed with a decisive victory. Today, Watson applies its advanced capabilities to the medical field, aiding in cancer diagnosis and treatment planning by analysing a patient's symptoms against a database of over 10 million health records. Additionally, Watson accelerates research by processing information far faster than any human. With a new medical paper published every 41 seconds, no doctor could possibly keep up with this volume of data—but Watson can.

In addition to diagnostics, AI is playing a crucial role in predictive healthcare, which involves using data to anticipate health issues before they become severe. By analysing a patient's medical history, genetic information, and lifestyle factors, AI can identify patterns and predict the likelihood of developing certain conditions, such as heart disease, diabetes, or even mental health issues. This type of predictive analysis allows healthcare providers to intervene early, offering preventive treatments or lifestyle recommendations that can reduce the risk of complications. For example, AI algorithms can monitor a patient with cardiovascular risk factors and alert their healthcare provider if there are signs of an impending heart attack, allowing for timely intervention.

Researchers at the Weizmann Institute of Science in Israel have uncovered how individuals respond differently to various foods. By analysing millions of data points— including participants' dietary habits, physical activity, and gut microbiome—a machine learning model identified 137 factors that predict glycaemic response, or how much a person's blood sugar rises after eating specific foods. Using these insights, 26 participants were provided with personalized diet plans based on their predicted glycaemic responses. This group experienced significantly improved blood sugar levels after meals compared to the control group. These findings are critical, as large glycaemic spikes are linked to conditions such as diabetes, obesity, and heart disease.

Wearable devices and remote monitoring technologies have also played a key role in making predictive healthcare a reality. Devices like smartwatches and fitness trackers are equipped with sensors that collect data on a user's heart rate, physical activity, sleep patterns, and more. AI systems analyse this data to detect irregularities and potential health risks. If a wearable device notices an abnormal heart rhythm, for instance, it can notify the user and prompt them to seek medical attention. This capability not only empowers individuals to take control of their health but also helps reduce the burden on healthcare systems by catching potential problems early.

The Migraine Alert app uses machine learning algorithms to predict the onset of migraines with 85% accuracy. This enables users to take preventative measures rather than only addressing the migraine after it begins.

AI's potential in predictive healthcare extends beyond individual patient care to public health. By analysing large datasets that include information about population health trends, environmental factors, and disease outbreaks, AI can help predict and manage public health crises. During the COVID-19 pandemic, AI models were used to predict virus spread, identify high-risk populations, and even aid in the development of vaccines. The ability to predict and prepare for health challenges on a larger scale could be invaluable in preventing future pandemics and managing chronic disease burdens more effectively.

Despite its promise, the integration of AI in diagnostics and predictive healthcare is not without challenges. One major concern is the quality of data that AI systems rely on. AI algorithms are only as good as the data they are trained on, and if the data is incomplete, biased, or inaccurate, it can lead to incorrect predictions or diagnoses. Ensuring the quality and diversity of medical datasets is essential for AI systems to provide reliable and equitable healthcare solutions.

AI relies completely on the quality of its data, as it uses this information to learn and make predictions. However, medical data is often unstructured and narrative-based. Inaccurate or incorrect labels can easily disrupt an algorithm's results.

Another challenge is the issue of patient privacy. AI systems require access to sensitive health information, which raises concerns about data security and the potential misuse of patient data. It is crucial that healthcare providers and technology companies implement robust security measures and adhere to strict data privacy regulations to protect patient information and maintain trust in AI technologies.

Additionally, while AI can enhance diagnostic accuracy, it is important to recognize that it cannot replace human judgment. Medical professionals bring context, empathy, and a holistic understanding of a patient's needs that AI cannot replicate. The most effective use of AI in healthcare is as a complementary tool that assists doctors in making more informed decisions, rather than a replacement for their expertise.

In the United States, the average clinic visit lasts just seven minutes. This may contribute to the

> *approximately 12 million significant misdiagnoses annually, as well as the fact that up to one-third of medical procedures performed are unnecessary.*

AI diagnostics and predictive healthcare represent a paradigm shift in the way healthcare is delivered. By providing more accurate diagnoses, anticipating health risks, and enabling early interventions, AI has the potential to improve patient outcomes, reduce healthcare costs, and empower individuals to take control of their health. However, realizing this potential requires addressing challenges related to data quality, privacy, and the integration of AI with human expertise. As these issues are resolved, AI will become an increasingly vital part of a healthcare system that is more proactive, personalized, and efficient.

The Role Of AI In Public Health

AI is increasingly being recognized as a powerful tool in the field of public health and crisis management. By harnessing the capabilities of AI, public health officials can make better-informed decisions, respond more quickly to emergencies, and develop effective strategies to prevent the spread of diseases. The integration of AI into public health has the potential to revolutionize the way societies prepare for, respond to, and recover from health crises, ultimately improving health outcomes on a global scale.

One of the most promising uses of AI in public health is in the area of disease surveillance and outbreak prediction. AI algorithms can analyse vast amounts of data from a variety of sources, including social media posts, health records, travel patterns, and environmental factors, to identify potential outbreaks before they become widespread. For example, during the early stages of the COVID-19 pandemic, AI models were instrumental in detecting unusual patterns of pneumonia in

Wuhan, China, which allowed health authorities to take early action. AI-powered tools can also help track the spread of infectious diseases by monitoring real-time data and creating predictive models, which can assist in allocating resources effectively and implementing timely containment measures.

Contact tracing is another area where AI has made a significant impact. During the COVID-19 pandemic, AI-powered contact tracing apps were developed to identify and notify individuals who had been in close proximity to confirmed cases. By automating this process, AI made it possible to trace contacts more efficiently and accurately, thereby reducing the transmission of the virus. AI-driven contact tracing also helped overcome the limitations of manual methods, which can be time-consuming and prone to human error, especially during large-scale outbreaks.

AI is also proving invaluable in resource allocation and crisis response. In times of public health emergencies, such as natural disasters or disease outbreaks, AI can analyse data to predict the demand for medical supplies, hospital beds, and healthcare personnel. This helps decision-makers allocate resources where they are most needed, ensuring that healthcare systems are not overwhelmed. For instance, during the COVID-19 crisis, AI was used to predict patient influx in hospitals and optimize the distribution of ventilators and personal protective equipment (PPE) to regions with the greatest need. By providing real-time insights, AI can help ensure that limited resources are used effectively, ultimately saving lives.

Beyond immediate crisis response, AI is also being used to analyse long-term public health trends and develop strategies to improve overall population health. By examining data on chronic diseases, social determinants of health, and environmental factors, AI can identify patterns and risk factors that contribute to poor health outcomes. Public health officials can use this information to design targeted interventions and policies that address the root causes of health disparities. For example, AI analysis of air quality data and its correlation with respiratory illnesses can help policymakers implement measures to reduce pollution and improve public health.

AI's role in vaccine development and drug discovery has also been transformative in crisis management. Traditional vaccine development can take years, but AI can significantly speed up the process by analysing large datasets to identify potential vaccine candidates and predict their efficacy. During the COVID-19 pandemic, AI was used to analyse the genetic sequence of the virus, identify potential targets for vaccines, and even simulate clinical trials. This accelerated timeline was crucial in developing vaccines that helped curb the spread of the virus and save countless lives.

Mental health is another area where AI is making a difference in crisis management. Public health crises, such as pandemics or natural disasters, often lead to increased levels of stress, anxiety, and depression among affected populations. AI-powered chatbots and virtual therapists can provide mental health support to individuals in need, offering coping strategies and connecting them to appropriate resources. These AI tools can help bridge the gap in mental health services, particularly in situations where healthcare professionals are overwhelmed or where access to mental health services is limited.

AI has the potential to assist in diagnosing mental health conditions like depression, which affects over 10% of the global population. For example, an algorithm called DeepMood demonstrated high accuracy in predicting depression by analysing a person's smartphone keyboard patterns.

Despite its potential, the use of AI in public health and crisis management is not without challenges. One of the primary concerns is the ethical use of data. AI systems rely on large amounts of data, often including sensitive health information, which raises concerns about privacy and data security. Ensuring that data is collected, stored, and used in an ethical and transparent manner is essential to maintaining public trust in AI technologies. Additionally, algorithmic bias is a significant issue that must be addressed, as biased data can lead to inequitable health outcomes and disproportionately impact vulnerable populations.

Another challenge is the digital divide, which can limit the effectiveness of AI-driven public health initiatives. Not all individuals have equal access to technology, and those in underserved communities may be left behind if public health interventions rely heavily on AI tools that require internet connectivity or smartphone access. To ensure that AI benefits everyone, efforts must be made to bridge this divide and provide equitable access to technology and digital health services.

A humanoid robot named "Pepper" has become a fixture in some Belgian hospitals, assisting patients and visitors. At Ostend's AZ Damiaan hospital, Pepper, developed by Belgian company Zora Bots, speaks 19 languages and serves as a receptionist. Its role includes greeting visitors, providing information, and guiding them to the correct floor and room, enhancing both social interaction and healthcare efficiency.

AI has the potential to play a transformative role in public health and crisis management by enabling early detection of outbreaks, optimizing resource allocation, accelerating vaccine development, and providing mental health support. By harnessing the power of AI, public health officials can respond more effectively to crises and improve the health and well-being of populations. However, to fully realize the benefits of

AI, it is essential to address challenges related to data privacy, algorithmic bias, and equitable access to technology. By doing so, AI can become an integral part of a more resilient and responsive public health system.

Climate Modelling And Prediction

AI has the potential to be a game-changer in addressing one of the most critical challenges facing humanity today: climate change. AI's ability to process vast datasets, identify patterns, and make predictions offers significant opportunities for climate modelling. However, questions remain about the challenges of scalability and the unintended consequences that could arise from the widespread use of AI for environmental purposes.

One of the most promising applications of AI in combating climate change lies in its ability to enhance climate modelling and prediction. Traditional climate models are based on complex mathematical representations of the Earth's systems, which require intensive computational resources to analyse various climate-related factors, such as atmospheric temperature, ocean currents, and greenhouse gas emissions. AI is enhancing these traditional methods by making them faster, more efficient, and more accurate.

Computers have seen an extraordinary growth in power. Between 1950 and 2000, their performance increased by a factor of ten billion. From 2000 to 2024, it surged again by another factor of a billion. Remarkably, each state-of-the-art supercomputer now generates more floating-point data in a single second than all the digital data stored globally just two decades ago.

Machine learning algorithms excel at identifying patterns

within large, complex datasets—a perfect match for the vast amounts of data involved in climate research. For example, AI models can sift through decades of historical climate data and satellite imagery to identify patterns that human researchers may overlook. These models can then be used to predict future climate scenarios with increased precision. By using neural networks, AI can also refine existing models and provide real-time predictions, giving scientists better tools to understand how extreme weather events, such as hurricanes, floods, or droughts, might unfold.

AI is also helping scientists develop more localized climate predictions, which are crucial for understanding the unique challenges faced by specific regions. Predictive models that use AI are now capable of providing insights at the level of individual cities, enabling local governments and communities to make informed decisions about infrastructure, agriculture, and emergency preparedness. For example, AI can be used to predict the impact of sea-level rise in coastal cities, enabling them to plan for flood defences or evacuation routes. By offering more granular climate data, AI empowers policymakers and stakeholders to respond proactively, which is essential in the fight against climate change.

Another key advantage of AI in climate modelling is the ability to integrate various data sources—such as satellite images, sensor data, and meteorological records—to create a holistic view of the climate system. AI's capacity for deep learning means that these diverse inputs can be processed together, revealing interconnections that might be missed using traditional methods. This interdisciplinary approach is particularly useful for understanding complex phenomena like the interaction between the atmosphere and ocean currents, which play a critical role in regulating global temperatures.

A challenge lies in data availability and quality. Climate modelling and energy optimization require high-quality data from diverse sources, often collected over long periods. Unfortunately, such data is not always available, or it may be incomplete or inconsistent. This data scarcity limits the ability of AI models to make accurate predictions or optimize systems effectively. Moreover, access to data is often restricted due to privacy concerns or national regulations, further complicating the development of globally scalable AI solutions.

There is also the challenge of equity and accessibility. AI-driven climate solutions may benefit countries and regions that have the infrastructure and technological capacity to deploy these advanced tools. Developing nations, which are often the most vulnerable to the impacts of climate change, may lack access to the necessary technology and expertise to implement AI-based solutions. Bridging this gap requires international collaboration, funding, and policy interventions to ensure that AI-driven climate solutions are equitable and inclusive.

IBM's Deep Thunder is a high-resolution weather forecasting system that provides precise, localized predictions to support weather-sensitive operations. By analysing over 100 terabytes of data daily, including information from more than 195,000 personal weather stations, Deep Thunder generates hyper-local forecasts at resolutions ranging from 300 – 2000 meters or 0.2 to 1.2 miles.

Finally, there is the issue of public trust and ethical considerations. AI applications in climate solutions often require access to sensitive data, such as energy usage patterns or geographical information. Ensuring data privacy while making AI effective is a delicate balance. Public concerns over data security, surveillance, and the potential misuse of AI for commercial gain can also hinder the adoption of AI-driven solutions. Building public trust through transparency, clear regulations, and responsible AI use is essential if these technologies are to be adopted at scale.

AI'S Own Energy Footprint

AI is revolutionizing industries and transforming everyday life, but this innovation comes with a cost that is increasingly hard to ignore: energy consumption. AI systems, particularly advanced models like generative AI, require vast amounts of computational power to train and operate. This power demand is creating a significant environmental footprint, adding complexity to the promise of AI as a tool for progress.

A single interaction with an AI system, such as asking a question on ChatGPT, can consume approximately ten times more electricity than a simple Google search. With millions of weekly users, the cumulative energy demand quickly escalates. This is just one platform in a rapidly growing industry.

The energy intensity of AI stems primarily from the data centres that house the infrastructure for training and deploying AI models. These centres are responsible for a significant portion of the technology sector's carbon emissions. For instance, Microsoft reported a nearly 30% increase in CO_2 emissions since 2020, driven by its expanding data centre operations to support AI tools. Similarly, Google's emissions in 2023 were almost 50% higher than in 2019, largely attributed to AI-driven energy demand.

Training generative AI models is particularly energy intensive. Training GPT-3, for example, consumed nearly 1,300 megawatt hours of electricity—equivalent to the annual power consumption of 130 U.S. homes. GPT-4, an even more advanced model, required approximately 50 times more energy. AI's energy use currently is estimated to be around 2-3% of total global emissions, but this fraction is expected to increase fast. As AI systems become more sophisticated, their computational needs are doubling roughly every three months, placing additional strain on global electrical grids.

While the potential of AI to help address climate change is immense, there are significant challenges to scaling AI solutions for widespread environmental impact. One concern is the energy consumption required to train and run AI models. The computational resources involved in machine learning, especially for large-scale neural networks, are substantial, and the energy required to power these systems often relies on carbon-intensive electricity. This paradox—using energy-intensive technologies to solve energy efficiency problems—is a hurdle that must be addressed to make AI a genuinely sustainable tool.

Efforts are being made to develop more energy-efficient AI algorithms and leverage renewable energy for data centres, but these solutions are still in their infancy. Researchers are exploring approaches such as federated learning, which distributes the computational load across multiple devices, reducing the carbon footprint associated with centralized AI training. However, balancing AI's benefits against its environmental costs remains a complex challenge.

The environmental impact of AI is deeply tied to the mining of critical resources like lithium, a key component in the batteries powering our devices. Places like Silver Peak, Nevada, with its vast lithium deposits and eerie green evaporation ponds, are just one part of a global web of resource extraction. Rare earth mines in Inner Mongolia and tin-rich islands in Indonesia further illustrate the hidden costs, including ecosystem destruction, dangerous working conditions, and community displacement. Much like the resource booms of the past, the AI industry's sleek image often obscures the environmental and human toll behind its technological advancements.

Despite these challenges, the AI industry is exploring ways to enhance energy efficiency. New technologies, such as specialized accelerators and 3D chips, promise better performance with lower energy costs. Companies like Nvidia are developing advanced hardware that can reduce energy consumption significantly while delivering superior results. Data centres, too, are adopting innovative cooling techniques and optimizing operations to align with sustainable energy sources.

The speed and power of computer hardware have grown exponentially since the invention of the microchip 65 years ago. To put this into perspective: if smartphones had been built back then, they would have been the size of a 100-story building and required 30 times the electricity produced by the entire world at that time!

Reducing AI's energy consumption also involves rethinking how and where it is used. Employing smaller, task-specific models for certain applications can lower resource demands. Addressing the issue of "dark data"—unused data that still occupies storage and consumes energy—is another step toward sustainability.

AI has the potential to help mitigate global greenhouse gas emissions by optimizing processes and resources, but achieving this potential requires balancing its benefits against its environmental costs. Regulators are beginning to take notice, with initiatives such as energy consumption tracking for AI systems gaining traction. By advancing efficiency and making strategic choices about AI deployment, the industry can aim for a future where innovation and sustainability coexist.

The use of AI for climate solutions holds both promise and challenges. AI's capabilities in climate modelling, energy optimization, and resource management present real opportunities to mitigate climate change and adapt to its impacts. However, realizing the full potential of AI for environmental purposes will require overcoming significant hurdles related to energy consumption, data quality, equity, and public trust. To make AI a sustainable and effective tool for combating climate change, collaboration between governments, industry, and civil society is essential. By navigating these challenges, AI could become a cornerstone of humanity's effort to protect the planet and secure a sustainable future.

General Energy Efficiency

Beyond modelling, AI is also playing a crucial role in enhancing energy efficiency, which is vital for reducing greenhouse gas emissions. Smart technologies powered by AI can optimize energy consumption across various sectors, including industrial manufacturing, transportation, and residential energy use. By reducing waste and improving efficiency, AI-driven technologies help to decrease the overall carbon footprint.

In smart buildings, for example, AI is being used to manage energy consumption more effectively. Smart thermostats, lighting systems, and HVAC units equipped with AI algorithms can learn the behaviour patterns of occupants and adjust settings accordingly. This allows these systems to optimize energy usage based on real-time conditions—like reducing heating or cooling when rooms are unoccupied—thereby minimizing energy waste. Google's DeepMind, for instance, was used to optimize the energy usage of its data centres, reducing cooling costs by up to 40%. Such applications demonstrate how AI can lead to significant reductions in energy consumption, contributing directly to climate mitigation efforts.

The integration of AI into the power grid is another significant development. Smart grids leverage AI to predict energy demand, manage load distribution, and integrate renewable energy sources more effectively. The unpredictability of renewable energy sources like wind and solar has often been a challenge; AI models can forecast fluctuations in energy supply and help balance the grid accordingly. This ensures that renewable energy is utilized efficiently, reducing the reliance on fossil fuels and promoting a cleaner energy mix.

AI is also being used to enhance energy efficiency in transportation. AI-driven route optimization software helps logistics companies reduce fuel consumption by planning more efficient delivery routes. Electric vehicle (EV) fleets also benefit from AI, with algorithms determining optimal charging schedules that maximize battery life while reducing demand on the electrical grid. AI can even assist in the development of autonomous electric vehicles, which have the potential to make transportation more energy-efficient by reducing traffic congestion and optimizing fuel use.

The Pattern

AI holds immense potential for improvement across countless domains, offering transformative capabilities that can revolutionize industries, markets, and societies. However, its implementation consistently reveals familiar challenges and limitations. The quality of data remains a critical factor —"garbage in, garbage out" continues to define AI's reliance on accurate, unbiased datasets for training. Alongside this, the use of data at inference inevitably raises issues of privacy, security, and trust, demanding careful navigation.

Human involvement is indispensable in this journey. Supervising AI, ensuring ethical considerations, and incorporating creativity and ingenuity are areas where human strengths complement AI's capabilities. This synergy highlights the concept of co-intelligence, where AI and humans together achieve outcomes far superior to what either could accomplish alone. Balancing potential and risk while fostering collaboration between AI and human intelligence is the best way forward for leveraging AI's transformative power.

Life 3.0 refers to a hypothetical stage of life characterized by the ability to design and modify both its hardware (physical form) and software (knowledge and behaviour). Unlike Life 1.0 (biological organisms like bacteria that cannot change during their lifetime) or Life 2.0 (cultural beings like humans that can adapt their software but not their hardware), Life 3.0 represents a form of technological life, such as advanced AI, that could potentially self-evolve in both structure and capability. This concept suggests a transformative leap in intelligence and adaptability beyond biological constraints.

ARTIFICIAL CREATIVITY

Can AI Be Creative?

Creativity is often considered one of the last frontiers of human uniqueness, a defining trait that seems unattainable for machines. But as AI advances, the question arises: Can AI truly be creative? Creativity, in its essence, is about exploring, combining, and transforming existing structures to make something new. It is about breaking rules, imagining novel possibilities, and expressing ideas that resonate with others. The rise of AI in the creative domain challenges our traditional understanding of creativity, blurring the lines between human ingenuity and machine-generated innovation.

In the 1960s and 70s, American psychologist George Land conducted a study on 1,600 children and found striking results about creativity. At age five, an impressive 98% of the children exhibited genius-level creativity. However, by age ten, only 30% still showed such creativity, and by age fifteen, the number had dropped sharply to just 12%. These findings highlight a troubling reality: traditional education often suppresses creative thinking. By prioritizing analytical

*skills and a structured approach to finding one correct
answer, schools leave little space for creativity to thrive.*

To understand whether AI can be creative, it is helpful to examine what we mean by creativity. According to cognitive scientist Margaret Boden, creativity can be broken down into three categories: combinatorial creativity, exploratory creativity, and transformational creativity.

Combinatorial creativity involves merging existing ideas in novel ways, creating something that feels fresh while still being familiar. An example of this can be found in architecture, where forms and styles from different cultures or time periods are combined to create something new. AI is particularly good at this type of creativity because it can analyse vast datasets, identify patterns, and synthesize elements in unexpected ways. For instance, AI algorithms have been used to design new fashion styles, merging influences from different eras to create innovative garments.

Exploratory creativity refers to generating new ideas by exploring the possibilities within a given set of rules or constraints. This type of creativity is similar to how artists like Claude Monet transformed painting by exploring the effects of light and colour through impressionism. AI also excels at exploratory creativity, particularly in artistic fields like music and visual arts. Software like DeepArt or Emmy (EMI), a musical AI developed by composer David Cope, can produce works in the style of classical artists by exploring various creative combinations within specific artistic boundaries.

---

*In 1993, classical composer David Cope unveiled
"Bach by Design", an album of original piano
compositions reminiscent of the style of 18th-century
composer Johann Sebastian Bach. The pieces were*

composed by the software program Emmy.

Transformational creativity goes further by breaking or modifying the existing rules to create something completely new. This kind of creativity is often the hardest to achieve, even for humans, as it requires a deep understanding of the current framework and a willingness to redefine it. While AI can modify existing structures to some extent, true transformational creativity often involves an intuitive leap, something machines struggle to replicate without human guidance. One prominent example of an AI approaching transformational creativity is Google's DeepDream, which creates surreal, dream-like images by amplifying certain features of a photograph—an approach that diverges significantly from traditional artistic practices.

AI has demonstrated its creative capabilities in many fields, from visual arts to music and even literature. In the world of music, AI systems have composed classical pieces indistinguishable from the works of Bach or Mozart. Emmy, for instance, analysed Bach's compositions to generate new pieces that fooled even trained musicians into thinking they were listening to an authentic Bach original. In visual arts, systems like Creative Adversarial Networks (CANs) have produced paintings that have been exhibited in prestigious galleries and even sold for substantial amounts at auction. These AIs use algorithms to generate art that goes beyond simple imitation, creating works that are judged by critics and audiences to be unique and inspiring.

In literature, AI has also made strides, producing stories and poetry that mimic the styles of famous writers. Tools like GPT-4, developed by OpenAI, can generate prose that captures the nuances of human language, crafting narratives that can be both coherent and emotionally resonant. For example, GPT-4 can write a story in the style of Ernest Hemingway, using short, impactful sentences that convey a powerful sense of atmosphere. These achievements suggest that AI is capable of producing content that humans recognize as creative.

However, it is important to note that AI's creativity is fundamentally different from that of humans. AI lacks the intentionality that defines human creativity. It does not create art or music because it has an emotional urge or an intrinsic motivation to express something. Instead, AI generates creative outputs, when we ask it to, based on patterns, probabilities, and the vast datasets it has been trained on. AI lacks the subjective experience that drives human artists to explore their inner thoughts, emotions, and cultural influences, which are often the foundation of meaningful art.

Human creativity is deeply intertwined with personal experiences, emotions, and the desire for self-expression. When a painter like Van Gogh creates a masterpiece, it is not just a technical process of combining colours and shapes—it is an expression of his internal struggles, worldview, and emotional depth. This kind of deeply personal and self-motivated creativity is something that AI, as it currently stands, cannot replicate. AI can generate outputs that mimic creativity, but it does not have the ability to create with intention, emotion, or consciousness.

Another limitation of AI creativity is its reliance on data. AI can only create based on what it has been trained on—it cannot generate something entirely outside of its dataset. While AI can produce novel combinations and sometimes surprise even its creators, its outputs are still bounded by the data it has been fed. This makes AI-generated creativity more of an extension or reinterpretation of existing works rather than a radical departure from them.

Despite these limitations, AI has proven to be a valuable collaborative tool for human creators. Many artists, musicians, and writers are using AI as a partner to enhance their creative processes, exploring new ideas and pushing the boundaries of their disciplines. For example, musician Taryn Southern used AI to co-compose her album "I AM AI," using AI-generated melodies and harmonies as the basis for her songs. Visual artists have also embraced AI to generate unique styles and forms that they can then refine or incorporate into their own work.

"As machines become more and more efficient and perfect, so it will become clear that imperfection is the greatness of man." - Ernst Fischer.

While AI can certainly exhibit behaviours that we recognize as creative, it lacks the consciousness, intentionality, and emotional depth that characterize true human creativity. AI's creativity is impressive and has the potential to revolutionize the fields of art, music, and literature, but it is ultimately an extension of the human creativity. As AI continues to evolve, it will undoubtedly become an even more powerful tool for assisting and inspiring human creators, but the essence of creativity—the desire to express, connect, and innovate—remains uniquely human, at least for now.

AI-Generated Art And Music

AI-generated art and music challenges our conventional notions of creativity and artistry, prompting us to reconsider what it means to create and who—or what—can be considered an artist. The question arises is whether the creations of AI hold the same value as human-made art, and whether they can evoke the same emotional resonance.

One of the earliest breakthroughs in AI-generated art came in the form of algorithmic art, which involved computers generating images based on mathematical algorithms. Artists like Harold Cohen pioneered this field with his program AARON, which could create drawings autonomously. Initially,

AARON's outputs were abstract, focusing on shapes and colours, but over time, the program evolved to create more complex and sophisticated works. Today, AI has moved far beyond simple algorithmic art, utilizing advanced techniques such as neural networks and generative adversarial networks (GANs) to produce stunning visual pieces.

Generative Adversarial Networks (GANs), introduced by researcher Ian Goodfellow in 2014, have been instrumental in advancing AI-generated art. GANs consist of two neural networks—a generator and a discriminator—that work in tandem to create new images. The generator produces images, while the discriminator evaluates them against real images, providing feedback that helps the generator improve. This adversarial process continues until the generated images are nearly indistinguishable from those made by humans. The result is AI-generated art that is often stunningly lifelike or profoundly abstract, pushing the boundaries of what we consider possible in visual creativity.

One notable example of GAN-generated art is "Portrait of Edmond de Belamy," created by the Paris-based collective Obvious. The portrait was generated by feeding a GAN a dataset of historical portraits, and the resulting artwork was eventually auctioned at Christie's for an astounding $432,500. This sale sparked debates about the value of AI-generated art and whether it could be considered truly original or merely a reflection of the dataset on which the AI was trained. Nevertheless, it highlighted the growing acceptance of AI as a creative force in the art world.

AI-generated art is not limited to paintings and drawings; it also extends to sculpture, animation, and digital installations. Artists like Refik Anadol use AI to create immersive digital installations that respond to real-time data, creating a dynamic and interactive experience for viewers. By analysing vast amounts of data and transforming it into visual art, Anadol's works explore the relationship between technology, perception, and creativity, offering audiences a glimpse into the possibilities of AI as a medium of artistic expression.

"Data is still the pigment — But now, the brush can think." – Refik Anadol

---

In the realm of music, AI has also made significant strides. AI-generated music can be traced back to early experiments in algorithmic composition, where composers used computers to generate musical sequences based on mathematical formulas. Today, AI-generated music has become more sophisticated, capable of composing entire symphonies, pop songs, and even jazz improvisations. One well-known AI music program is AIVA (Artificial Intelligence Virtual Artist), which has been used to compose music for films, video games, and commercials. AIVA employs deep learning techniques to analyse a vast library of musical compositions and generate new pieces that adhere to specific styles or moods.

Another prominent example of AI-generated music is OpenAI's MuseNet, which can compose music in various genres and styles, from classical to rock. MuseNet uses a deep neural network to predict the next note in a sequence, allowing it to create complex and coherent musical pieces. The program has even been able to blend styles, such as composing a piece that combines Mozart's classical elements with the rhythms of jazz or electronic music. This ability to merge genres and create novel musical experiences is one of the unique contributions of AI to the world of music.

AI-generated music has also found its way into mainstream pop culture. In 2016, musician Taryn Southern released an album titled "I AM AI," which was co-composed using AI software called Amper Music. The album featured tracks that blended electronic and pop elements, showcasing how AI could be used as a creative partner in the music-making process. Rather than replacing human musicians, AI served as a tool for enhancing creativity, allowing Southern to experiment with new sounds and compositions that she might not have arrived at on her own.

Jazz and improvisational music are other areas where AI has demonstrated its creative potential. AI systems like the Continuator, developed by François Pachet, can listen to a musician's performance and generate improvised responses in real-time, effectively "jamming" with human players. This kind of collaboration between AI and human musicians blurs the line between human and machine creativity, as the AI adapts to the musician's style and creates music that feels spontaneous and expressive.

'People can always have fears. I have exactly the opposite feeling – when you have new technology it opens the door for many more people.' – François Pachet

---

While AI-generated art and music have garnered significant attention and acclaim, they have also raised important questions about authorship, originality, and the role of the artist. If an AI creates a painting or composes a song, who should be credited as the artist? Is it the programmer who designed the AI, the person who curated the training data, or the AI itself? These questions challenge our traditional notions of authorship and force us to rethink the role of human creativity in an age where machines can produce works of art.

Another concern is the potential for algorithmic bias in AI-generated art and music. AI systems are trained on existing datasets, which means they are influenced by the biases present in those datasets. If an AI is trained on a dataset that predominantly features Western classical music, for example, it may struggle to create music that reflects other cultural traditions. This raises important ethical considerations about the diversity and inclusivity of AI-generated content and the need to ensure that AI systems are trained on representative datasets that reflect a wide range of artistic styles and cultural perspectives.

Despite these challenges, AI-generated art and music have opened up new possibilities for collaboration and experimentation. Many artists and musicians see AI not as a threat but as a powerful tool that can enhance their creative processes. By using AI to generate ideas, explore new styles, or overcome creative blocks, human creators can push the boundaries of their own work and discover new artistic possibilities. AI can serve as a source of inspiration, providing unexpected insights and novel combinations that spark new ideas and drive artistic innovation.

In conclusion, AI-generated art and music represent a fascinating convergence of technology and creativity, challenging our understanding of what it means to create and who can be considered an artist. While AI lacks the emotional depth, intentionality, and personal experience that characterize human creativity, it has demonstrated an impressive ability to produce works that are both aesthetically compelling and thought-provoking. As AI continues to evolve, it will likely play an increasingly important role in the creative arts, not as a replacement for human artists, but as a collaborator and a tool that expands the possibilities of artistic expression. The future of art and music is one in which humans and machines work together, each contributing their unique strengths to the creative process.

Creative Authenticity

Creativity has always been a hallmark of human ingenuity, enabling us to explore, combine, and transform existing structures into something new and meaningful. While AI continues to advance, raising existential questions about its ability to replicate human creativity, we must ask: what defines creative authenticity, and how do humans maintain their unique creative edge in an era increasingly influenced by machines?

"AI will change the nature of creativity, so it's important that we develop new ways to interact with these machines." — Yves Behar

---

Creativity is about more than just novelty; it involves producing something new, surprising, and valuable. Whether it is Claude Monet's transformative impressionism, Arnold Schönberg's bold invention of atonality, or Zaha Hadid's seamless fusion of abstract art with architecture, human creativity thrives on breaking or bending existing rules to inspire fresh perspectives.

Human creativity does not occur in a vacuum—it emerges from an interplay of learned structures, intuition, and personal experiences. Creativity is not confined to traditional art forms —it permeates disciplines like mathematics, where thinkers push boundaries and discover new insights. Mathematicians like Andrew Wiles and Grigori Perelman demonstrate that creative leaps are essential for solving complex problems, such as Fermat's Last Theorem or the Poincaré Conjecture. These achievements often rely on intuition and the ability to combine unrelated concepts into innovative solutions.

Modern tools amplify this creativity. Computers, once relegated to performing tedious calculations, now co-author papers and explore mathematical frontiers alongside their human counterparts. Israeli mathematician Doron Zeilberger's insistence on crediting his computer as a collaborator exemplifies how machines enhance human creativity, even in logical, rule-based fields like mathematics.

"AI has the potential to enhance human creativity, by providing us with new tools and perspectives that we can use to generate ideas and solve problems." — Gary Kasparov

Despite their capabilities, AI systems lack one critical aspect of creativity: intention. Machines cannot originate ideas or create with purpose—they rely on human-designed algorithms to guide their output. This absence of volition differentiates human and machine creativity. Artists like Monet or composers like Bach did not create out of obligation; they were driven by internal motivation and a desire to express something profound.

Furthermore, while AI excels at tasks like pattern recognition and generating variations, it struggles with ambiguity and context. For example, a machine might fail to interpret nuanced language or create a cohesive narrative. Similarly, visual programs like DeepDream can produce intriguing art but lack the ability to contextualize their creations within broader artistic or cultural frameworks.

The true potential of creativity in the age of AI lies in collaboration. Machines can complement human creativity by automating repetitive tasks, enhancing efficiency, and expanding the range of possibilities. This symbiotic relationship can elevate both human and machine contributions, as seen in fields like architecture, music, and computational art.

For instance, the Heydar Aliyev Centre by Zaha Hadid showcases how human ingenuity, aided by advanced computational tools, can achieve architectural feats previously thought impossible.

As AI becomes more sophisticated, preserving creative authenticity requires addressing several key challenges. AI's creativity depends on the quality of its training data. Biased or low-quality inputs can lead to uninspired or problematic outputs, undermining the value of AI-generated work. But if the quality of the training data is so important, who can claim authorship and ownership. Who owns a piece of art or music created by an AI system? How should credit be shared between the programmers, the training-data providing artists, the end-users, and the AI itself?

As AI-generated content becomes more prevalent, audiences may struggle to distinguish between human and machine-made works, leading to a potential devaluation of human-authored creations.

Creativity thrives on curiosity, experimentation, and serendipity—qualities machines cannot replicate. In the face of advancing AI, creativity remains one of humanity's most vital superpowers. Unlike machines, humans possess the ability to infuse their work with meaning, emotion, and intentionality. Creativity is not just about producing output—it is a means of exploring our shared humanity and gaining deeper insights into the world.

Moreover, creativity is not limited to innate talent or artistic pursuits. It can be nurtured and developed through curiosity, learning, and collaboration. By embracing diverse experiences and perspectives, humans can continue to innovate and maintain their creative edge in an increasingly automated world.

So, the age of AI presents both opportunities and challenges for creativity. While machines can mimic certain aspects of the creative process, they lack the intentionality and emotional depth that define human artistry. By leveraging AI as a tool rather than a replacement, humans can enhance their creative endeavours and explore uncharted possibilities.

Ultimately, creative authenticity lies in our ability to innovate with purpose, express individuality, and find meaning in our work. As we navigate the evolving relationship between humans and machines, creativity will remain a defining trait of what it means to be human—and a powerful force for shaping the future.

AI As A Tool For Artists

AI has come a long way in recent years, evolving from a mere computational aid to a partner in the creative process. For many artists, AI is now seen as a versatile tool that can augment, inspire, and transform creative practices across disciplines like visual arts, music, writing, and even architecture. This emerging collaboration between humans and AI opens up exciting possibilities for exploring the very nature of creativity. Rather than seeing AI as a competitor, artists are beginning to harness it as an innovative assistant that expands the boundaries of their own imagination and creative capabilities.

Adobe Project Scene Stitch leverages AI's creative capabilities to enhance photo editing. Imagine working on a photo where unwanted elements—like a distracting road cutting through a serene grassy mountain—need to be removed and replaced with matching scenery. This AI tool scans a vast library of images to find suitable graphic elements and seamlessly integrates them, creating a cohesive and visually appealing result.

The role of AI in the creative arts is akin to that of a new, powerful tool in an artist's toolbox. Just as the invention of the camera gave rise to new forms of artistic expression, AI offers creative practitioners new methods to generate, analyse, and manipulate content. The possibilities are diverse. AI can help artists visualize abstract concepts, suggest new colour palettes, or generate unexpected forms and textures that may have otherwise remained undiscovered.

For instance, artists using tools like DeepDream or Artbreeder can produce surreal visuals that blend the known with the imagined—creating stunning dreamscapes or entirely new forms of representation. These tools allow artists to input parameters, such as colour schemes or preferred subjects, and see what AI generates based on these guidelines. By serving as a partner in the generative process, AI gives artists the ability to see beyond the boundaries of their own minds, introducing serendipity into their creative workflows.

AI as a tool is not just about providing new brushes or mediums; it is about co-creation. Unlike traditional tools that simply follow the artist's lead, AI can offer unexpected suggestions, sometimes even deviating from the artist's intent and offering something entirely novel. This characteristic brings an element of collaboration to the table. For example, AI-generated artworks using Generative Adversarial Networks (GANs) can create images that are strikingly different from traditional human concepts, often surprising the artist in positive ways. The dynamic interplay between artist and machine opens up pathways that neither could have envisioned alone.

"AI is going to change everything, but it's going to be a partnership between humans and AI, not a competition." —Mark Cuban.

Take, for instance, the work of artist Mario Klingemann, known for using neural networks in his creative practice. Klingemann often starts with an idea, but he uses AI to generate variations and explore the boundaries of that idea. This back-and-forth process is akin to having a dialogue with another artist, one that constantly challenges your expectations and leads you toward surprising and often thrilling outcomes.

Musicians are also exploring these collaborative opportunities. AI tools like Google's Magenta, Amper Music, or OpenAI's

MuseNet can help create musical compositions, generate melodies, and even fill in missing parts of a piece. A musician might start with a basic idea and ask an AI to riff on it, offering new harmonies, counterpoints, or even entire sections of a song. This co-creative process is much like having a second, tireless collaborator who can generate novel suggestions, which the human artist can curate, refine, and incorporate.

AI-driven tools also excel at mining vast amounts of data and identifying patterns that may be difficult for the human mind to discern. This ability is particularly powerful for writers or visual artists seeking fresh ideas. Imagine being a poet struggling with writer's block—AI language models, such as GPT-4, can assist by generating sentences, offering new metaphors, or providing thematic suggestions that can act as prompts to get the creative juices flowing again. Writers have used such tools to create novels, screenplays, and poetry, sometimes as direct collaborators, and other times as inspiration sources.

In visual art, AI can produce entirely new genres by taking inspiration from vast libraries of past styles and artworks. For example, Google's DeepArt can take any image and apply the stylistic elements of a famous painter to it. Artists like Refik Anadol utilize machine learning to create mesmerizing data visualizations that are interactive and immersive, turning data into a form of abstract expressionism that pushes our understanding of aesthetics.

"I see AI becoming this extension of the human mind." – Refik Anadol

---

These AI-generated suggestions are not meant to replace human intuition—rather, they serve as inspiration, a starting point from which human artists can adapt, reimagine, and evolve the work. They act as muses that present ideas without the limitations of a conscious creative process, opening a world of unconventional possibilities and fostering an environment where creativity can flourish.

The integration of AI in artistic practice is also blurring the lines between disciplines. An architect might use an AI model trained on abstract paintings to inspire new building forms, while a painter could use AI-generated data visualizations to explore social issues on canvas. This cross-pollination of disciplines is where AI's true power as a creative tool shines. It allows for connections between seemingly unrelated domains, fostering hybrid forms of artistic expression.

The democratizing effect of AI in the arts is also significant. Traditionally, one might have needed years of training to master an instrument or a particular visual technique. AI tools, however, enable artists to overcome technical barriers more quickly, allowing them to focus on high-level creative decision-making rather than mechanical execution. For instance, people who may not have formal training in composition can use AI to compose beautiful pieces of music, allowing them to express their creativity without being limited by their technical skills.

In this way, AI becomes an enabler of creativity rather than a threat to it. It gives more people access to tools that allow them to express themselves, leading to a more diverse range of voices and ideas contributing to the global artistic tapestry. AI-generated art, far from diminishing the role of human artists, amplifies their abilities, offering new techniques, insights, and even whole genres of art.

In 2016, a team of art historians, engineers, and data scientists collaborated on "The Next Rembrandt" project, aiming to create a new painting in Rembrandt's style using artificial intelligence. They began by analysing 346 of Rembrandt's works, digitized through 3D scans, to extract data on his use of geometry, composition, and painting materiuls. The AI identified a common subject in Rembrandt's oeuvre: a white, middle-aged man with facial hair, dressed in black with a white collar and hat. Using this information, the system generated a new portrait, incorporating over 148 million pixels and 150 gigabytes of rendered data. The final image was then brought to life through 3D printing techniques that replicated the texture and brushstrokes characteristic of Rembrandt's oil paintings. This project exemplifies the intersection of technology and art, demonstrating how AI can be utilized to study and emulate the techniques of historical artists, potentially offering new insights into their creative processes.

While AI can generate visual art, music, or writing, it is essential to remember that these creations are still deeply connected to human intention. AI is not truly creative on its own—it lacks emotions, experience, and a subjective perspective, all crucial elements that give art its meaning and value. A painting by Claude Monet is cherished not just for its visual beauty, but for the story behind it, for the intent of capturing a fleeting moment of light in a world that was becoming increasingly industrialized. Similarly, AI-generated works of art are valuable because of the human input behind them: the artist's decisions, the themes they explore, and the human experience they communicate.

Ultimately, AI is best thought of as a creative assistant. It can help an artist break through creative blocks, introduce randomness or complexity, and provide new perspectives. But it is the human artist who takes these elements and gives them coherence, intention, and purpose. AI is a powerful tool that can augment human creativity, but it cannot replace the uniquely human qualities of empathy, emotional depth, and a personal connection to the work.

Consider the example of Italy's leading newspaper, "Il Secolo XIX", which embraced AI to support its creative writing and journalism. Faced with the challenge of producing high-quality, cost-effective content in the digital age, the newspaper introduced a virtual assistant powered by AI. This tool streamlined the creative process by scanning vast archives and the internet to uncover unique connections and references for stories, while also proofreading drafts for grammatical errors and consistency. Journalists at "Il Secolo XIX" could focus their energy on writing engaging, in-depth pieces, leaving the labour-intensive research and editing to the AI. Rather than replacing its human writers, the virtual assistant elevated their work, enabling "Il Secolo XIX" to deliver expansive, high-quality journalism that set it apart from competitors.

As AI continues to evolve, so too will its role in the creative process. Artists, musicians, writers, and creators across disciplines will find new and innovative ways to integrate AI into their work, leading to unexpected forms of art and expression. The lines between human creativity and machine contribution will continue to blur, resulting in an artistic landscape that is richer, more diverse, and more reflective of both human and technological progress.

AI-driven creativity is not about competition between humans and machines—it is about partnership. It is about expanding what is possible, pushing the limits of our imagination, and finding new ways to explore and express the complexities of the human experience. By embracing AI as a tool for human artists, we open up a future where creativity knows no bounds, where every idea can be explored, and where the beauty of art is amplified through the collaboration of human and machine.

THE ETHICAL DILEMMA

AI Bias

AI holds the potential to enhance various aspects of our lives, from personalized recommendations to automated decision-making. However, with this power comes significant ethical concerns, one of the most critical being bias in AI systems. Bias in AI can occur in numerous ways, often mirroring and amplifying the biases already present in human society. The consequences of biased AI are profound, affecting everything from hiring practices to criminal justice, and raising important ethical questions about fairness, accountability, and equality. Understanding how AI bias happens, as well as the far-reaching consequences it can have, is key to addressing this pressing issue.

AI bias is primarily rooted in the data used to train machine learning models. AI systems learn from vast amounts of historical data, and if this data contains biases, the AI will inherit and even magnify those biases. For instance, if an AI system is trained on historical hiring data that reflects gender discrimination, it will likely perpetuate that discrimination by favouring certain applicants over others based on gender. This phenomenon is known as "data bias," where the quality and composition of the data directly influence the outputs of the AI model.

Another major source of bias is the lack of diversity in training datasets. When the data used to train an AI model is not representative of the population it will serve, the resulting model may perform poorly for underrepresented groups. For example, facial recognition systems have been found to be far less accurate for people with darker skin tones because the training datasets often contain a disproportionate number of images of light-skinned individuals. This type of bias can lead to significant real-world consequences, such as wrongful identification or exclusion from services.

"Ethics should not be something that we think about after we've built the technology. It should be something that is part of the design process from the very beginning." - Timnit Gebru.

Human biases also play a role in how AI systems are developed and deployed. The choices made by developers—such as which data to use, how to label it, and which metrics to optimize—are all influenced by their own perspectives, consciously or unconsciously. This can introduce what is known as "algorithmic bias," where the design and decision-making process of creating the AI model embeds certain biases into the system. Even the goals set for an AI can reflect biases; for instance, a model optimized solely for profit might inadvertently harm vulnerable groups by not taking their needs into consideration.

Bias can also be introduced through the feedback loop that occurs when AI systems interact with users. When AI systems make predictions or recommendations, they influence human behaviour, which in turn generates new data that feeds back into the system. If an AI model has a bias towards certain outcomes, its recommendations can lead users to reinforce that bias, creating a self-perpetuating cycle. For example, if a content recommendation algorithm favours sensationalist news, users are more likely to engage with such content, leading to even more sensationalist recommendations in the future.

The consequences of AI bias are far-reaching and can significantly impact individuals and communities. One of the most troubling areas where AI bias manifests is in the criminal justice system. AI tools are increasingly used to assess the likelihood of reoffending, inform sentencing decisions, or even determine parole eligibility. However, if these tools are trained on biased historical data, they may reinforce existing inequalities, disproportionately labelling certain racial or socioeconomic groups as higher risk. Such biased outcomes can lead to unfair sentencing, further entrenching systemic discrimination.

AI bias also has significant implications for employment. Many companies use AI-powered tools to screen job applications and identify suitable candidates. If the data used to train these models reflects historical biases—such as a preference for male candidates in certain industries—then qualified individuals from underrepresented groups may be systematically overlooked. This not only limits opportunities for individuals but also perpetuates the lack of diversity in the workforce, ultimately affecting innovation and productivity.

In healthcare, AI bias can lead to unequal treatment and outcomes. AI models used for diagnostic purposes or treatment recommendations may not work as effectively for minority groups if those groups are underrepresented in the training data. For instance, studies have shown that some AI systems are less effective at diagnosing skin conditions on people with darker skin tones, simply because the training data lacked sufficient diversity. Such disparities in healthcare can have life-or-death consequences, exacerbating health inequities that already exist.

AI bias can also impact access to financial services. Algorithms used by banks and lending institutions to assess creditworthiness may be biased against certain demographics, leading to unjust denials of loans or credit. If an AI model is trained on data that reflects historical disparities in access to credit, it may continue to disadvantage marginalized communities, making it harder for them to break free from cycles of poverty.

In addition to these specific domains, AI bias can have broader societal implications. When biased AI systems are deployed at scale, they can amplify stereotypes and reinforce harmful narratives. For example, AI language models that are trained on large text corpora from the internet may reflect and propagate sexist, racist, or other prejudiced views. These biases can influence public perception and perpetuate harmful stereotypes, particularly when AI-generated content is used in news articles, social media, or other influential platforms.

Addressing AI bias is a complex but essential task. One key approach is to ensure that training datasets are diverse and representative of the populations the AI will serve. This requires actively seeking out data that includes underrepresented groups and ensuring that the data is of high quality. Efforts should also be made to identify and remove biases from the data before it is used for training.

Another important step is to involve a diverse group of stakeholders in the AI development process. This includes not only developers but also ethicists, social scientists, and representatives from communities that may be impacted by the AI. A diverse team is more likely to identify potential biases and address them before they become embedded in the system.

Transparency and accountability are also crucial. AI developers should be transparent about the data used, the design choices made, and the limitations of their models. This allows for greater scrutiny and helps build trust with the public. In addition, mechanisms for accountability should be established to ensure that organizations deploying AI are held responsible for the impacts of their systems, particularly when those impacts are harmful.

Regular audits and impact assessments can also help identify and mitigate bias. These assessments should be conducted throughout the lifecycle of the AI system, from development to deployment. By continuously monitoring the performance of AI models, developers can identify biases that may emerge over time and take corrective action.

Finally, fostering public awareness and education about AI bias is essential. As AI becomes more integrated into daily life, it is important for the general public to understand the potential risks and limitations of these technologies. An informed public is better equipped to demand fairness and accountability from organizations that develop and deploy AI.

AI bias is a significant ethical issue that has the potential to perpetuate and even amplify existing inequalities in society. Understanding how bias occurs and the consequences it can have, is the first step in addressing this complex problem. While there is no simple solution, a combination of diverse data, inclusive development practices, transparency, accountability, and ongoing monitoring can help mitigate bias and ensure that AI systems are fair and equitable. As AI continues to play an increasingly prominent role in our lives, addressing bias is not just a technical challenge—it is a moral imperative to ensure that AI serves all of humanity, not just a privileged few.

Recognizing And Mitigating Bias

As AI continues to weave itself into the fabric of society, ensuring that it operates without perpetuating harmful biases is becoming increasingly crucial. To prevent AI from amplifying existing inequities, we need to focus on recognizing sources of bias and adopting strategies to mitigate it effectively.

Recognizing bias in AI systems starts with understanding the different types of bias that can arise throughout the lifecycle of AI development and deployment. Bias in AI generally falls into three main categories: data bias, algorithmic bias, and user interaction bias.

Data bias occurs when the dataset used to train an AI system is not representative of the population it is intended to serve. For instance, if a facial recognition system is primarily trained on light-skinned individuals, it will likely be less accurate when identifying people with darker skin tones. This type of bias often stems from historical inequalities that are reflected in the data, causing AI systems to replicate and even exacerbate existing prejudices. Recognizing data bias involves careful examination of training datasets to assess whether they include balanced and representative samples.

Algorithmic bias refers to biases introduced during the design and development of an AI model. Developers make choices that determine how the AI system is structured, including what metrics to optimize and how to label data. These choices can inadvertently introduce bias if developers are not mindful of potential ethical issues. Algorithmic bias can also emerge if an AI model overemphasizes certain features in the data, leading to biased predictions. Recognizing this bias requires examining the algorithms and the design choices that went into creating the model.

Bias can also arise from how users interact with AI systems. For example, recommendation algorithms used in social media platforms tend to amplify content that generates high engagement, which may lead to the propagation of extreme views or misinformation. This bias results from the feedback loop that occurs when users' behaviours reinforce the AI's existing biases. Recognizing user interaction bias involves analysing how AI models change and adapt over time based on user feedback and ensuring that these changes do not contribute to harmful outcomes.

Mitigating bias in AI systems is a multifaceted challenge that requires interventions at multiple stages of the AI lifecycle —from data collection and model development to testing, monitoring, and deployment. Many techniques can help minimize bias in AI systems.

One of the most effective ways to mitigate bias is to ensure that the datasets used to train AI models are diverse and representative. This means collecting data that includes a wide variety of demographic groups, ensuring balanced representation in terms of gender, race, age, and other characteristics. By incorporating diverse data, AI models are more likely to perform equitably across different groups. This approach also involves auditing datasets for historical biases and actively working to remove or counteract those biases.

Developers can use fairness-aware machine learning algorithms that are specifically designed to mitigate bias during training. These algorithms can adjust model parameters to ensure that predictions are not disproportionately skewed against any particular group. Techniques such as re-weighting data points, adjusting decision thresholds, or using fairness constraints can help achieve more balanced outcomes. The goal is to ensure that the AI system's performance metrics, such as accuracy or error rates, are equitable across different demographic groups.

Regular testing and auditing are critical for identifying and mitigating bias in AI systems. Bias testing involves evaluating how an AI model performs across different demographic categories to identify disparities. This can include measuring metrics such as false positive rates and false negative rates for various groups. By conducting these tests regularly, organizations can identify biases early and take corrective actions. Auditing also plays a key role in maintaining transparency and accountability, providing an independent assessment of how well the AI system is meeting fairness standards.

Incorporating human oversight into AI decision-making can help mitigate bias by allowing human experts to review and validate the AI's outputs. Human-in-the-loop (HITL) approaches are particularly useful in high-stakes scenarios, such as hiring, healthcare, or criminal justice, where biased outcomes can have serious consequences. By having human reviewers check the AI's decisions for fairness and correctness, organizations can reduce the risk of biased outcomes and ensure that the AI system aligns with ethical standards.

Making AI systems more transparent and explainable can help mitigate bias by allowing stakeholders to understand how decisions are being made. Explainable AI (XAI) involves developing models that provide interpretable insights into how they arrived at a particular decision. By making the decision-making process more transparent, developers and users can identify potential sources of bias and take appropriate action. This transparency also helps build trust among users, as they can better understand the rationale behind the AI's outputs.

Diversity in the teams that design and develop AI systems is an important factor in mitigating bias. When development teams are composed of individuals from diverse backgrounds, they are more likely to identify and address potential biases that may be overlooked by a homogenous group. Including ethicists, social scientists, and representatives from communities that may be affected by AI in the development process ensures that the AI system is designed with broader perspectives in mind.

AI systems are dynamic and can evolve based on new data and user interactions. To prevent biases from emerging or worsening over time, it is essential to continuously monitor AI models and gather feedback from users. This includes tracking the system's performance over time and identifying any deviations that may indicate bias. Continuous monitoring allows organizations to respond promptly to new biases and make adjustments to maintain fairness.

Recognizing and mitigating bias in AI systems is not just a technical challenge—it also involves ethical and regulatory considerations. Governments and regulatory bodies are increasingly recognizing the importance of addressing AI bias and are developing guidelines and standards to ensure fairness and accountability. For example, the European Union has introduced regulations aimed at promoting transparency, accountability, and fairness in AI systems.

Organizations must also adopt ethical principles to guide the development and deployment of AI systems. These principles should emphasize fairness, accountability, and the protection of individual rights. Establishing internal ethics boards or committees can help organizations navigate the ethical complexities of AI and ensure that their systems align with societal values.

Bias in AI systems is a significant challenge that requires concerted efforts to recognize and mitigate. By understanding the various sources of bias and implementing strategies to address them, we can build AI systems that are fairer and more equitable. Mitigating bias is not just a technical endeavour—it requires diverse teams, transparent practices, and a commitment to ethical principles. As AI becomes more integrated into our daily lives, addressing bias is crucial to ensure that these systems benefit all of humanity and do not perpetuate or amplify existing inequalities.

The Role Of Diverse Teams

In the pursuit of fairness and equity in artificial intelligence, one factor stands out as particularly crucial: the role of diverse teams in the development of AI systems. The diversity of the team designing and implementing an AI system can significantly influence how biases are recognized, addressed, and ultimately mitigated. A homogenous team is more likely to miss certain perspectives and potential pitfalls, whereas a diverse group brings varied experiences, viewpoints, and insights that can help create AI technologies that work better for everyone.

"As we create AI, we have to make sure that we're building AI for all, which means the AI has to really understand, respect, and include everyone." - Satya Nadella.

Artificial Intelligence is increasingly being integrated into systems that directly affect people's lives, from healthcare and education to hiring and law enforcement. When AI systems are developed by a narrow group of individuals, they often reflect the limited perspectives and inherent biases of that group. This is where the importance of diversity comes into play—diverse teams are more capable of identifying the blind spots and biases that may be present in the data or the algorithms themselves.

Diverse teams bring a range of lived experiences to the table. These experiences are invaluable when it comes to understanding the varied ways in which an AI system might impact different groups of people. For example, a team with members from different ethnic backgrounds may be more attuned to the potential racial biases that could emerge in a facial recognition system. Similarly, gender-diverse teams are more likely to recognize and address biases that may disadvantage women in hiring algorithms. By incorporating multiple perspectives, diverse teams can help ensure that AI systems are designed to be fairer and more inclusive.

One of the primary benefits of having diverse teams is the ability to identify blind spots that might otherwise go unnoticed. Blind spots occur when developers lack awareness of the experiences of different demographic groups, leading to biases that manifest in AI systems. For example, a team composed exclusively of individuals from urban areas might not fully understand the needs of rural communities, resulting in AI models that are less effective for those populations.

These blind spots can have significant consequences. In healthcare, for example, AI systems used for diagnosing diseases may be trained primarily on data from certain populations, leading to poorer outcomes for underrepresented groups. If the development team lacks members who understand the specific health challenges faced by those groups, these biases are likely to go unnoticed. By involving team members who have diverse backgrounds and expertise, these blind spots can be identified and addressed early in the development process.

Diverse teams are also more likely to engage in ethical decision-making when developing AI systems. When individuals from different backgrounds work together, they bring a wider range of moral and ethical perspectives to the table. This diversity of thought encourages deeper discussions about the potential societal impacts of AI, helping to ensure that ethical considerations are embedded into the design of the technology.

For example, when developing an AI model for hiring, a diverse team may be more likely to ask critical questions about fairness. Are the features being used in the model—such as educational background or employment history—likely to disadvantage certain groups? Are there historical inequities that need to be accounted for in the data? By fostering an environment in which these kinds of questions are encouraged, diverse teams can help create AI systems that are not only effective but also ethical and equitable.

Algorithmic bias often stems from unrepresentative data. If the training data used to build an AI system does not reflect the diversity of the population it will serve, the resulting model will likely be biased. Having a diverse team helps ensure that the data used is representative and that the model's outputs are evaluated from multiple perspectives.

Diverse teams are more likely to recognize when certain groups are underrepresented in the training data and take steps to address this imbalance. For instance, if a facial recognition model is being developed, a team that includes members from different racial backgrounds is more likely to notice if the training dataset lacks sufficient representation of people with darker skin tones. This awareness can prompt efforts to gather more representative data, ultimately leading to a more equitable AI system.

Inclusive design is a critical aspect of building fair AI systems, and it starts with having diverse teams. Inclusive design processes involve actively seeking input from a broad range of stakeholders, including those who are likely to be most impacted by the AI system. Diverse development teams are more likely to recognize the importance of involving stakeholders from different backgrounds and communities, ensuring that the AI system is designed with everyone in mind.

For example, when developing a language model, a diverse team might involve speakers of different dialects or individuals who speak languages that are often underrepresented in technology. By involving these stakeholders, the team can ensure that the AI system works well for a wider range of users, rather than just those who speak the most commonly represented languages.

Trust is a crucial component of the successful deployment of AI systems, and diverse teams can play a key role in building that trust. When users see that an AI system has been developed by a team that reflects their own experiences and backgrounds, they are more likely to trust that the system has been designed with their needs in mind. This trust is particularly important in areas such as healthcare, finance, and law enforcement, where the consequences of biased AI can be severe.

Moreover, diverse teams are better equipped to communicate

the limitations and potential biases of AI systems to the public. By being transparent about the challenges and actively working to address them, these teams can help build public confidence in AI technologies. This transparency is essential for fostering a sense of accountability and ensuring that AI systems are used responsibly.

While the benefits of diverse teams are clear, achieving diversity in AI development is not without its challenges. The technology industry as a whole has struggled with diversity, and AI development is no exception. Addressing this issue requires concerted efforts from organizations, including creating inclusive hiring practices, providing mentorship and support for underrepresented groups, and fostering a culture that values diverse perspectives.

However, the opportunities presented by diverse teams are immense. By bringing together individuals with different backgrounds, experiences, and expertise, we can create AI systems that are not only more effective but also more equitable. Diverse teams are better equipped to recognize and address bias, engage in ethical decision-making, and build AI systems that work for everyone, not just a privileged few.

The role of diverse teams in algorithm development cannot be overstated. Diversity is not just a nice-to-have; it is essential for creating AI systems that are fair, ethical, and equitable. By bringing together individuals with varied perspectives, experiences, and expertise, diverse teams can help identify and mitigate bias, ensure that AI systems are designed with all users in mind, and build public trust in these technologies. As AI continues to shape our world, the need for diverse teams in its development will only become more pressing. Creating fair and equitable AI systems is a collective responsibility, and it starts with ensuring that the teams building these systems reflect the diversity of the society they aim to serve.

Data Privacy Concerns

As AI continues to evolve data privacy concerns are taking centre stage. AI systems rely heavily on data—collected, processed, and analysed—to function effectively. This dependence on data raises significant questions about how personal information is being used, who has access to it, and what protections are in place to ensure the privacy of individuals. In a world increasingly driven by AI, understanding, and addressing data privacy concerns is crucial to maintain trust and safeguard personal freedoms.

AI systems are powered by massive amounts of data. Machine learning models, for instance, require large datasets to train effectively. These datasets often contain personal information, such as purchasing habits, browsing history, medical records, or even biometric data. By analysing this data, AI can make predictions, generate personalized recommendations, and automate decision-making processes. However, the use of such data raises important questions about privacy and consent.

In 2000, only 20% of the world's information was stored digitally. Today, that figure has soared to nearly 99.9%. Remarkably, the total data generated by humanity up to the year 2000 is now produced every single day.

The collection and storage of data are often done without explicit consent or clear understanding from the individuals whose data is being used. Many people are unaware of how much information they are sharing or the ways in which it could be used. AI systems can aggregate data from various sources, painting a detailed picture of an individual's behaviour, preferences, and even health conditions. This level of information can be used to improve services, but it also poses significant risks if it falls into the wrong hands or is used for unintended purposes.

One of the main challenges in data privacy is the issue of consent. AI systems often collect data passively, through devices such as smartphones, smart home appliances, and wearables. Users may not fully understand the extent to which their data is being collected or how it will be used. Consent is frequently obtained through long, complex terms of service agreements that few people read or understand. This lack of informed consent raises ethical concerns about whether individuals are truly agreeing to the use of their data.

In the digital economy, data is the new oil—an invaluable resource fuelling corporate power and influence. Data is extracted from everyday activities: every search, click, and interaction feeds into vast databases. Smart devices and assistants collect details about your health, habits, and home life, while smart cities track movement and behaviour on a grand scale. Tech giants like Amazon and Google are the barons of this data age, using centralized information to predict trends, shape decisions, and influence societies. This isn't just about ads; it's about power—reshaping markets and reinforcing inequalities. By recognizing this exchange of convenience for personal information, individuals can make more thoughtful choices in navigating the digital world.

Another privacy challenge involves data anonymization. Many organizations attempt to anonymize personal data before using it for AI training. However, true anonymization is difficult to achieve. Advanced AI algorithms can often re-identify individuals from supposedly anonymized datasets by cross-referencing multiple sources of information. This re-identification risk means that even data that has been stripped of obvious identifiers can still pose a privacy threat.

The vast amounts of data required by AI systems make them attractive targets for cyberattacks. A breach of an AI system can expose sensitive personal information on a massive scale. Data breaches not only compromise individual privacy but also erode public trust in AI technologies. Ensuring robust data security measures are in place is essential to protect against unauthorized access and prevent sensitive information from falling into the wrong hands.

Questions of data ownership are also central to privacy concerns in an AI-driven world. Who owns the data collected by AI systems? Is it the individual who generated the data, the company that collected it, or the AI system that processes it? The lack of clear legal frameworks around data ownership can lead to misuse of personal information and limit individuals' ability to control how their data is used.

AI's capabilities in surveillance and monitoring have significant implications for privacy. Facial recognition technology, for instance, is increasingly being used for surveillance purposes. While such technologies can enhance security, they also raise concerns about the erosion of privacy and the potential for misuse by governments or corporations. The ability of AI to monitor individuals' movements and behaviours in real-time can create a surveillance society where personal freedoms are compromised.

To address the growing concerns around data privacy in AI, a combination of technological, regulatory, and ethical approaches is required. Different strategies can help mitigate the risks associated with data privacy.

One approach to safeguarding data privacy is to adopt a "privacy by design" framework. This means that privacy considerations are built into the AI system from the very beginning, rather than being added as an afterthought. Privacy by design involves minimizing data collection, using encryption to protect data, and ensuring that only necessary information is collected and stored.

Governments and regulatory bodies have a key role to play in addressing data privacy concerns. Regulations such as the General Data Protection Regulation (GDPR) in the European Union have set a high standard for data protection by giving individuals greater control over their data and imposing strict requirements on organizations that collect and process personal information. Similar regulations should be developed and enforced worldwide to ensure that AI systems are held accountable for how they handle data.

Ensuring transparency in data collection and use is essential for building trust. AI developers should provide clear, accessible information about what data is being collected, how it will be used, and who will have access to it. Simplified consent processes, such as providing users with easy-to-understand summaries of data usage, can help individuals make informed decisions about sharing their data.

Differential privacy is a technique that allows AI models to learn from data without revealing specific information about individual data points. By adding statistical noise to the data, differential privacy ensures that the privacy of individuals is maintained, even while the AI system gains insights from the overall dataset. This approach can help mitigate the risks associated with data re-identification.

Federated learning is another technique that can help address data privacy concerns. Instead of collecting data in a centralized location, federated learning allows AI models to be trained on data stored locally on users' devices. This means that personal data never leaves the user's device, reducing the risk of data breaches and ensuring that individuals retain greater control over their information.

Establishing ethical guidelines for AI development is crucial for ensuring data privacy. Organizations should adopt ethical principles that prioritize user privacy and data protection.

These principles should guide decision-making throughout the AI lifecycle, from data collection to model deployment. Ethical AI development also involves conducting privacy impact assessments to identify and mitigate potential risks before deploying AI systems.

While organizations and governments have a significant role to play in addressing data privacy concerns, individuals also have a responsibility to protect their own privacy. This includes being mindful of the data they share, understanding the privacy policies of the apps and services they use, and taking steps to secure their personal information. Using privacy-enhancing tools, such as virtual private networks (VPNs) and encrypted messaging apps, can help individuals maintain control over their data in an AI-driven world.

Data privacy is one of the most pressing concerns in an AI-driven world. As AI systems become more powerful and more integrated into our lives, the need to protect personal information becomes increasingly important. Addressing data privacy concerns requires a multi-faceted approach, involving stronger regulations, privacy-conscious design, transparency, and the use of privacy-preserving technologies. By prioritizing data privacy, we can build AI systems that respect individual rights, maintain public trust, and ensure that the benefits of AI are realized without compromising personal freedoms.

In 2024, global digital activity reached unprecedented levels, with 5.5 billion people online. Each minute, users conducted 5.9 million Google searches, Netflix streamed 363 thousand hours of content, TikTok users uploaded 16 thousand videos, Microsoft Teams facilitated 229 million meeting minutes, and 251 million e-mails were sent. However, increased digital activity brought security challenges, with 4,080 records compromised in data breaches every minute, underscoring the need for robust cybersecurity measures.

Who's Responsible For AI Decisions?

As AI becomes embedded in decision-making processes across industries, the question of accountability is becoming increasingly important. Who should be held responsible when an AI system makes a mistake, or when its decisions lead to unintended consequences? This issue is particularly complex because AI systems are often developed and operated by multiple stakeholders, including developers, companies, and users. Establishing clear lines of accountability is essential to ensure that AI systems are used responsibly and that their impacts are appropriately managed.

AI systems, especially those based on machine learning, operate in ways that are often opaque even to their developers. These systems learn from large datasets and make decisions based on patterns they identify, but the exact logic behind these decisions may not always be transparent. This lack of transparency, often referred to as the "black box" nature of AI, makes it difficult to determine who is accountable when something goes wrong.

For example, if an AI system used for hiring makes discriminatory decisions, who should be held responsible? Is it the developers who created the algorithm, the company that deployed it, or the data scientists who provided the training data? The answer is not always straightforward, as each of these stakeholders plays a role in the development and use of the AI system. This complexity makes accountability a challenging issue to navigate.

Accountability in AI decision-making can be approached from both legal and ethical perspectives. Legally, there are ongoing debates about whether existing laws are sufficient to address the unique challenges posed by AI. In many cases, laws that govern product liability are being adapted to cover AI systems. For instance, if an autonomous vehicle causes an accident, existing liability laws may hold the manufacturer responsible. However, the dynamic nature of AI, which can evolve and learn after deployment, complicates the application of traditional legal frameworks.

Ethical accountability, on the other hand, involves considering the broader societal impacts of AI decisions. Developers and companies have an ethical responsibility to ensure that their AI systems are fair, transparent, and do not cause harm. This includes taking proactive steps to identify and mitigate biases, ensuring that AI systems are explainable, and being transparent about the limitations of the technology. Ethical accountability also means involving stakeholders who may be affected by AI decisions in the development process, ensuring that their perspectives are considered.

Developers play a crucial role in ensuring that AI systems are designed responsibly. They are responsible for choosing appropriate training data, selecting algorithms that minimize bias, and conducting thorough testing to identify potential issues before deployment. Developers must also work to make AI systems more interpretable, so that their decisions can be understood and audited by others. However, developers alone cannot be held fully accountable, as they often work within the constraints set by the organizations that employ them.

Companies that deploy AI systems also bear significant responsibility. They are the ones who decide how and where AI is used, and they must ensure that the systems they deploy are used ethically and responsibly. This includes conducting impact assessments to understand the potential consequences of AI deployment, as well as establishing mechanisms for monitoring and addressing any negative outcomes. Companies should also be transparent with users about how AI is being used and provide avenues for recourse if individuals are negatively affected by AI decisions.

In some cases, users of AI systems also have a role to play in accountability. For example, if a healthcare provider uses an AI tool to assist in diagnosing patients, they must understand the limitations of the tool and use their professional judgment to make final decisions. Users should be educated about the strengths and weaknesses of the AI systems they interact with, so that they can use them appropriately and recognize when a decision might need further review.

To address the challenges of accountability in AI decision-making, regulatory bodies around the world are beginning to develop frameworks specifically for AI. The European Union's proposed AI Act, for example, seeks to establish clear guidelines for the development and deployment of AI systems, with a focus on high-risk applications. The Act includes requirements for transparency, risk management, and human oversight, and it assigns specific responsibilities to different stakeholders involved in the AI lifecycle.

Another regulatory approach is the concept of "human-in-the-loop" (HITL), which ensures that human oversight is maintained in critical decision-making processes. By requiring that a human be involved in reviewing and approving certain AI decisions, HITL aims to prevent the misuse of AI and ensure that accountability remains with a human operator rather than being shifted entirely to an automated system.

Explainability is a key component of accountability in AI. If an AI system makes a decision that has significant consequences, it is important to be able to understand how that decision was reached. This is particularly important in sectors such as healthcare, finance, and criminal justice, where AI decisions can have life-altering impacts. Explainable AI (XAI) aims to make the decision-making process of AI systems more transparent, allowing stakeholders to understand the factors that influenced a particular outcome.

Without explainability, it is difficult to assign accountability, as it is unclear whether a poor decision was the result of flawed data, a biased algorithm, or inappropriate use of the AI system. By making AI systems more interpretable, developers and companies can help ensure that accountability is maintained and that individuals affected by AI decisions have a clear path to understanding and challenging those decisions if necessary.

Given the complexity of AI systems and the number of stakeholders involved, accountability for AI decisions must be viewed as a shared responsibility. Developers, companies, regulators, and users all have roles to play in ensuring that AI is used responsibly. This collective approach to accountability helps ensure that no single entity is unfairly blamed for the negative consequences of AI, while also ensuring that all stakeholders are motivated to act ethically and responsibly.

For example, developers should strive to create fair and transparent algorithms, companies should ensure that these algorithms are used appropriately, and regulators should provide oversight to ensure that standards are being met. Users, too, must be educated about the limitations of AI and use their judgment to complement AI decisions. By sharing accountability across all stakeholders, we can create a system in which AI is used in a way that benefits society while minimizing harm.

Accountability in AI decision-making is a complex but essential issue. As AI systems continue to influence more aspects of our lives, it is crucial to establish clear lines of accountability to ensure that these systems are used responsibly and ethically. This requires a collective effort, involving developers, companies, regulators, and users, as well as the implementation of regulatory frameworks and practices that prioritize transparency and human oversight. By fostering a culture of shared accountability, we can ensure that AI serves the interests of all members of society, while minimizing the risks associated with its use.

Ensuring AI Is Safe

Another pressing question dominates discussions around the technology: how can we ensure that AI is safe for everyone? The development and implementation of AI systems have enormous potential to transform industries, optimize services, and improve the quality of life for billions. However, the vast power of AI also presents challenges, particularly in the realms of safety, ethics, and inclusivity. Ensuring AI is safe for everyone means adopting comprehensive strategies to prevent harm and unintended consequences while maximizing benefits across diverse communities.

The importance of ensuring AI is safe cannot be understated. Unsafe AI can have disastrous consequences—such as biased decision-making, privacy violations, unsafe interactions, and even physical harm in areas like autonomous vehicles or robotic systems. When an AI system makes incorrect decisions, the impacts can ripple across society, affecting individuals, businesses, and governments. Mistakes in healthcare diagnostics, flawed credit ratings, wrongful arrests due to facial recognition errors, or even AI-driven misinformation can have devastating personal and societal consequences.

Addressing these challenges requires a multi-faceted approach to developing AI that is reliable, transparent, and aligned with human values. Safety must be baked into AI from the ground up—from the initial data collection and training phases to deployment and post-deployment monitoring. A key question remains: what specific measures are required to make AI safe for everyone, regardless of their background or circumstances?

The principle of "safety-by-design" in AI development is akin to building a structurally sound house from the foundation up. It means designing AI systems with safety protocols, rigorous testing, and ethical considerations embedded throughout the entire development process. The goal is to minimize harm and reduce the likelihood of unintended consequences.

"Secrecy is the underlying mistake that makes every innovation go wrong in Michael Crichton novels and films! If AI happens in the open, then errors and flaws may be discovered in time... perhaps by other, wary AIs!" – David Brin.

High-quality data forms the backbone of any AI system. Ensuring that training datasets are diverse, balanced, and representative of all segments of society is critical to minimizing algorithmic bias. Without addressing biases in the data, AI systems will inevitably make decisions that reflect and perpetuate existing inequalities.

Testing and evaluation are crucial to identifying any flaws or inconsistencies in AI models before they are deployed. This includes extensive pre-launch testing in real-world scenarios to ensure that the AI behaves as intended. Testing must be done under varied and challenging circumstances to uncover how the system handles unpredictable situations—ensuring robustness and reliability.

AI systems often function as opaque "black boxes," making decisions without providing clear explanations. Ensuring AI is transparent and explainable is crucial to building trust and accountability. An explainable AI provides insights into how it reaches its decisions, which is especially important in critical domains like healthcare, criminal justice, and finance. Stakeholders, including users, developers, and regulators, should have a clear understanding of why an AI system is behaving the way it is.

A practical way of ensuring AI safety is to integrate human oversight into AI systems—particularly in high-stakes environments. By keeping humans in the loop (HITL), decisions made by AI can be reviewed, corrected, or overridden by human experts. This approach can be instrumental in situations where moral or ethical considerations play a significant role, as it ensures that human judgment is part of the decision-making process.

Ensuring AI is safe is not a one-time effort but an ongoing process. After an AI model is deployed, it is essential to continuously monitor its performance and outcomes. If any issues arise—such as discriminatory behaviour, reduced accuracy, or harmful unintended effects—they must be addressed promptly through updates and retraining.

AI is a global technology, but its development and impact are deeply influenced by local contexts. As such, it is imperative to establish global standards for AI safety and ethics, while also respecting regional cultures, laws, and values. Regulatory measures can help ensure that AI developers, organizations, and users comply with best practices for safety.

Governments and regulatory bodies must enact comprehensive policies that outline the safety standards for AI systems. Regulations that establish clear guidelines for data privacy, accountability, bias mitigation, and ethical use of AI can promote the responsible deployment of AI while safeguarding citizens' rights.

AI certification programs can ensure that only AI systems that pass rigorous safety and ethical benchmarks are deployed. Independent audits and assessments by third-party entities can help verify that AI systems are functioning safely and within legal and ethical boundaries.

Organizations, governments, and researchers must collaborate to share best practices for AI safety. By working together, stakeholders can create a shared understanding of the challenges and solutions related to AI safety, avoiding repeated mistakes, and improving AI governance.

Ensuring AI is safe for everyone also involves addressing the diverse needs of different groups of people. Historically marginalized and underrepresented communities often face the highest risks of being negatively impacted by AI—whether it is due to biased datasets, systemic discrimination, or reduced access to technology. Inclusivity must be at the core of AI safety efforts to ensure that everyone can benefit from AI without suffering harm.

A diverse AI development team brings varied perspectives, which can help in identifying potential pitfalls or biases that might not be apparent to a homogenous group. Representation in AI development is essential for ensuring that the systems being built address the needs of diverse populations and do not perpetuate harmful stereotypes.

AI systems should be context-aware and adaptable to the specific cultural and social contexts in which they operate. This requires careful consideration of factors such as language, local customs, and socio-economic conditions to ensure that AI remains effective and safe for everyone, regardless of their environment.

Including the voices of communities most affected by AI technologies is critical to ensuring safety and fairness. Community involvement in discussions around AI deployment helps identify concerns early on, leading to more responsible and inclusive technology.

Finally, ensuring AI is safe for everyone means building public trust. This involves educating the general population about AI— how it works, its benefits, and its potential risks. Transparency around AI development and use is essential for fostering public trust. When people understand how AI is being used in their lives, they can make informed decisions about how to engage with it.

AI literacy initiatives can empower individuals to understand AI's capabilities and limitations, thereby reducing fear and uncertainty. For example, helping users recognize the difference between AI-generated content and human-created content can combat misinformation and increase awareness of AI's impacts on society.

Ensuring AI is safe for everyone is an ongoing, multi-dimensional challenge that requires collaboration, regulation, and an unwavering commitment to ethical principles. It involves building diverse teams, designing AI systems with safety as a core feature, developing transparent regulatory frameworks, and engaging with communities to ensure inclusivity. With proper safeguards and a concerted global effort, AI can truly benefit all of humanity while minimizing the risks and unintended consequences. The journey toward safe and equitable AI is complex, but it is essential to building a future where AI serves society in a fair, ethical, and responsible manner.

The Role Of Human Oversight

AI systems are becoming increasingly pervasive in our everyday lives, from virtual assistants in our smartphones to recommendation algorithms on streaming platforms and decision-support tools in healthcare. As AI takes on a greater role in making decisions that impact individuals and society at large, one critical issue looms larger than ever: the role of human oversight. Ensuring human oversight in AI systems is essential to keeping these technologies aligned with our values, minimizing harm, and guaranteeing accountability.

AI systems are designed to learn from data, adapt, and even make autonomous decisions. However, these systems, as sophisticated as they may be, lack the kind of common sense, ethical considerations, and broader context that come naturally to human beings. Human oversight is necessary to counterbalance AI's limitations—from understanding the subtleties of language and human behaviour to handling unpredictable real-world situations. In situations where AI might make decisions based solely on data correlations, human intervention can bring in the nuances of ethics, fairness, and empathy.

"It's important that we have human oversight in AI decision-making, to ensure that it is aligned with our values and that it benefits society as a whole." -Max Tegmark

---

AI systems have already demonstrated the risks of operating without adequate human oversight. Take the case of facial recognition technologies that were adopted by law enforcement agencies, which led to misidentifications and false arrests. These incidents often occurred because the systems failed to account for biases in the training data, particularly with regard to racial and gender representation. This kind of bias might have been mitigated if humans were involved in continuously monitoring and validating the output of these systems, ensuring their accuracy and fairness.

Human oversight can take many forms, depending on the context in which the AI is being used. One of the most common methods is "human-in-the-loop" (HITL), where human intervention is required before the AI makes critical decisions. This approach is especially beneficial in areas where the consequences of an incorrect decision are severe, such as healthcare or criminal justice. For instance, an AI system might analyse medical scans for potential signs of illness, but a human doctor ultimately reviews and confirms the diagnosis. This not only helps improve the accuracy of the system but also instils trust among patients and healthcare providers.

Another model is "human-on-the-loop" (HOTL), where humans oversee the AI's functioning in real-time but do not intervene in every decision. This is commonly used in autonomous systems, such as drones or self-driving cars, where human operators monitor the overall performance and can step in if something goes wrong. In this model, humans act as supervisors, ensuring that the AI does not deviate from its intended goals or safety parameters.

The "human-out-of-the-loop" (HOOTL) model represents fully autonomous systems where no real-time human intervention is involved, but even here, oversight plays an essential role. For these systems, human oversight occurs during the development phase, where rigorous testing and validation processes are implemented to ensure that the AI behaves safely and ethically. For example, automated financial trading systems are heavily monitored and tested before deployment, ensuring that they adhere to regulatory requirements and do not pose risks to market stability.

While the importance of human oversight is clear, implementing it effectively poses several challenges. One of the primary challenges is the complexity of modern AI systems. Deep learning models, for instance, are often described as "black boxes" because even their developers cannot always explain how they arrive at a particular decision. This lack of transparency can make it difficult for human overseers to detect errors or biases, let alone intervene effectively.

Furthermore, the scale and speed at which AI operates can overwhelm human supervisors. In areas like financial trading or real-time content moderation on social media platforms, decisions are made in milliseconds, far faster than a human can react. This necessitates innovative oversight mechanisms that combine automated checks with human intuition. Techniques such as explainable AI (XAI) are being developed to make AI decision-making more transparent, thus facilitating better human oversight.

Another challenge is the potential for over-reliance on AI, often referred to as "automation bias." When humans are tasked with overseeing AI systems that are perceived as highly accurate or sophisticated, there is a risk that they may become complacent and fail to intervene, even when the system is making errors. This issue underscores the need for training and awareness among human supervisors to ensure they remain engaged and critical of AI decisions.

Ensuring effective human oversight in AI systems requires a delicate balance. On one hand, excessive human intervention can limit the efficiency gains promised by automation, potentially leading to bottlenecks and delays. On the other hand, insufficient oversight can lead to ethical lapses, safety hazards, and public distrust in AI technologies. Finding the right balance involves determining the appropriate level of human involvement based on the context and potential impact of the AI's decisions.

One approach is to develop oversight frameworks that are dynamic and adaptable. Instead of rigid rules about when humans should intervene, these frameworks can use risk assessment to determine the appropriate level of oversight. For example, an AI system used in healthcare might require continuous human oversight when diagnosing life-threatening conditions, while an AI used for non-critical administrative tasks might only need periodic reviews.

As AI systems continue to evolve, the role of human oversight will also need to adapt. Advances in explainable AI, ethical AI frameworks, and regulatory measures are all contributing to more robust oversight mechanisms. However, the ultimate responsibility lies with the humans who design, deploy, and interact with these systems. Developers must be proactive in building AI systems that are transparent and interpretable, making it easier for human supervisors to understand and oversee their operation.

In the future, we may see hybrid systems where AI assists human supervisors in overseeing other AI systems, creating a layered approach to oversight. This could help mitigate the challenges of scale and speed, ensuring that even highly complex and fast-moving AI systems remain under effective human control.

The role of human oversight is fundamental to ensuring that AI systems serve humanity's best interests. By thoughtfully integrating human judgment into AI workflows, we can harness the benefits of automation while safeguarding against the risks. Ultimately, human oversight is not just about preventing mistakes—it's about ensuring that AI remains aligned with human values, ethics, and aspirations.

THE SHADOW SIDE

Widening Economic Inequality

The rise of AI and automation is reshaping industries, labour markets, and the global economy. While these technologies hold the promise of efficiency, innovation, and economic growth, they also bring a significant risk: widening economic inequality. As AI-driven systems become more advanced and more widely implemented, the gap between those who benefit from these technologies and those who do not is growing, potentially leading to serious social and economic consequences.

AI and automation are transforming the nature of work by replacing or significantly altering jobs across various industries. While many white-collar jobs that involve repetitive data processing are susceptible to automation, it is also affecting blue-collar work, such as manufacturing, logistics, and customer service. This trend poses a significant risk to workers whose roles can be automated, resulting in job displacement and a shrinking pool of available employment opportunities for lower-skilled workers.

Historically, technological advances have led to the creation of new jobs, but the speed and scale of AI-driven automation may exceed society's ability to adapt. In the past, workers displaced by machines often found employment in new industries created by those same technological advancements. However, with

AI, the skills required for the new jobs being created—often involving coding, data analysis, or advanced technical abilities—are significantly different from those required for the jobs that are disappearing. This shift has left many workers unprepared, contributing to a widening gap between highly skilled and lower-skilled workers.

AI is also accelerating economic inequality by concentrating wealth in the hands of those who own and develop these technologies. Large technology companies, predominantly based in wealthier countries, are at the forefront of AI research and implementation. As these companies dominate the AI landscape, the profits generated from increased efficiency, automation, and new AI products tend to benefit a small group of individuals—primarily investors, executives, and highly-skilled workers—while the economic opportunities for the broader population dwindle.

The economic divide is also apparent on a global scale. Wealthier nations, with the resources to invest in AI research and development, are benefiting from the economic advantages of automation, whereas developing countries that rely on low-cost labour may find themselves left behind. Industries such as textile manufacturing, where developing nations often have a competitive advantage, are increasingly being automated. This trend could lead to diminished economic prospects for countries that depend on labour-intensive industries, exacerbating the global inequality gap.

"The future is here – it's just not evenly distributed." – William Gibson

---

AI-driven automation is contributing to the polarization of the labour market. Jobs are increasingly split between high-skill, high-wage positions that require advanced technical skills and low-skill, low-wage positions that cannot easily be automated, such as care work, cleaning, or certain types of manual labour. The middle-skill, middle-wage jobs that traditionally supported the middle class are increasingly disappearing, leading to a hollowing out of the labour market. This polarization exacerbates economic inequality, as those at the top see their incomes grow, while many others struggle to make ends meet.

AI undermines established growth models, particularly in manufacturing and services. In Bangladesh, AI integration into garment production could displace up to 60% of jobs in the sector by 2030. Similarly, automation in call centres and IT services is reducing the labour-intensity of industries that have driven growth in countries like India and the Philippines, threatening their competitive edge in global markets.

Moreover, the jobs that are least likely to be automated often involve interpersonal skills, empathy, and physical presence—traits that are inherently human and cannot be easily replicated by AI. However, these roles are frequently undervalued and underpaid, leading to further disparities in income and job security.

Addressing the risks of widening economic inequality requires proactive policies and initiatives aimed at ensuring that the benefits of AI are distributed more equitably. One proposed solution is the implementation of a Universal Basic Income (UBI), which would provide all citizens with a guaranteed income, regardless of employment status. This safety net could help those who are displaced by automation to meet their basic needs while they retrain or transition to new roles. However, UBI remains a controversial solution, with concerns about its cost and potential disincentive for work.

In 1954, union leader Walter Reuther visited a Ford Motors plant that had recently introduced robotic machines on its assembly line. When a Ford employee asked how Reuther planned to collect union dues from the robots, he cleverly responded, "How do you plan to get them to buy Fords?"

Education and retraining programs are crucial in helping workers adapt to the changing job landscape. Governments, educational institutions, and private companies must collaborate to provide accessible and affordable training opportunities that equip workers with the skills needed for emerging industries. Emphasizing lifelong learning and reskilling can help bridge the gap between displaced workers and the new opportunities created by AI.

Another approach is the implementation of progressive taxation and wealth redistribution policies. Taxing large technology companies that benefit most from automation and using those funds to invest in social safety nets, education, and community support programs can help mitigate the negative impacts of AI-driven inequality. Governments should also consider incentivizing companies to invest in their workers by providing training and upskilling opportunities, thereby ensuring that the workforce can adapt to technological changes.

Inclusive AI development is also essential. Ensuring that AI technologies are developed with diverse teams and taking into account the needs and perspectives of different communities can help create solutions that benefit a broader cross-section of society. Ethical AI practices that prioritize fairness, transparency, and inclusivity can reduce the risk of exacerbating existing inequalities.

Ultimately, addressing the risks of widening economic inequality due to AI requires both social and political will. Policymakers must recognize the potential dangers of unchecked automation and take steps to ensure that the benefits of AI are widely shared. This will require collaboration between governments, private companies, and civil society to create a framework that promotes equitable growth and protects vulnerable populations.

AI offers opportunities to reduce inequality if leveraged for social good. Precision farming powered by AI can significantly boost crop yields for smallholder farmers in regions like sub-Saharan Africa.

The rise of AI and automation has the potential to bring about significant economic and social benefits, but without thoughtful intervention, it also risks deepening existing inequalities. By investing in education, promoting inclusive development, and implementing fair economic policies, society can work towards an AI-driven future that benefits everyone, rather than a privileged few.

The Digital Divide

AI is rapidly transforming economies, industries, and societies, bringing new opportunities for growth and innovation. However, the benefits of AI are not accessible to everyone. The digital divide—the gap between those who have access to technology and those who do not—is becoming an increasingly critical issue as AI becomes more prevalent. This divide not only limits individual opportunities but also has far-reaching implications for inequality, both within and between countries.

The digital divide in the context of AI is about more than just having a smartphone or an internet connection. It extends to access to the resources necessary for developing and benefiting from AI technologies, such as computing power, data, digital skills, and infrastructure. Access to these resources is distributed unevenly, often favouring wealthier individuals, communities, and countries.

For individuals and communities without access to high-speed internet, advanced computing devices, and reliable electricity, the opportunities to benefit from AI are extremely limited. For example, remote learning platforms that use AI for personalized education are of little use in regions without stable internet access or where people lack the necessary digital literacy skills. This lack of access can prevent communities from gaining the skills needed to participate in the modern workforce, further entrenching existing inequalities.

AI risks amplifying the divide between rich and poor countries. In 2023, the United States alone attracted $67 billion in private AI investments—9 times more than China, the second-highest recipient. Wealthier nations, with 80–93% internet penetration, dominate AI innovation, leaving countries with limited access —just 27% in low-income regions—struggling to keep pace. These disparities make it increasingly difficult for poorer nations to compete in AI-driven economies.

On a larger scale, the divide is evident between countries. Wealthier nations that have the resources to invest in AI research and development are at the forefront of technological advancements, while developing nations, which may lack the necessary infrastructure and investment, risk falling behind. This disparity limits the ability of developing countries to compete in the global economy, exacerbating the economic divide between nations.

Access to AI technologies is closely tied to access to education and digital skills. In regions where quality education is lacking, individuals are less likely to acquire the skills necessary to engage with AI technologies. This can create a cycle of exclusion, where communities that lack access to technology also lack the skills needed to take advantage of it, thereby perpetuating their disadvantaged status.

The rise of AI is also creating new demands for skills in areas such as data science, machine learning, and computer programming. These are highly specialized skills that require access to quality education and training, which are often not available in underserved communities or developing nations. As a result, those who are unable to access the education needed to work in AI-related fields are left out of the economic opportunities that these industries create.

AI-enabled educational tools can bring quality learning to remote areas. For instance, programs in Viet Nam aim to integrate AI and digital literacy into all levels of education by 2025, equipping future generations with the skills to thrive in an AI-driven world.

Efforts to bridge this skills gap are critical for ensuring that AI technologies benefit a broader spectrum of society. Initiatives that focus on digital literacy, coding, and STEM education can help equip individuals with the skills they need to participate in an AI-driven economy. However, these initiatives require significant investment and political will, particularly in regions that have been historically underserved.

The economic consequences of the digital divide are significant. As AI technologies continue to drive economic growth, those without access to these technologies are increasingly excluded from the benefits. In many cases, this exclusion is not just about missing out on new opportunities; it is about losing access to existing ones. As industries adopt AI-driven automation, jobs that require less technical skill are at greater risk of being replaced by machines, while new jobs being created are often out of reach for those without the necessary digital skills.

This shift has the potential to deepen economic inequality, both within and between countries. In wealthier nations, communities with limited access to technology may find themselves excluded from economic growth and upward mobility. Meanwhile, developing nations that are unable to invest in AI may find their industries becoming less competitive on the global stage, leading to a widening economic divide between rich and poor countries.

The digital divide also has social implications. Communities that lack access to AI technologies may miss out on advancements in healthcare, education, and public services that are increasingly being driven by AI. For example, AI-powered diagnostic tools have the potential to improve healthcare outcomes, but only for those who have access to the necessary technology and infrastructure. Without targeted efforts to expand access, the gap in quality of life between those who have access to AI technologies and those who do not will continue to grow.

Addressing the digital divide requires coordinated efforts from governments, private companies, and civil society. One important step is to expand access to the internet and digital infrastructure, particularly in underserved regions. Investment in broadband infrastructure, affordable devices, and reliable electricity can help ensure that more people have the tools they need to benefit from AI technologies.

Targeted policies can bridge the AI gap. For example, India's Digital India initiative connected over 600,000 villages to high-speed broadband, laying the groundwork for AI-driven education and agriculture solutions.

In addition to expanding physical access, it is essential to invest in education and training programs that equip individuals with the skills they need to participate in an AI-driven economy. This includes not only technical skills, such as coding and data analysis, but also digital literacy and critical thinking skills that can help individuals understand and engage with AI technologies in meaningful ways.

The private sector also has a role to play in bridging the digital divide. Technology companies can work to make their products and services more accessible to underserved communities, both by lowering costs and by providing training and support. Public-private partnerships can be particularly effective in addressing the digital divide, combining the resources and expertise of the private sector with the reach and public mission of government institutions.

The digital divide is not just a local or national issue; it is a global one. Addressing the disparities in access to AI technologies will require international cooperation and support. Wealthier nations that are leading the development of AI have a responsibility to support efforts to expand access to technology in developing countries. This can be done through funding for infrastructure projects, support for educational initiatives, and the sharing of knowledge and best practices.

Organizations such as the United Nations and the World Bank can play an important role in coordinating these efforts, helping to ensure that the benefits of AI are distributed more equitably. By working together, countries can help bridge the digital divide and create a more inclusive global economy where everyone has the opportunity to benefit from the advancements brought about by AI.

The digital divide poses a significant challenge to the equitable distribution of the benefits of AI. Without targeted efforts to expand access to technology and education, the gap between those who benefit from AI and those who do not will continue to widen, exacerbating existing inequalities. By investing in infrastructure, education, and international cooperation, it is possible to bridge the digital divide and create a future where the benefits of AI are accessible to all, not just a privileged few.

The challenge of the digital divide is a reminder that technology alone cannot solve social and economic inequality. Ensuring that AI serves as a force for good will require not only technological innovation but also a commitment to fairness, inclusion, and social justice. By working together, we can create an AI-driven future that benefits everyone, regardless of where they live or what resources they have access to.

China And Catching Up

In the early 2000s, Chinese entrepreneurs often emulated successful Silicon Valley products, a strategy that many in the West dismissed as mere imitation. However, this approach served as a learning platform, enabling these entrepreneurs to develop world-class products tailored to the Chinese market.

Wang Xing exemplifies this trajectory. He initially created Chinese versions of platforms like Friendster, Facebook, Twitter, and Groupon, which allowed him to master product design and navigate China's competitive business environment. This experience was instrumental when he launched Meituan, a group discount service that evolved into a comprehensive platform offering services such as food delivery, hotel bookings, and travel arrangements.

Meituan's growth has been remarkable. In 2024 the company reported a 22% increase in revenue, reaching $13 billion. This success is attributed to Meituan's ability to adapt and innovate beyond its initial group-buying model, effectively catering to the evolving needs of Chinese consumers.

Wang's strategy differed from his Western counterparts by customizing services to fit local preferences. He avoided early overspending to attract customers, focusing instead on long-term investments such as securing exclusive deals with vendors and developing a reliable payment system. This approach enabled Meituan to outperform competitors, including Groupon, whose valuation declined significantly after its initial public offering.

Its success underscores the effectiveness of learning through imitation, followed by strategic adaptation to local markets, challenging the notion that early-stage copying hinders innovation.

Didi Chuxing, often called the "Uber of China," differs from its Silicon Valley counterpart with a "heavy touch" approach. While Uber focuses on connecting drivers and riders, Didi controls multiple aspects of its ecosystem, including gas stations and repair shops. This strategy not only deters copycat startups but also generates vast amounts of data, enhancing its AI capabilities. Operating in 16 countries and serving hundreds of millions of users, Didi's integrated model has made it a leader in the global ride-hailing industry. So, different regions may lean towards different models. While bike-sharing might not be something Uber would thrive on, it worked for Didi to extend their business.

And lastly another data goldmine generating innovation in China, WeChat. WeChat is a super-app that has become an indispensable part of daily life in China, integrating countless services into one seamless platform. Its rise is closely tied to China's mobile-first internet culture, where most people's first online experiences came through affordable smartphones rather than PCs.

WeChat allows users to do everything they might traditionally do on a computer, and more, all within a single app. Beyond chatting with friends, users can order food, unlock shared bikes, buy movie tickets, book doctor appointments, and even trade stocks. These functions are supported by WeChat Wallet, a mini-app introduced in 2014, which revolutionized payments played a significant role in transforming China into a cashless society. By centralizing services and financial transactions, it has amassed an unparalleled trove of user data, offering insights into consumer behaviour, travel habits, and more. Considering the 1.4 billion monthly users of the app, the amount of data is staggering.

So, will China surpass the US and take the lead in AI? It is a close call for the coming decade. AI can be divided into different categories: in internet AI, the competition will be tight; in business AI—such as managing financial portfolios and making decisions on bank loans—the US is likely to maintain its lead for a long time. On the other hand, in the field of perception AI, China has an advantage due to cultural factors, such as a greater willingness to trade privacy for convenience. Lastly, in autonomous AI, the US currently leads, but China is making significant efforts to catch up quickly. In the end, it is too close to call, but both the US and China will strive relentlessly to assert their dominance in the AI race.

Facial Recognition

Facial recognition technology has emerged as one of the most prominent and contentious applications of artificial intelligence in recent years. Imagine walking down a busy street, perhaps in Beijing, London, or New York. You look up at a streetlight, and there it is — a small camera quietly capturing your image, analysing it, and cross-referencing it with vast databases in real time. This is not science fiction; this is the new normal in many cities worldwide. AI has supercharged the capabilities of these surveillance systems, making it possible for governments and corporations alike to identify individuals within seconds, monitor movements, and predict behaviours.

Facial recognition technology is being deployed for a variety of purposes: from border control to enhancing public safety, catching criminals, and even in schools to track attendance. In countries like China, facial recognition is integral to its nationwide surveillance system, monitoring citizens and feeding data into the social credit system. This system assigns citizens scores based on their behaviour, directly impacting access to public services, transportation, and employment opportunities.

To highlight how easily technology can be repurposed, consider Google's image recognition AI software. Initially trained by users identifying trees and streetlights in CAPTCHAs, the same technology could be adapted to identify individuals in conflict zones. This potential for misuse sparked significant protests from Google employees when the company decided to sell its software to the U.S. military.

While facial recognition can certainly help in catching criminals and ensuring security, its implications for privacy are immense. The technology does not differentiate between those with good intentions and those without, resulting in a blanket form of surveillance that tracks everyone — potentially even at their most vulnerable moments. Citizens under constant watch may alter their behaviours to avoid scrutiny, chilling free expression, and stifling creativity. Facial recognition thus becomes a powerful tool for social control, one that is particularly worrisome in authoritarian regimes.

Moreover, the accuracy of facial recognition technology is inconsistent. Numerous studies have shown that AI-based facial recognition systems are prone to bias, often performing worse on individuals with darker skin tones or women, leading to misidentification and false accusations. This reinforces and amplifies existing societal inequalities. Innocent people, particularly from minority communities, may be unjustly targeted, which could have serious consequences for their safety and trust in law enforcement.

Facial recognition technology has also spread into the corporate world. Retailers use it to monitor customer behaviour, and tech companies employ it for device authentication. This has sparked debates about consent and data ownership. How much of our biometric information are we comfortable sharing with corporations? Who holds these facial data, and what are they doing with it? Without strict regulations, the line between safety and intrusion blurs, leaving privacy increasingly vulnerable in this new surveillance age.

Government vs. Corporate Surveillance

Government surveillance and corporate surveillance are two sides of the same coin, both relying on AI to collect, analyse, and exploit vast amounts of data. The key difference is their purpose: governments use AI surveillance ostensibly to ensure security and maintain order, whereas corporations use it to maximize profit, often by manipulating consumer behaviour.

Government surveillance, in its most extreme form, can transform into an Orwellian nightmare. AI enables mass monitoring of citizens, tracking their locations, social interactions, online activities, and even predicting their potential actions. Take China's extensive use of surveillance systems, including facial recognition and social credit scores, as a glaring example. These tools empower the government to punish behaviour deemed undesirable, making privacy a casualty of state control. Even in democracies, AI-powered surveillance has raised concerns. Initiatives justified by the need to combat terrorism or crime can gradually creep into regular law enforcement and everyday life, expanding the scope of what is being monitored, often without public consent or oversight.

The Stasi, the intelligence agency of former East Germany, was one of the most efficient and oppressive in history. They maintained detailed files on the majority of East German households, monitoring phone calls, intercepting letters, and even installing hidden cameras in homes. All of this was managed by human operatives and documented on paper, requiring an enormous bureaucracy and massive storage facilities for billions of physical records. Now, imagine the Stasi equipped with AI. AI could automatically monitor phone calls, messages, and online activities. Surveillance cameras and satellite data could track people's movements in real-time, effectively assigning every individual a virtual operative observing them 24/7.

Corporate surveillance, though different in scope, is just as invasive. Companies like Google, Facebook, and Amazon collect staggering amounts of data from users — every click, search, and interaction is recorded and analysed. AI systems then predict user behaviour, target ads, and shape consumer habits. The motivations here are profit-driven: the more a company knows about you, the more effectively it can market products and keep you engaged. However, the consequences are significant. User data is treated as a commodity, often bought, and sold without explicit consent, resulting in a loss of control over one's own personal information.

The intertwining of government and corporate surveillance raises further concerns. Governments may access corporate data to monitor individuals without directly implementing mass surveillance themselves, effectively outsourcing this responsibility. Conversely, corporations may lobby for policies that allow greater data collection, reducing regulatory constraints. This creates an ecosystem where surveillance is not just pervasive but normalized, and citizens lose sight of who is watching and why.

These blurred lines underscore the need for transparency and regulation. Governments should not have unchecked power to surveil citizens, and corporations must be held accountable for how they collect and use data. Establishing boundaries that protect individual privacy while ensuring that security needs are met is essential if we are to safeguard fundamental rights in an AI-driven world.

Balancing Security And Privacy

The balance between security and privacy is a perennial debate, intensified by the rise of AI technologies. As surveillance capabilities grow, so do concerns about how far governments and corporations should be allowed to go in the name of security. Is it possible to achieve a balance where citizens feel safe without giving up their fundamental rights?

The argument in favour of enhanced surveillance is grounded in its potential to prevent crime, terrorism, and ensure public safety. AI's ability to process vast datasets quickly makes it a powerful tool for detecting threats in real time. Governments argue that these measures are necessary in an increasingly digital world where bad actors operate across borders. AI surveillance can help track suspicious behaviour, disrupt planned attacks, and respond to threats before they escalate. In a time where cyber threats and domestic terrorism are real and evolving dangers, many see these tools as necessary for maintaining public order.

AI has supercharged surveillance, enabling real-time monitoring of vast populations. While it detects fraud and predicts health risks, it also raises profound concerns about privacy and autonomy. From governments enforcing social control to corporations trading personal data, the stakes are high. Balancing innovation with individual rights demands informed discourse, robust regulations, and conscious choices about our digital footprints.

Yet, the risks of these surveillance measures encroaching upon individual freedoms cannot be ignored. Privacy is not just about keeping personal information confidential; it is about maintaining autonomy and the right to live without undue interference. Constant monitoring can lead to a society where people self-censor, reluctant to express opinions or explore ideas that might be deemed controversial. This, in turn, erodes democratic freedoms and stifles innovation.

Finding the right balance involves placing clear limits on what data can be collected, how it can be used, and how long it is retained. Privacy advocates suggest regulations that mandate transparency in AI decision-making, ensuring that citizens know when and why they are being surveilled. Governments should also provide mechanisms for accountability, such as independent oversight bodies that review surveillance practices and address misuse.

Around 130 cities in the United States have adopted a sensor system called ShotSpotter, which detects the sound of gunfire and instantly relays the exact coordinates to the police, enabling a rapid response.

Technology can also be part of the solution. Privacy-preserving AI methods, like differential privacy and federated learning, allow data to be analysed without directly exposing individual information. Using such tools, we can harness AI's power without sacrificing personal privacy. In addition, encryption and decentralized data storage are key technologies that can help mitigate the risks associated with data centralization and potential abuse.

Public participation in these discussions is equally crucial. Citizens need to understand what is at stake and be involved in the conversations about how AI surveillance should be regulated. The fear of terrorism or crime should not be exploited to create a surveillance state where fundamental rights are compromised. Striking the balance between security and privacy means making informed choices that do not merely react to fear but reflect a commitment to democratic values, individual freedoms, and the right to privacy. By demanding transparency and accountability from both governments and corporations, citizens can help ensure that AI serves as a force for safety and progress rather than a tool of unchecked control.

In today's digital age, "free" often comes at a hidden cost: your data. From social media to fitness apps, platforms collect and monetize personal information, transforming user habits into profit. Store loyalty cards track purchases, free email accounts scan messages for targeted ads, and fitness apps log health and location data. This system, described as surveillance capitalism, turns human experiences into a valuable commodity sold to multiple buyers simultaneously. While these services offer undeniable convenience, they've enabled tech giants to amass unprecedented wealth and influence. Opting out entirely might seem impractical, but awareness is key. By choosing privacy-focused alternatives, limiting what you share, or supporting businesses with ethical data practices, you can navigate this digital landscape more thoughtfully.

DIGITAL DECEPTION

What Are Deepfakes?

Deepfakes are a form of synthetic media where artificial intelligence is used to manipulate or generate images, audio, or video content to make it appear authentic. The term "deepfake" is a combination of "deep learning" and "fake," emphasizing the role of AI in creating these deceptive pieces of content. Deepfakes have rapidly gained attention in recent years, both for their impressive capabilities and for the concerning ethical implications they bring. They can be entertaining when used to create funny or artistic mashups, but they also pose serious risks when used to spread misinformation or defame individuals.

Deepfakes are hyper-realistic manipulations of audio and video content, making it increasingly difficult to distinguish between genuine and fabricated media.

One of the most famous early examples of a deepfake surfaced in 2018, when a video of former President Obama calling President Trump a "total dipshit" went viral. The catch? It was not real. The video was created by BuzzFeed to demonstrate just how convincing deepfakes could be and to warn people of the need to question what they see online. In this way, deepfakes have shown themselves to be a powerful tool for deception, and as the technology advances, they will become increasingly difficult to distinguish from genuine footage.

The technology behind deepfakes relies heavily on artificial intelligence, specifically a type of machine learning known as Generative Adversarial Networks (GANs). GANs consist of two neural networks working in tandem to create highly realistic, but ultimately fake, content. To understand GANs, imagine two artificial intelligence agents: a "forger" and a "detective." The forger's job is to create an image or video, while the detective's role is to determine if that creation is authentic or not. The forger generates content, and the detective analyses it, comparing it to real examples.

This process happens millions of times in a feedback loop, with each network improving its ability to generate or detect fake content. The forger constantly adjusts and refines its creations to fool the detective, while the detective becomes increasingly sophisticated at spotting flaws. Over time, the forged images or videos become so realistic that they can successfully deceive not only the detective but also human viewers. This is how GANs enable deepfakes to achieve such a convincing level of realism.

To create a deepfake video, developers need a large dataset of images or videos of the person they intend to replicate. The more data available, the better the quality of the resulting deepfake. The AI analyses countless frames, picking up on unique features such as facial structure, expressions, and subtle movements. For instance, if someone wants to create a deepfake of a celebrity, they would gather thousands of video clips, enabling the AI to learn the person's mannerisms, voice, and even micro-expressions.

Once enough data has been collected, the AI can then generate new content where this person appears to be saying or doing things they never actually did. The potential implications of this technology are vast. It can be used for harmless entertainment, like creating a humorous video of a celebrity singing a popular song, but it can also be weaponized for more nefarious purposes, like creating fake political speeches or spreading disinformation during elections.

Deepfake technology has already been misused in troubling ways. In 2019, a wave of deepfake pornographic videos featuring celebrities' faces emerged on adult websites. These non-consensual videos were a gross invasion of privacy and highlighted how dangerous deepfakes could be when used to harass or intimidate. Furthermore, deepfakes can also serve as political weapons, discrediting candidates or influencing public perception. The ability to create convincing fake videos could lead to serious consequences, from damaging reputations to impacting global political stability.

Developers and researchers are actively working to counter the spread of deepfakes, creating tools and techniques to detect them. Deepfake detection algorithms are designed to spot inconsistencies that the human eye might miss, such as unnatural blinking patterns or subtle digital artifacts. However, as deepfake technology continues to evolve, so do the methods to bypass these detection tools, resulting in an ongoing cat-and-mouse game between creators and detectors.

The emergence of deepfakes also raises questions about the future of authenticity and trust in a digital age. As deepfakes become increasingly realistic, the challenge of discerning what is real from what is fake will grow ever more complex. In the future, mixed reality and augmented reality may blur the lines between fact and fiction even further, making it essential to establish digital literacy as a core competency. It is crucial for individuals to develop the ability to critically evaluate content, understand the technology behind digital manipulation, and question the authenticity of the media they consume.

Deepfakes are emblematic of the double-edged nature of artificial intelligence. On one hand, they can be used creatively, providing new opportunities for storytelling, entertainment, and artistic expression. On the other hand, their capacity to deceive poses significant risks to privacy, security, and the very notion of truth in the digital age. As the technology progresses, society must grapple with how to harness its potential while mitigating its dangers. Legislation, public awareness, and advancements in detection technology will all play critical roles in navigating the challenges presented by deepfakes.

The Threat Of Misinformation

Deepfakes are not merely an amusing novelty; they are a potent tool in the spread of misinformation, which has profound implications for society. Misinformation, or false information spread regardless of intent, has always been a part of human communication, but deepfakes take it to a new, dangerous level. By manipulating the very fabric of visual and audio evidence, deepfakes can create convincing falsehoods that can easily deceive even the most discerning viewers. The threat of misinformation becomes amplified in an environment where trust in media and institutions is already fragile.

One of the primary dangers of deepfakes lies in their ability to manufacture fake events or statements, particularly those involving public figures. Imagine a video of a world leader making threatening statements toward another country. Such a deepfake could provoke international tensions, leading to diplomatic crises or even military actions. The rapid dissemination of such fake content across social media platforms can lead to real-world consequences before the truth has a chance to surface. This immediacy and reach make deepfakes a powerful weapon for those who seek to manipulate public opinion or destabilize political systems.

The influence of deepfakes extends beyond politics. Fake videos can be used to spread false narratives about individuals, ruin careers, or damage reputations. For instance, a deepfake showing a prominent CEO admitting to unethical practices could lead to stock market volatility and financial losses, even if the video is later proven to be fake. The consequences of such misinformation are not limited to the individual; they can have ripple effects throughout entire industries and markets.

The psychological impact of deepfakes also cannot be ignored. The erosion of trust in what people see and hear undermines the foundations of informed decision-making. When people can no longer trust their senses, they become more susceptible to conspiracy theories and less likely to engage with legitimate news sources. This creates fertile ground for those who wish to sow discord and confusion, as individuals retreat into echo chambers where their beliefs are reinforced, and opposing views are dismissed as fake. This cycle of mistrust and misinformation poses a significant threat to democratic societies, which rely on an informed electorate to function effectively.

Combatting the threat of deepfake-driven misinformation is a multifaceted challenge. It requires technological, educational, and regulatory responses. On the technological front, researchers are developing sophisticated algorithms to detect deepfakes by analysing digital artifacts, such as inconsistencies in lighting, shadows, or facial movements. These detection tools are essential for identifying deepfakes before they spread widely. However, the creators of deepfakes are continually improving their techniques, making it a constant battle to stay ahead of the technology.

Jorge Luis Borges' "The Library of Babel" (1941) envisions a universe as an infinite library of hexagonal rooms, filled with books containing every possible arrangement of characters. While the library holds all conceivable texts, from coherent books to future predictions, the overwhelming randomness renders most of them meaningless. The story highlights the paradox of infinite knowledge

*buried in chaos and resonates today as a reflection on
information overload, where sifting through vast data
to find meaning remains a significant challenge.*

Education is another critical component in addressing misinformation. Digital literacy programs that teach individuals how to critically evaluate online content and recognize signs of manipulation can help mitigate the impact of deepfakes. People need to be aware of the existence of deepfakes and understand that not everything they see online is genuine. By fostering a culture of scepticism and critical thinking, society can become more resilient to the influence of false information.

Regulation also has a role to play in mitigating the threat of deepfakes and misinformation. Governments around the world are beginning to explore legal frameworks to address the malicious use of deepfakes. This includes laws that criminalize the creation and distribution of deepfakes intended to harm others, as well as regulations that require social media platforms to take proactive steps in identifying and removing fake content. However, creating effective legislation is challenging, as it must balance the need to protect free expression with the imperative to prevent harm.

Social media platforms have a particularly important role in controlling the spread of deepfake-driven misinformation. Companies like Facebook, X, and YouTube have begun to implement policies aimed at detecting and removing manipulated media. While these efforts are a step in the right direction, they are not foolproof. The volume of content uploaded to these platforms every day makes it difficult to catch every deepfake, and the line between parody, satire, and malicious intent can often be blurred, complicating moderation efforts.

AI's potential for weaponization poses unprecedented risks. Autonomous drones, scalable to massive fleets controlled by just a few individuals, could unleash devastating attacks at the push of a button. But easier weapons can be built with AI. AI can manipulate public opinion, as seen with Cambridge Analytica's use of Facebook data in 2016. To counter these threats, robust regulations and proactive safety measures are critical.

The threat of misinformation fuelled by deepfakes is a pressing concern that requires a coordinated effort from technology developers, governments, social media platforms, and the public. As deepfake technology becomes increasingly sophisticated, the challenge of maintaining trust in information will only grow. It is crucial to develop robust systems for identifying and mitigating misinformation while also educating the public on the risks and encouraging responsible use of technology. Only through a collaborative and multifaceted approach can we hope to navigate the challenges posed by deepfakes and preserve the integrity of truth in the digital age.

Ways To Detect Deepfakes

Detecting and combating deepfakes is a dynamic and challenging process, as the technology behind deepfakes continues to evolve and improve. Researchers, governments, and technology companies are all working on multiple fronts to address the growing threat of deepfakes and to protect individuals and societies from their harmful effects. This requires a combination of technological solutions, regulatory frameworks, public awareness, and collaboration across sectors.

One of the most important ways to detect deepfakes is through the use of AI-driven detection tools. These tools analyse various features of a video or image, looking for subtle signs that indicate manipulation. For example, early deepfakes often had noticeable issues with blinking patterns, as the AI models were not trained to accurately replicate natural blinking behaviours. Although deepfake creators have since overcome this particular weakness, detection tools have evolved to identify other telltale signs, such as inconsistencies in lighting, shadows, and facial movements. Algorithms can also analyse image compression artifacts, irregularities in audio, or even physiological signals, such as heart rate, which may be reflected in slight skin colour variations.

Deepfake detection technologies continue to advance rapidly, but they face a significant challenge: the creators of deepfakes are also constantly improving their techniques. This ongoing battle between detection and generation is often described as a cat-and-mouse game, with each side striving to stay ahead of the other. The most effective detection tools are those that utilize deep learning models capable of analysing a wide range of features, as well as continuously adapting to new deepfake techniques.

Another critical aspect of combating deepfakes is the role of social media platforms and technology companies. Platforms like Facebook, X, and YouTube are implementing policies to identify and remove deepfake content. These companies use both automated detection tools and human moderators to review flagged content and determine whether it violates community guidelines. Additionally, some platforms have begun labelling manipulated content to alert viewers that a video or image may not be authentic. While these measures are not foolproof, they represent an important step toward mitigating the spread of harmful deepfakes.

Public awareness and education are also essential in the fight against deepfakes. By increasing digital literacy, individuals can learn to recognize signs of manipulation and become more sceptical of content that seems suspicious. Education initiatives can teach people how to critically evaluate online media, cross-check information from multiple sources, and question the authenticity of videos or images that could be deepfakes. This cultural shift toward scepticism and critical thinking is crucial for reducing the impact of misinformation and minimizing the influence of malicious actors.

Another promising approach to combating deepfakes is the use of blockchain technology for content verification. Blockchain can be used to create a digital record of the origin and history of a video or image, making it easier to verify its authenticity. By embedding metadata that records when and where a piece of content was created, and by whom, blockchain can help establish a chain of custody that ensures the integrity of digital media. This approach, known as "content provenance," could provide a powerful tool for combating deepfakes by allowing individuals to trace the origin of a piece of content and verify its authenticity.

On the regulatory front, governments around the world are beginning to recognize the need for legal frameworks to address the malicious use of deepfakes. Some countries have already introduced laws that criminalize the creation and distribution of deepfake content intended to harm others, while others are exploring regulations that require social media platforms to take proactive measures in identifying and removing manipulated media. However, crafting effective legislation is challenging, as it must strike a balance between protecting free expression and preventing harm. It is also important for regulations to be adaptable, as the technology behind deepfakes is constantly evolving.

Collaboration between governments, technology companies, academic researchers, and civil society is crucial for addressing the challenges posed by deepfakes. Governments can play a role in funding research into deepfake detection and supporting public awareness campaigns, while technology companies can share data and collaborate on developing detection tools. Academic researchers can contribute by advancing the scientific understanding of deepfakes and developing innovative approaches to detection and prevention. By working together, these stakeholders can create a comprehensive and effective response to the deepfake threat.

In conclusion, combating deepfakes requires a multifaceted approach that includes technological innovation, public awareness, regulatory action, and cross-sector collaboration. While deepfake technology is advancing rapidly, so too are the tools and strategies for detecting and mitigating its harmful effects. By investing in detection technologies, educating the public, implementing effective regulations, and fostering collaboration, we can minimize the risks associated with deepfakes and protect the integrity of information in the digital age. The fight against deepfakes is ongoing, but with a coordinated effort, it is possible to reduce their impact and safeguard the truth in an increasingly complex digital landscape.

AI VS. HUMAN INTELLIGENCE

Why AI Is Not Conscious Yet

Consciousness is one of the most mysterious and debated concepts in both philosophy and science. It is what allows us to have subjective experiences, to perceive the world, and to reflect on ourselves and our surroundings. Consciousness is often described as the awareness of one's own thoughts, feelings, and sensations, a continuous experience that forms the core of what it means to be human. The question of whether machines can ever achieve consciousness is a major topic in the discourse around AI. Despite the rapid advancements in AI, the consensus remains that current AI systems are far from possessing true consciousness.

"The question of whether machines can think is about as relevant as the question of whether submarines can swim." – Edsger Dijkstra

---

To understand why AI is not yet capable of consciousness, it helps to delve into what consciousness entails. Human consciousness arises from the intricate interplay of billions of neurons in the brain, which create a dynamic and evolving internal model of the world. This model is not static; it is continuously updated as we interact with our environment. Our brains are constantly learning, adapting, and making sense of the vast array of sensory inputs that we receive every moment. Moreover, human consciousness is deeply connected to our emotions, memories, and experiences, making it a highly personal and subjective phenomenon.

The neocortex, the brain's outermost layer, plays a key role in memory, thinking, and pattern recognition. It organizes information hierarchically, reflecting the sequential nature of our actions and thoughts. This is why tasks like reciting the alphabet backward or starting a memorized song mid-way feel unnatural—the brain stores and retrieves information in structured, sequential order. A strength and a weakness at the same time.

The brain stores information in cortical columns, or uniformly organized groupings of neurons found in the neocortex. There are about 500,000 such columns in the neocortex, each containing about 60,000 neurons. Within each cortical column are pattern recognizers, comprising of about 100 neurons. All in all, there are approximately 300 million pattern recognizers in the neocortex

---

AI, on the other hand, operates on fundamentally different principles. At its core, AI is based on algorithms and data. Machine learning models, including the most sophisticated neural networks, learn by identifying patterns in massive datasets and using those patterns to make predictions or decisions. AI can be trained to perform tasks with remarkable accuracy, from recognizing faces in images to generating realistic text. However, these abilities are limited to specific tasks and are rooted in data-driven processing rather than genuine understanding. AI lacks self-awareness, the ability to reflect on its actions, and the capacity for subjective experiences.

One of the key differences between human consciousness and AI lies in the nature of learning. Humans are capable of abstract reasoning, learning from minimal data, and applying knowledge across different domains. Our learning process is inherently flexible and context-driven, allowing us to adapt to new situations and environments with ease. AI, by contrast, relies heavily on large quantities of data and is limited to the specific domain for which it has been trained. Even the most advanced AI systems, such as those using deep learning, struggle to generalize knowledge beyond their training data. They lack the intuitive understanding that humans possess, which allows us to make sense of novel experiences and unfamiliar contexts.

The concept of consciousness also involves a sense of self. Humans are aware not only of the external world but also of their own thoughts, emotions, and existence. This self-awareness is a crucial aspect of consciousness that AI lacks. While AI can simulate conversation, generate creative content, and even mimic emotional responses, these abilities are purely superficial. AI does not possess an internal subjective experience; it does not "know" that it is performing these tasks. The responses generated by AI are based on pre-defined patterns and statistical correlations rather than an understanding of the meaning behind them.

The brain's sensory processing begins in the sensory cortex, passing through the thalamus—a midbrain structure that filters sensations as pleasing or not—before reaching the neocortex. The neocortex, crucial for memory and thinking, relies on the hippocampus to identify new or noteworthy information, such as recognizing faces or changes. Movement control is shared between the neocortex and the cerebellum, with the latter handling both instinctive and refined actions like catching a ball or dancing. Together, these regions of the brain form a dynamic network essential for sensory perception, memory, motor coordination and our consciousness somehow.

Another important aspect of consciousness is the ability to have free will or intentionality—the capacity to make decisions based on desires, goals, or intentions. Humans can set their own goals, reflect on their motivations, and make choices that are influenced by a complex interplay of rational thought, emotions, and personal values. AI, however, operates entirely based on the instructions and objectives provided by its human developers. It has no desires, no intrinsic motivations, and no understanding of the consequences of its actions. It executes tasks according to its programming, without any sense of purpose or intentionality.

"I think, therefore I am" – Rene Descartes

But what does thinking and being mean with regards to AI?

One of the most significant limitations of current AI systems is their inability to understand context in the way that humans do. AI can analyse data and recognize patterns, but it does not truly understand the context or the underlying meaning of the information it processes. For instance, an AI language model can generate coherent sentences, but it does not understand the meaning of the words it uses. It lacks the common sense and real-world knowledge that humans rely on to navigate complex social situations and interpret nuanced information. This lack of contextual understanding is a major barrier to achieving anything resembling human-like consciousness.

In 1988, roboticist Hans Moravec highlighted a paradox: AI systems can rival adults in complex intellectual tasks but struggle with basic perceptual skills innate to infants. A contemporary example is AI's difficulty in counting the letter 'r' in the word 'strawberry.' When prompted, models like GPT-4 and Claude often assert there are only two 'r's, overlooking the correct count of three.

This limitation stems from the way AI processes language. Large Language Models (LLMs) utilize tokenization, breaking words into subword units or tokens. For instance, 'strawberry' might be divided into 'straw' and 'berry,' causing the model to miss individual letters. This tokenization approach, while effective for understanding context and generating coherent text, can lead to errors in tasks requiring precise letter-level analysis.

The debate around AI and consciousness often leads to discussions about Artificial General Intelligence (AGI), which refers to an AI system that possesses the ability to understand, learn, and apply knowledge across a wide range of tasks —much like a human being. AGI would require not only advanced computational power but also the ability to integrate information from diverse sources, reason abstractly, and possess a form of self-awareness. While AGI is a long-standing goal in the field of AI research, we are still far from achieving it. The current generation of AI, known as narrow AI, is designed to perform specific tasks and lacks the general intelligence and consciousness that characterize human cognition.

Computational power is not the answer to all challenges. Consider a school principal tasked with scheduling students, classes, and teachers. With ten rooms and 15 classes, there are 3,003 possible arrangements per hour. Over an eight-hour day, this balloons to over six octillion possibilities—a six followed by 27 zeros. Even a computer processing a billion operations per second would take over 200 billion years of time to evaluate them all. AI needs to use heuristics to get the job done. Maybe not the best solution, but good enough.

It is also important to consider the philosophical questions surrounding AI and consciousness. Some argue that consciousness is more than just a complex computational process; it may involve aspects of human biology that cannot be replicated in machines. The philosopher David Chalmers refers to this as the "hard problem" of consciousness—the challenge of explaining why and how subjective experiences arise from physical processes in the brain. If consciousness is indeed tied to the biological and chemical processes of the human brain, it may be impossible to recreate it in a machine, no matter how advanced the technology becomes.

Impossible? In September 1933, physicist Ernest Rutherford publicly dismissed the potential of nuclear energy, reportedly calling it "moonshine." The following day, while walking in London, Leó Szillárd conceived the idea of a neutron-induced nuclear chain reaction, laying the foundation for nuclear energy.

So, while AI has made remarkable progress in recent years, it remains fundamentally different from human intelligence in terms of consciousness. AI lacks self-awareness, subjective experience, intentionality, and the ability to understand context in a meaningful way. The human brain's capacity for abstract reasoning, emotional understanding, and self-reflection sets it apart from even the most advanced AI systems. Until we have a deeper understanding of the nature of consciousness and how it arises, the prospect of creating truly conscious AI will remain beyond our reach. For now, AI can be seen as a powerful tool that complements human intelligence, but it is not a replacement for the rich and complex phenomenon of human consciousness.

Strengths And Weaknesses Of AI

Artificial intelligence has transformed numerous aspects of modern life. AI's capabilities have evolved rapidly, often surpassing human abilities in certain tasks, but there are still areas where human intelligence holds distinct advantages. To fully understand the implications of AI's development, it is crucial to compare the strengths and weaknesses of AI with those of humans, highlighting the areas where each excels and falls short.

One of the key strengths of AI lies in its ability to process and analyse vast amounts of data with incredible speed and accuracy. AI systems can sift through enormous datasets, identify patterns, and make data-driven decisions much faster than any human. This capability makes AI invaluable in fields such as medical diagnostics, financial analysis, and scientific research, where large volumes of information must be analysed to draw meaningful conclusions. For instance, AI has been used to identify early signs of diseases in medical images, achieving levels of accuracy that often match or even exceed those of human specialists. The ability to perform repetitive and data-intensive tasks without fatigue is a significant advantage that AI has over humans.

AI also excels in consistency and reliability. Unlike humans, who are prone to errors due to fatigue, stress, or distractions, AI can perform the same task repeatedly with a high degree of precision. This makes AI ideal for tasks that require meticulous attention to detail, such as quality control in manufacturing or processing large volumes of transactions in banking. The absence of emotional and psychological factors allows AI to operate without the biases or inconsistencies that can affect human decision-making. This objectivity is particularly valuable in areas where impartiality is critical, such as legal analysis or hiring processes.

According to the United Kingdom's communications regulator, the average person checks their phone every two minutes.

Another strength of AI is its capacity for scalability. Once an AI model has been trained, it can be deployed across multiple systems and scaled to handle increasing workloads without requiring additional training. This is in stark contrast to humans, who require extensive training and experience to perform specialized tasks. AI's scalability makes it an attractive solution for businesses looking to automate processes and improve efficiency, as it can be applied to various contexts with minimal additional cost or effort.

The Associated Press (AP) produces 40,000 of its 730,000 annual articles using AI, particularly for repetitive tasks like reporting on company earnings. Lisa Gibbs, AP's Director of News Partnerships and AI News Lead, explains: "It frees our journalists from routine tasks, to do higher-level work that uses their creativity; allows us to create more content that serves new audiences more efficiently; and improves our ability to discover news".

However, despite these impressive strengths, AI has notable weaknesses that limit its capabilities compared to human intelligence. One of the most significant weaknesses of AI is its lack of common sense and contextual understanding. AI systems operate based on the data they have been trained on and the algorithms that guide their behaviour. They lack the ability to understand the broader context of a situation or to apply knowledge in a flexible, adaptive manner. Humans, on the other hand, excel at understanding context, making intuitive judgments, and drawing on a wealth of experiences to navigate complex, ambiguous situations. This ability to reason abstractly and adapt to new circumstances is something that current AI systems struggle to achieve.

Embrace AI as a tool to enhance your abilities, not to replace them.

Creativity is another area where humans hold a distinct advantage over AI. While AI can generate art, music, or even write text based on patterns it has learned from existing data, it does not possess the same creativity as humans. Human creativity is driven by emotions, imagination, and the ability to think outside the box—qualities that AI lacks. For example, a human artist can create a painting that conveys deep emotions or tells a unique story, drawing on personal experiences and cultural influences. AI, by contrast, can only generate content based on the data it has been exposed to, without any genuine understanding or emotional connection. This limitation makes AI-generated content impressive but often lacking in depth and originality.

Emotional intelligence is another key area where humans surpass AI. Humans are capable of understanding and responding to emotions, both their own and those of others. This emotional intelligence is essential for effective communication, empathy, and building relationships. AI, on the other hand, can simulate emotional responses or recognize basic emotional cues, but it does not truly understand emotions or have the capacity to empathize. This limitation makes AI poorly suited for roles that require a deep understanding of human emotions, such as counselling, caregiving, or leadership. The inability of AI to genuinely connect with people on an emotional level is a significant barrier to its use in many human-centred fields.

Learning is another area where AI and human intelligence differ significantly. While AI can learn from large datasets and improve its performance over time, its learning is limited to the specific task for which it has been trained. Humans, by contrast, are capable of lifelong learning from relatively small datasets, adapting to new challenges, and applying knowledge across different domains. Human learning is not only about acquiring information but also about understanding complex concepts, making connections between different ideas, and applying knowledge creatively. AI's learning is constrained by the data it receives and the algorithms that define its behaviour, making it less adaptable and versatile compared to human learning.

AI also lacks the ability to set its own goals or act with intentionality. Human intelligence is characterized by the capacity for self-reflection, goal-setting, and purposeful action. Humans can decide what they want to achieve, reflect on their progress, and adjust their actions accordingly. AI, on the other hand, operates based on the objectives provided by its developers or users. It has no intrinsic motivations or desires, and it cannot make decisions beyond the scope of its programming. This lack of autonomy means that AI is ultimately a tool that requires human guidance and direction, rather than an independent agent capable of making its own choices.

Ethical decision-making is another area where AI falls short compared to humans. Human decision-making is influenced by moral values, cultural norms, and ethical considerations. People can weigh the potential consequences of their actions, consider the impact on others, and make decisions that align with their sense of right and wrong. AI, however, lacks an inherent understanding of ethics. While AI can be programmed to follow ethical guidelines or to make decisions based on predefined criteria, it does not possess an understanding of morality. This raises concerns about the use of AI in situations that require complex ethical judgments, such as autonomous vehicles or medical decision-making.

In conclusion, AI and human intelligence each have their own unique strengths and weaknesses. AI excels in processing large amounts of data, performing repetitive tasks with precision, and scaling across multiple applications. It is a powerful tool that can enhance productivity, improve decision-making, and solve complex problems. However, AI's limitations—including its lack of common sense, creativity, emotional intelligence, and ethical reasoning—mean that it cannot replace the richness and complexity of human intelligence. Instead, AI should be viewed as a complement to human abilities, enhancing what we can achieve while leaving the uniquely human aspects of intelligence, such as creativity, empathy, and ethical decision-making, in our hands. The future of AI lies in collaboration with humans, leveraging the strengths of both to create a better and more innovative world.

Augmented Intelligence

In recent years, the concept of augmented intelligence has gained traction as an alternative to the idea of artificial intelligence entirely replacing human roles. Augmented intelligence emphasizes collaboration between humans and machines, combining the analytical power of AI with the creativity, emotional intelligence, and contextual understanding that humans bring to the table. Rather than viewing AI as a competitor, augmented intelligence envisions a future where technology enhances human capabilities, enabling us to achieve more together than either could alone.

---

*Knowledge is nonrival, meaning its value
remains undiminished when shared. In fact, it
becomes more valuable as it reaches more people
and grows through collective sharing.*

At its core, augmented intelligence is about using AI as a tool to enhance human decision-making and problem-solving. AI systems excel at processing large volumes of data, identifying patterns, and making data-driven recommendations. By leveraging these strengths, humans can make more informed decisions, particularly in fields where vast amounts of information must be analysed. For instance, in healthcare, AI can analyse medical records, imaging data, and research findings to assist doctors in diagnosing diseases and recommending treatment options. However, the ultimate decision lies with the healthcare professional, who can integrate AI insights with their clinical expertise and understanding of the patient's unique circumstances.

---

*Keeping up with the world's current level of
publication on scientific research would require
200,000 people reading full-time.*

Augmented intelligence also plays a significant role in creative fields, where AI can act as a collaborator that inspires new ideas. Artists, writers, and musicians have begun using AI to generate creative content, such as visual art, music, or even story prompts. These AI-generated pieces serve as a starting point for human creativity, sparking new ideas and pushing creative boundaries. By working together, humans and AI can produce innovative works that blend the precision of machine learning with the emotional depth and originality of human artistry. This symbiotic relationship allows artists to explore new possibilities while retaining full control over the creative process.

One of the key benefits of augmented intelligence is its ability to enhance productivity by automating repetitive or mundane tasks. In industries such as finance, customer service, and logistics, AI-powered systems can handle routine tasks, such as data entry, answering customer inquiries, and managing inventory. This frees up human workers to focus on more complex and meaningful work, such as building relationships with clients, solving strategic problems, and driving innovation. By automating the more monotonous aspects of their jobs, augmented intelligence enables workers to be more engaged and fulfilled, ultimately leading to higher job satisfaction and better outcomes.

Standardization prevents errors and promotes the reuse of templates and information by establishing clear norms and protocols, making processes more efficient with each repetition. As information continues to accumulate, it becomes increasingly difficult for professionals to manage it all effectively. Standardized routines address this challenge by ensuring that key processes are performed correctly, freeing professionals to concentrate on more complex or unique tasks that require higher levels of intellectual effort.

In addition to improving productivity, augmented intelligence also enhances decision-making by providing humans with insights that they might not otherwise have access to. AI algorithms can analyse complex datasets, detect trends, and identify correlations that are not immediately apparent to human analysts. In fields such as finance, AI can help investors make informed decisions by analysing market trends, economic indicators, and historical data. In law, AI can assist lawyers by reviewing large volumes of legal documents, identifying relevant precedents, and summarizing key points. However, in both cases, the human professional remains in control, using their expertise to interpret AI-generated insights and make informed judgments.

In 2016, BakerHostetler, one of the largest law firms in the United States, added Ross, a "robotic lawyer," to its team. Powered by IBM's Watson supercomputer, Ross can analyse thousands of legal documents across hundreds of databases and independently determine which ones are most relevant for building a strong case.

Augmented intelligence is particularly valuable in scenarios that require a combination of technical expertise and emotional intelligence. For example, in customer service, AI chatbots can handle basic inquiries and provide quick responses, while human agents can step in to address more complex or sensitive issues that require empathy and a personal touch. This division of labour allows for a more efficient use of resources, with AI handling high-volume, low-complexity tasks, and humans focusing on interactions that require emotional understanding and relationship-building. By working together, AI and human agents can provide a better overall customer experience, balancing efficiency with empathy.

Virgin Trains has used natural language processing to automate 85 percent of its complaint processing.

Moreover, augmented intelligence has the potential to democratize access to information and expertise. AI-powered tools can help individuals with limited knowledge or experience in a particular field gain insights and make informed decisions. For instance, AI-driven platforms can help small business owners manage their finances, develop marketing strategies, or optimize their supply chains, even if they lack formal training in these areas. By providing access to advanced tools and insights, augmented intelligence empowers individuals and small organizations to compete on a more level playing field with larger, more resource-rich competitors.

However, for augmented intelligence to reach its full potential, it is essential to foster a collaborative mindset that values the unique contributions of both humans and machines. This involves recognizing the strengths and limitations of AI and understanding how to effectively integrate technology into human workflows. Training and education are critical components of this process, as workers need to be equipped with the skills to interact with AI systems, interpret their outputs, and leverage them to enhance their work. By building a culture of collaboration and continuous learning, organizations can ensure that their workforce is prepared to embrace augmented intelligence and harness its benefits.

"As artificial intelligence evolves, we must remember that its power lies not in replacing human intelligence, but in augmenting it. The true potential of AI lies in its ability to amplify human creativity and ingenuity." – Ginni Rometty

Ethical considerations are also crucial in the development and deployment of augmented intelligence systems. It is important to ensure that AI is used responsibly, with appropriate safeguards in place to protect privacy, prevent bias, and maintain transparency. Augmented intelligence should be designed to empower humans rather than replace them, with a focus on enhancing human decision-making and creativity. By prioritizing ethical AI development, we can create systems that are not only powerful but also aligned with human values and needs.

"AI has the potential to augment human intelligence, not replace it. It can help us make better decisions, solve complex problems, and tackle tasks that are too difficult or time-consuming for humans to do on their own." – Fei-Fei Li

---

Augmented intelligence represents a vision of the future where humans and machines work together to achieve more than either could alone. By combining the analytical power of AI with the creativity, emotional intelligence, and contextual understanding of humans, augmented intelligence has the potential to transform industries, enhance productivity, and improve decision-making. Rather than fearing AI as a threat, we should embrace it as a partner that can help us unlock new possibilities and create a better, more innovative world. The future of intelligence is not about replacing humans with machines but about augmenting our abilities to solve the complex challenges of the 21st century.

"True collaboration is not about dividing work between machines and people but about bringing the strengths of both together to solve problems and achieve more than either could alone." – Garry Kasparov,

---

What Happens If AI Becomes Smarter Than Humans?

"People worry that computers will get too smart and take over the world, but the real problem is that they're too foolish

and they've already taken over the world." – Pedro Domingos.

The idea of artificial intelligence surpassing human intelligence has long been a staple of science fiction, but with recent advances in AI, the prospect of AI becoming smarter than humans no longer seems purely hypothetical. This scenario, often referred to as the development of Artificial General Intelligence (AGI) or even further with superintelligence, raises profound questions about what would happen if machines could outperform humans in all cognitive tasks. Such a development could bring both extraordinary benefits and significant risks, and it is crucial to explore the potential consequences of creating an intelligence that exceeds our own.

One of the most optimistic visions of superintelligent AI is that it could solve many of the world's most pressing challenges. With the ability to process information, learn, and innovate far beyond the capacity of any human, a superintelligent AI could accelerate scientific discoveries, create solutions to complex problems like climate change, eradicate diseases, and eliminate poverty. For example, AI with superior cognitive abilities could analyse massive datasets to discover new medical treatments, design more efficient energy systems, or predict and mitigate natural disasters with unprecedented accuracy. The potential for a superintelligent AI to transform society for the better is immense, provided that it is aligned with human values and goals.

However, the development of AI that surpasses human intelligence also comes with considerable risks. One of the primary concerns is the potential loss of human control over superintelligent systems. Unlike current AI, which operates under the guidance and control of human programmers, a superintelligent AI could become autonomous, making decisions, and pursuing goals without human intervention. If the goals of a superintelligent AI are not perfectly aligned with human values, it could act in ways that are harmful or even catastrophic. This misalignment problem, often referred to as the "control problem," is a major challenge for AI researchers and ethicists. Ensuring that an AI's motivations and actions are consistent with human well-being is an extremely complex task, especially when dealing with an intelligence that may be far beyond our own.

"There is no reason and no way that a human mind can keep up with an artificial intelligence machine by 2035." —Gray Scott.

Another risk associated with superintelligent AI is the potential for unintended consequences. Even if an AI's objectives are designed with the best intentions, the way it interprets and pursues those goals may lead to unexpected and undesirable outcomes. For example, an AI tasked with solving climate change might decide that the most efficient solution is to drastically reduce human activity, without considering the ethical implications of such an action. The difficulty lies in programming an AI to understand the nuances of human values and ethics, which are often subjective and context dependent. The potential for an AI to misinterpret its objectives and take actions that are harmful to humanity is a significant concern that must be addressed before the development of superintelligent systems.

The emergence of superintelligent AI also raises concerns about economic and social inequality. If a superintelligent AI were developed by a particular corporation or nation, it could give that entity an overwhelming advantage over others, potentially leading to a concentration of power and wealth. This could exacerbate existing inequalities and create a world where a small group of individuals or countries wield unprecedented influence over the rest of humanity. The ethical implications of who controls superintelligent AI and how it is used are critical considerations that must be addressed to prevent a future marked by extreme disparities in power and opportunity.

There is also the question of how superintelligent AI would affect the nature of work and human purpose. If AI becomes capable of outperforming humans in virtually all tasks, it could render many forms of employment obsolete, leading to widespread job displacement. While AI has the potential to improve productivity and create new opportunities, the transition to a world where most work is automated could be challenging. People derive a sense of purpose and identity from their work, and if AI were to take over most jobs, society would need to find new ways for individuals to find meaning and contribute. Some have proposed ideas like Universal Basic Income (UBI) as a way to support people in a highly automated future, but the social and psychological implications of such a shift would need to be carefully considered.

Moreover, the rise of a superintelligent AI could challenge our understanding of what it means to be human. Intelligence has always been a defining characteristic of humanity, and the development of a machine that surpasses us in this regard raises philosophical questions about our place in the world. Would we still be the dominant species, or would we need to coexist with a new form of intelligence that may have its own goals and values? The prospect of coexisting with an entity that is vastly more intelligent than us is both intriguing and unsettling, and it forces us to confront fundamental questions about our identity and future.

To mitigate the risks associated with superintelligent AI, many experts advocate for a cautious and collaborative approach to AI development. This includes establishing international regulations to ensure that AI research is conducted safely and responsibly, developing ethical frameworks to guide AI behaviour, and fostering transparency and cooperation among researchers, governments, and organizations. Additionally, efforts are being made to develop AI alignment techniques, which aim to ensure that AI systems remain aligned with human values and act in ways that are beneficial to humanity. By prioritizing safety and ethical considerations, it may be possible to harness the potential of superintelligent AI while minimizing its risks.

The prospect of AI becoming smarter than humans presents both incredible opportunities and significant challenges. On one hand, a superintelligent AI could help solve some of the most complex problems facing humanity, ushering in a new era of prosperity and advancement. On the other hand, the risks associated with loss of control, unintended consequences, inequality, and the disruption of work and human purpose are profound and must be carefully managed. As we move forward in the development of AI, it is essential to prioritize ethical considerations, safety, and international cooperation to ensure that the rise of superintelligent AI benefits all of humanity. The future of AI is not predetermined, and the choices we make today will shape whether it becomes a complement to human intelligence or a potential existential threat.

Humans Remain Essential In An AI World

In the midst of the rapid rise of AI, it's natural to wonder what role humans will play in an increasingly automated world. As we witness algorithms performing complex calculations, generating creative content, and even assisting in decision-making, some might question whether human intelligence is being pushed aside. Yet, there are profound reasons why humans remain essential in an AI-powered future – reasons rooted in qualities that AI, despite its incredible capabilities, cannot replicate.

In a 2023 experiment conducted with Boston Consulting Group, 800 management consultants were split into two groups: one using AI assistance and the other working without it. Participants were tasked with completing various work-related assignments within a set timeframe. The results showed that AI-assisted participants produced higher-quality, more creative work in less time than the "human-only" group. However, many relied heavily on AI outputs, often copying, and pasting without editing or verifying accuracy. Consequently, for tasks requiring critical thinking and accuracy checks, only 65% of AI-assisted participants provided correct answers, compared to 84% of those in the "human-only" group.

Artificial intelligence is extraordinary at processing vast amounts of data and extracting patterns. However, even the most sophisticated machine learning systems lack true emotional understanding. Empathy—the ability to understand and share the feelings of another—is fundamental to human connection. Whether it is comforting a grieving friend, providing motivation to someone who is struggling, or understanding the nuanced emotions of a child, empathy requires an appreciation of context, subtlety, and shared human experiences that AI lacks.

In fields such as healthcare, education, and counselling, this emotional connection is crucial. A doctor does not just treat a disease; they also provide reassurance to anxious patients. A teacher does not merely convey information; they inspire students, adapt to their moods, and support their dreams. AI might assist in analysing data or providing suggestions, but the human touch remains indispensable when it comes to offering true emotional support, understanding, and motivation.

Another critical distinction between humans and AI lies in our capacity for ethical judgment. AI systems operate based on data, algorithms, and programming—they can calculate probabilities, optimize for certain goals, or even simulate ethical dilemmas, but they lack a genuine moral compass. Human beings, on the other hand, draw on a rich tapestry of cultural norms, personal experiences, empathy, and ethical frameworks to make decisions that affect others.

"The future of work lies in the collaboration between humans and AI, where technology enhances our natural abilities, allowing us to think more strategically and creatively and empowering us to drive innovation in the workplace." - Demis Hassabis.

For instance, in law enforcement or the judicial system, decisions often involve complex moral considerations. Should a person receive leniency based on extenuating circumstances? How do we balance justice with mercy? While AI can provide data-driven insights, it is ultimately human judgment that must make the call, weighing not just the facts but the broader social implications, fairness, and humanity of the decision. Our moral reasoning is shaped not by static algorithms but by evolving ethical debates, experiences, and a sense of justice that emerges from our shared humanity.

AI-generated art, music, and writing have made headlines for their surprising ingenuity. Yet, while AI can imitate and even innovate within predefined constraints, true human creativity involves more than just the recombination of existing patterns. Creativity is about challenging conventions, seeing the world from new perspectives, and expressing something deeply personal and original. It often involves breaking rules and imagining possibilities that are entirely outside the box —something AI, which relies on established data and learned patterns, struggles to achieve.

A study of around four hundred college-educated professionals found that those using ChatGPT for writing tasks completed their work in half the time. Less experienced writers improved the quality of their output, while skilled writers maintained their standards but worked more efficiently.

The creative process is also fundamentally linked to the human condition. Artists, writers, musicians, and other creators draw on their emotions, personal experiences, and the desire to communicate something meaningful to others. AI might generate an impressive painting, but it cannot paint out of longing, joy, or heartbreak. Human creativity is about exploration, emotional depth, and the desire to connect—elements that transcend the capabilities of algorithms.

Humans are uniquely adaptable beings. Throughout history, we have faced and overcome countless challenges—natural disasters, pandemics, societal upheavals—often finding creative and unexpected solutions. This adaptability is fuelled not just by our problem-solving skills but by qualities like resilience, determination, and the ability to learn from failure. AI systems, on the other hand, excel in predictable environments where the rules are clearly defined. When conditions change dramatically, AI may struggle, whereas humans are capable of rethinking strategies, shifting perspectives, and finding new ways forward.

Consider the workplace. AI can optimize tasks, streamline processes, and even identify inefficiencies. However, when a crisis hits—whether it is a sudden market change, a pandemic, or a natural disaster—human adaptability and leadership become crucial. People can come together, innovate on the fly, and navigate uncertainty with an intuition and flexibility that

AI simply does not possess. It is this human spirit—our capacity to persevere, to hope, to adapt—that ensures we remain vital, even in a world transformed by technology.

Culture is another area where humans remain essential. Culture encompasses art, language, traditions, values, and the shared experiences of communities. It is deeply subjective and varies widely across the globe. AI can learn about cultural symbols and replicate styles, but it does not experience culture. It does not understand what it feels like to celebrate a festival, to mourn a loss, or to belong to a particular community. Humans provide context and meaning that AI simply cannot grasp because it lacks subjective experience.

In cross-cultural communication, for example, understanding nuances—such as humour, sarcasm, or gestures—requires an understanding that goes beyond data. It requires lived experience. This cultural competency is essential in diplomacy, international business, and community relations, where misunderstanding cultural context can lead to significant issues. Humans, with their lived experiences and shared histories, are irreplaceable when it comes to navigating the complexities of culture and meaning.

As AI continues to evolve, the importance of human oversight becomes even more critical. AI systems are powerful, but they are only as good as the data they are trained on and the parameters set by their creators. Bias in data, unintended consequences, and ethical dilemmas are all issues that require human intervention. Humans must ensure that AI is developed and deployed in ways that align with our values, which respect individual rights, and that benefit society as a whole.

This oversight is not just about preventing harm; it is also about ensuring that AI serves humanity in meaningful ways. It involves asking questions like: Who benefits from this technology? Are we inadvertently reinforcing inequalities? How do we ensure transparency and accountability in AI systems?

These are questions that require human empathy, ethical reasoning, and a commitment to the greater good qualities that machines do not possess.

"By far, the greatest danger of Artificial Intelligence is that people conclude too early that they understand it." — Eliezer Yudkowsky.

Ultimately, the future is not about AI replacing humans but about AI augmenting human capabilities. AI can handle repetitive tasks, analyse vast datasets, and provide insights that would take humans years to uncover. This frees us to focus on what we do best: caring for one another, thinking creatively, solving complex problems, and building meaningful connections. The goal is not to compete with AI but to collaborate with it, using its strengths to enhance our own abilities and improve our quality of life.

"The future of artificial intelligence is not about man versus machine, but rather man with machine. Together, we can achieve unimaginable heights of innovation and progress." - Fei-Fei Li

---

In fields like medicine, AI can assist doctors by analysing medical images or predicting health trends, but it is the doctor who will sit with the patient, explain the diagnosis, and provide comfort. In education, AI can help tailor learning experiences, but it is the teacher who will inspire students, adapt lessons to the unique dynamics of the classroom, and foster a love for learning. In these and countless other domains, humans and AI can work together to achieve outcomes that neither could achieve alone.

While AI is a powerful tool that is reshaping the world, humans remain at the centre of this transformation. Our empathy, ethical reasoning, creativity, adaptability, cultural understanding, and capacity for oversight ensure that we are not only relevant but essential in an AI-driven future. The challenge and opportunity ahead lie in embracing AI as a partner, one that enhances our abilities and allows us to focus on what makes us truly human.

Human Values And Ethical Frameworks

As AI technology continues to advance, it becomes increasingly clear that human values and ethical frameworks must guide its development and application. AI has immense power, and with great power comes great responsibility. Without a well-defined ethical compass, AI has the potential to cause significant harm —whether through biased algorithms, breaches of privacy, or unintended social consequences.

Human values—such as fairness, justice, empathy, and respect for individual rights—must be at the core of AI development. These values cannot be encoded into algorithms as simple instructions; they require continuous dialogue, reflection, and adaptation. Ethical frameworks help ensure that AI systems are developed with the intention of benefiting humanity, rather than serving narrow interests or exacerbating inequalities.

"The real danger is not that computers will begin to think like men, but that men will begin to think like computers." – Sydney Harris

---

One of the key challenges is ensuring that AI is inclusive and equitable. This means considering the impact of AI on different groups of people, especially those who are marginalized or vulnerable. AI systems must be designed to minimize bias, and there must be accountability mechanisms in place to address any harm that arises from their use. This requires human oversight, transparency in decision-making processes, and a commitment to the ethical use of technology.

Moreover, ethical considerations must extend beyond the initial design and deployment of AI systems. As AI learns and evolves, continuous monitoring and evaluation are necessary to ensure that it remains aligned with human values. This is particularly important as AI begins to play a larger role in areas such as law enforcement, healthcare, and finance, where decisions can have profound effects on individuals and communities.

The development of international ethical standards and regulations is also crucial. AI is a global technology, and its impact knows no borders. Collaborative efforts among governments, industry leaders, researchers, and civil society are needed to establish guidelines that promote the responsible use of AI. These guidelines should address issues such as data privacy, algorithmic transparency, and the prevention of harmful uses of AI, such as autonomous weapons or surveillance technologies that infringe on civil liberties.

Ultimately, the need for human values and ethical frameworks in AI is about ensuring that technology aligns with our values. It is about creating a future where AI enhances human well-being, supports social justice, and contributes to a more equitable world. This requires intentional action, vigilance, and a collective commitment to using AI as a tool for good.

While AI is reshaping the world, humans remain at the centre of this transformation. Our empathy, ethical reasoning, creativity, adaptability, cultural understanding, and capacity for oversight ensure that we are not only relevant but essential in an AI-driven future.

EMBRACING AI TO SHAPE OUR FUTURE

AI Shapes Our Society

The rapid rise of artificial intelligence has touched every facet of our society, from how we communicate and work to how we learn and make decisions. As AI becomes increasingly integrated into our daily lives, we face profound questions about its impact on our social structures, politics, ethics, and our shared future. How can we embrace AI responsibly and inclusively, ensuring it helps create a better society for all?

> *"We tend to overestimate the effect of a technology in the short run and underestimate the effect in the long run." – Roy Amara*

AI is reshaping society in countless ways, from transforming industries to altering the nature of human interaction. In education, personalized AI tutors are helping students learn in ways that cater to their unique needs and learning styles. In healthcare, AI assists in diagnosing diseases more accurately and helping doctors deliver personalized treatment plans. But beyond these obvious benefits, AI is also redefining societal norms and expectations, with implications that reach deep into our social and political lives.

In our political systems, AI is used for a range of applications, from data-driven policy decisions to enhancing public safety. AI-powered systems can analyse vast amounts of social and economic data, helping policymakers understand trends, identify challenges, and respond more effectively to crises. Yet, this same technology also poses challenges. For instance, the use of AI in surveillance can enhance security, but it can also lead to privacy concerns and potentially be abused by authoritarian regimes to monitor citizens and suppress dissent.

The development of AI must be navigated thoughtfully to ensure it serves as a force for good, rather than a tool for exploitation or control. As AI technologies advance, we need to consider their effects on employment, privacy, and social equity. If designed and implemented inclusively, AI can enhance societal well-being, but if left unchecked, it could deepen inequalities and erode trust in institutions.

In Edward Bellamy's 1888 novel "Looking Backward", the protagonist sleeps through 113 years, awakening in 2000 to a world where jobs no longer define people's identities. With technology handling the day-to-day operations of society, individuals focus on learning, teaching, and exploring personal interests. What Bellamy envisioned as science fiction now feels like a glimpse into the near future.

The Impact Of AI On Democracy And Decision-Making

AI's influence on democracy and decision-making is complex and multifaceted. On one hand, AI has the potential to enrich democratic processes by providing citizens and policymakers with deeper insights into societal issues. AI algorithms can analyse public sentiment, helping governments make informed decisions based on the needs and preferences of their citizens. Imagine a world where policy decisions are informed not only by politicians but also by the collective voice of the people, analysed through AI to ensure inclusivity and fairness.

However, the potential for AI to undermine democratic values is also a significant concern. AI-driven misinformation campaigns, as witnessed in several elections around the world, have the power to manipulate public opinion and sow discord. Deepfakes and AI-generated content can make it difficult for individuals to distinguish between truth and falsehood, eroding the very foundation of informed decision-making in democratic societies.

Moreover, the use of AI in decision-making processes raises questions about accountability. If an AI system makes a decision that adversely affects a person or community, who is responsible? Unlike human decision-makers, AI lacks moral reasoning and empathy, which are crucial for ensuring that decisions are just and humane. Therefore, the integration of AI into democratic processes must be accompanied by mechanisms that ensure accountability, transparency, and fairness.

Transparency And Understanding

To harness AI for the betterment of society, transparency and public understanding must be prioritized. AI systems are often seen as "black boxes," with decision-making processes that are opaque and difficult for even their creators to fully understand. This lack of transparency can lead to mistrust and resistance, particularly when AI is used in sensitive areas such as healthcare, law enforcement, or social services.

"Responsible AI is not just about liability — it's about ensuring what you are building is enabling human flourishing." – Rumman Chowdhury

---

Promoting transparency involves not only making AI systems more understandable but also engaging the public in conversations about how AI is developed and used. Public forums, citizen panels, and educational initiatives can help demystify AI and provide people with a voice in shaping its future. For example, some countries have already begun involving citizens in discussions about AI ethics and governance, ensuring that diverse perspectives are taken into account when setting policies.

"It is important that we ensure that the development of AI is aligned with human values, and that its use is transparent and accountable." – Margaret Court

---

In addition, tech companies have a role to play in promoting transparency. By clearly communicating how data is used, how decisions are made, and what limitations exist, these companies can help build trust and ensure that AI technologies are aligned with public interests. Transparency is not just about explaining algorithms; it is about fostering an open dialogue with society, inviting scrutiny, and being willing to adapt based on feedback.

Ethical AI Initiatives

The development of ethical AI initiatives and standards is critical to ensuring that AI technologies are used responsibly. As AI becomes more powerful, the risk of unintended consequences, bias, and misuse grows. Ethical frameworks are needed to guide the development and deployment of AI in ways that prioritize human well-being, fairness, and justice.

"AI is a mirror, reflecting not only our intellect, but our values and fears." — Ravi Narayanan

---

Many organizations, governments, and tech companies are already working on establishing ethical guidelines for AI. These initiatives aim to ensure that AI systems are free from bias, respect privacy, and are designed to enhance rather than harm human lives. For instance, the development of AI systems that are used in hiring processes must be carefully monitored to ensure that they do not reinforce existing biases or discriminate against certain groups.

"It's not a question of whether AI will change the world, but how. Ensuring that this change is positive requires that we take ethical considerations into account from the very beginning." - Demis Hassabis.

International collaboration is also essential in this endeavour. AI is a global technology, and its impact transcends national borders. Therefore, ethical standards must be established at an international level, involving stakeholders from diverse backgrounds, including policymakers, technologists, ethicists, and civil society. By creating a shared understanding of what constitutes ethical AI, we can work towards a future where technology serves the common good rather than the interests of a select few.

Inclusive AI Development

To ensure that AI benefits everyone, its development must be inclusive. This means involving diverse voices in the design, development, and deployment of AI technologies. Historically, the tech industry has lacked diversity, leading to technologies that do not adequately serve—or, worse, actively disadvantage—marginalized communities. Encouraging diversity in AI development is crucial to preventing these outcomes and ensuring that AI technologies are equitable.

Inclusive AI development involves not only diversifying the teams that create AI but also considering the needs and experiences of different communities during the design process. For example, involving individuals from various cultural, socioeconomic, and educational backgrounds can help identify potential biases and blind spots that might otherwise go unnoticed. By incorporating a wider range of perspectives, AI systems can be designed to be fairer and more effective for everyone.

Moreover, public engagement is essential to making AI development inclusive. People from all walks of life should have a say in how AI is used in their communities. This can be achieved through public consultations, educational initiatives, and community forums where people can share their experiences and concerns. By fostering a culture of inclusivity, we can create AI systems that are not only technologically advanced but also socially responsible.

"The ethical challenge of AI is to ensure that it serves humanity as a whole, not just a privileged few. This requires a human-centred approach that respects human dignity, human rights, and fundamental freedoms." — UNESCO Recommendation on the Ethics of Artificial Intelligence.

AI is reshaping our society in profound ways, offering both opportunities and challenges. By embracing AI responsibly, promoting transparency, establishing ethical standards, and ensuring inclusive development, we can harness its potential to create a better future. The key lies in recognizing that AI is not an end in itself but a tool that, when guided by human values, can help us address some of the most pressing challenges of our time. The journey towards a future where AI serves all of humanity requires collaboration, vigilance, and a commitment to equity and justice.

As we move forward, we must remember that the power of AI lies not in replacing human intelligence but in augmenting it. By working together—humans and machines—we can create a society that is more just, more prosperous, and more connected. It is up to us to shape this future, ensuring that AI serves as a force for good and contributes to the well-being of every individual and community.

Adapting Education Systems

As we navigate the rise of AI, education must be reimagined to address the changes brought about by this technology. Preparing our children, students, and workforce for an AI-driven future means developing skills that complement AI while focusing on what makes us uniquely human. The current model of rote learning and standardized testing is insufficient to meet the challenges posed by AI, instead, we need to pivot toward more dynamic, adaptive, and human-centric learning environments.

AI excels at tasks involving pattern recognition, rapid computation, and data analysis. Therefore, education systems should emphasize skills that are beyond the reach of AI: creativity, emotional intelligence, critical thinking, and complex problem-solving. Subjects such as philosophy, ethics, and the arts, which encourage divergent thinking and empathy, must play a greater role in our education curricula. These human traits will be indispensable in a future where machines handle much of the routine work.

"Every industry and job is being transformed by AI, and it's up to us to shape the outcome." - Stuart Russell.

In addition to fostering human-centric skills, education must also emphasize lifelong learning. AI will continue to evolve at a rapid pace, and job roles will change just as quickly. To keep up, individuals must constantly learn new skills and adapt to evolving industries. Reskilling and upskilling programs should be widely available to equip individuals for new job opportunities created by AI. Governments, educational institutions, and private enterprises must work together to provide continuous learning opportunities, ensuring that no one is left behind in the AI-driven economy.

"85% of employers plan to prioritize upskilling their workforce." — World Economic Forum Future of Jobs Report 2025.

AI can also be integrated into the learning process itself. AI-powered personalized learning systems can identify each student's unique learning style and pace, providing tailored support to help them succeed. Intelligent tutoring systems can help alleviate the burden on teachers by providing individualized instruction, while educators focus on the critical role of cultivating students' emotional and social development —areas where AI still falls short.

The Role Of Governments

Governments and policymakers have a critical role to play

in ensuring that AI benefits society as a whole. Effective governance can shape AI into a force for good, ensuring that its benefits are distributed equitably, its risks are minimized, and that it upholds fundamental human rights. Policymakers must approach AI with a mix of proactive regulation, ethical guidelines, and societal support.

"It's important that we consider the long-term implications of AI, to ensure that it is developed in a way that benefits humanity and that we are prepared for its potential impacts." – Mark Zuckerberg

---

One of the primary responsibilities of governments is to regulate AI development and usage to prevent misuse, discrimination, and harm. While AI can bring about immense benefits, its potential for privacy invasion, bias, and manipulation must be carefully managed. Governments should implement strong data protection regulations to ensure individuals' personal information is safeguarded and not exploited. Regulations must also ensure transparency in AI decision-making, allowing individuals to understand and contest decisions that impact their lives—whether in hiring, healthcare, or criminal justice.

AI governance should also focus on creating standards for ethical AI development. Policymakers must ensure that AI systems are built and deployed responsibly, avoiding biases that can perpetuate social inequities. Governments must incentivize companies to prioritize fairness and accountability, while also fostering collaboration between the private sector, academia, and civil society to establish ethical AI standards.

"As more and more artificial intelligence is entering into the world, more and more emotional intelligence

must enter into leadership." – Amit Ray.

To address the socioeconomic impacts of AI, policymakers must create safety nets and support mechanisms for those whose jobs are displaced by automation. Investments in education, retraining programs, and public services are essential to help individuals transition to new opportunities in an AI-driven economy. Policymakers must also consider innovative solutions, such as universal basic income (UBI) or a "robot tax," to redistribute the wealth generated by automation and ensure that economic gains are shared equitably.

What Individuals Can Do

AI is not only reshaping our institutions and economies—it is transforming the very nature of human society. As we adapt to these changes, every individual has a role to play in building an AI-ready society. To thrive in an AI-driven world, we must embrace lifelong learning, cultivate our uniquely human skills, and actively participate in shaping AI's impact on our lives.

"AI will not make us obsolete, but it will make us superhuman." – Max Tegmark.

Becoming informed about AI and its implications is an important first step. AI technology is rapidly advancing, and understanding its capabilities, risks, and societal impact is essential to making informed decisions. Individuals should take the time to learn about AI through online courses, workshops, and public discussions. With this knowledge, people can better understand how AI is being used in their workplaces, communities, and everyday lives—and advocate for its responsible use.

"Chance favours the prepared mind" – Louis Pasteur

Another critical aspect of preparing for the AI age is protecting one's digital identity. Every time we use a search engine, browse social media, or engage with digital services, we generate valuable data that is collected by corporations and used to train AI systems. Being mindful of how we share our data, scrutinizing privacy policies, and using services that respect user privacy can help individuals retain control over their personal information. By supporting privacy-focused technologies, individuals can also push companies to adopt more ethical data practices.

Collaboration is also essential for shaping AI's impact. AI development should be inclusive, with input from people of diverse backgrounds, communities, and experiences. Individuals can contribute by participating in public consultations on AI policy, joining local tech ethics groups, or sharing their experiences with AI technologies. Just as public engagement shaped the regulations of previous transformative technologies, like nuclear energy and IVF, a diverse, informed public is crucial to creating responsible AI policies that align with societal values.

Ultimately, preparing for an AI-driven world requires both individual and collective action. We must work together to shape a future where AI complements human potential rather than replacing it—where it serves humanity's best interests and enhances our quality of life. By embracing learning, cultivating our human qualities, and actively participating in AI-related discussions, we can shape a future where AI is a powerful tool for positive change, fostering a fairer, more equitable society for all.

"AI is a tool, not a destination." – Ginni Rometty.

APPENDIX: REFERENCES FOR FURTHER READING

1. **A World Without Work** (2020), Daniel Susskind, *Automation will change the future of work, potentially making human labour obsolete, but it can also create new jobs and increase overall productivity.*
2. **AI 2041** (2021), Kai-Fu Lee and Chen Qiufan, *Fiction about how AI will change our world in the next twenty years.*
3. **AI for Business Leaders** (2023), Michael Ramsay, *AI is essential for competitive business transformation, offering strategic advantages in operations, customer experiences, and market positioning.*
4. **AI Needs You** (2024), Verity Harding, *Public engagement is crucial in shaping AI's development.*
5. **AI Snake Oil** (2024),Arvind Narayanan, Sayash Kapoor, *AI's limitations highlight that many challenges are societal rather than purely technological, requiring a combination of artificial and human intelligence.*
6. **AI Superpowers** (2018), Kai-Fu Lee, *China is determined to become the world superpower in AI and has heavily subsidized AI-tech start-ups to pave the way for a booming AI industry.*

7. **All-in On AI** (2018), Tom Davenport and Nitin Mittal, *A supportive culture that promotes experimentation and data literacy among staff is essential for leveraging AI in business processes.*

8. **Architects of Intelligence** (2018), Martin Ford, *A collection of interviews with experts in the field of AI exploring the potential impact on society and the economy.*

9. **Artificial Intelligence** (2019), Melanie Mitchell, *AI excels at specific tasks but struggles with basic perceptual and common-sense skills that humans easily possess.*

10. **Artificial Intelligence & Generative AI for Beginners** (2023), David M. Patel, *Generative AI is transforming industries like healthcare, entertainment, and retail, offering enhanced efficiency, deeper personalization, and groundbreaking innovation.*

11. **Atlas of AI** (2021), Kate Crawford, *The AI industry relies heavily on the extraction of minerals, data, and human labour, leading to significant environmental destruction and social inequality.*

12. **Co-Intelligence** (2024), Ethan Mollick, *AI's adaptability allows users to customize its persona for different tasks, enhancing creativity and efficiency in the workplace, though human oversight remains crucial for accuracy and quality control.*

13. **Competing in the Age of AI** (2020), Marco Iansiti and Karim R. Lakhani, *Digital technologies are breaking down traditional business boundaries, allowing companies to scale, broaden their scope, and enhance learning capabilities through AI.*

14. **Deep Medicine** (2019), Eric Topol, *Doctors can use AI to improve their diagnoses, as AI can assist in pattern recognition and help identify specific illnesses.*

15. **Deep Thinking** (2017), Garry Kasparov, *Computers*

have surpassed human intelligence … when it comes to playing chess.

16. **How to Create a Mind** (2012), Ray Kurzweil, *If machines can emulate the brain enough to think, future machines could perform acts of free will.*

17. **How We Learn** (2020), Stanislas Dehaene, *Human learning outpaces artificial intelligence in complexity and efficacy, especially in areas like data efficiency, abstract reasoning, and social learning.*

18. **Human + Machine** (2018), Paul R. Daugherty and H. James Wilson, *AI is automating routine tasks, allowing employees to focus on more complex and judgment-requiring activities.*

19. **Human Compatible** (2019), Stuart Russell, *The potential dangers of superintelligent artificial intelligence makes us need to rethink its design in order to ensure it remains beneficial to humanity.*

20. **Human/Machine** (2019), Daniel Newman and Olivier Blanchard, *Emotional intelligence and other human-centric skills are becoming increasingly valuable in the job market as technology cannot replicate these qualities.*

21. **IRREPLACEABLE** (2024), Pascal Bornet, *View AI as a partner rather than a competitor to enhance your capabilities and work more efficiently.*

22. **Life 3.0** (2017), Max Tegmark, *Intelligence, memory, computation, and learning are not exclusively human attributes and can exist in machines.*

23. **Marketing Artificial Intelligence** (2022), Paul Roetzer and Mike Kaput, *AI is transforming marketing by making strategies smarter, more efficient, and more effective, leveraging technologies like machine learning and deep learning.*

24. **Novacene** (2019), James Lovelock, *The Novacene is characterized by the emergence of a new form of life*

produced by artificial intelligence.

25. **Power And Prediction** (2018), Ajay Agrawal, Joshua Gans and Avi Goldfarb, *AI has become adept at making precise predictions, which should be used to inform human judgment rather than replace it.*

26. **Prediction Machines** (2018), Ajay Agrawal, Joshua Gans and Avi Goldfarb, *The future of effective prediction involves a synergistic collaboration between human intuition and machine precision, optimizing outcomes by leveraging the comparative strengths of both.*

27. **Rewired** (2023), Eric Lamarre, Kate Smaje and Rodney Zemmel, *Talent is central to digital transformation, requiring recognition of individual goals, provision of continuous learning opportunities, and guidance for newcomers to create a robust and adaptable workforce.*

28. **Superhuman Innovation** (2019), Chris Duffey, *AI can improve customer experiences by providing personalized service and smoothing over friction points in the buying process.*

29. **Superintelligence** (2014), Nick Bostrom, *To prevent unintended catastrophes, superintelligence can be programmed to learn human values and align its actions with them, either by determining core human values or inferring intentions based on majority values.*

30. **The Age of AI** (2021), Henry Kissinger, Eric Schmidt and Daniel Huttenlocher, *AI's integration into daily life, such as through social media algorithms and content curation, presents challenges around accountability and the potential to influence democracy and social divisions.*

31. **The AI Economy** (2019), Roger Bootle, *The AI revolution is unlikely to cause massive job loss and will lead to higher productivity and economic*

growth.

32. **The Automation Advantage** (2021), Bhaskar Ghosh, Gayathri Pallail and Rajendra Prasad, *Successful automation requires a clear strategy, including defining automation projects and continuous improvement.*

33. **The Coming Wave** (2023), Mustafa Suleyman, *Technologies often have unintended side effects, known as "revenge effects," which can lead to significant societal changes and challenges.*

34. **The Creativity Code** (2019), Marcus du Sautoy, *While AI can generate creative output, it lacks the human element of intention and free will, making it a creative tool rather than a creative agent.*

35. **The Economic Singularity** (2016), Calum Chase, *Machines and automation have historically generated more jobs and increased a nation's wealth, rather than threatening human employment.*

36. **The End of Marketing** (2020), Carlos Gil, *Traditional marketing strategies are becoming less effective compared to social media, where engagement and personal connections drive consumer behaviour.*

37. **The Future of the Professions** (2015), Richard Susskind and Daniel Susskind, *Professional roles are evolving rather than becoming obsolete, as the vast amount of knowledge today cannot be managed by one person alone.*

38. **The Future of Work** (2018), Darrell M. West, *To prepare for the transition to a digital economy, we need to broaden our definition of which jobs are worthy of receiving a wage and benefits, including volunteer work and activities that benefit society.*

39. **The Human Edge** (2019), Greg Orme, *AI is changing the workplace and taking over some human jobs, but it falls short in areas where*

humans excel: Creativity, Curiosity, Consciousness, and Collaboration (the 4Cs).

40. **The Mind's Mirror** (2024), Gregory Mone, Daniela Rus, *AI-generated responses were rated as more empathetic than human doctors' responses in some studies.*

41. **The Robots Are Coming!** (2019), Andrés Oppenheimer, *Up to 47 percent of current US jobs could be eliminated by 2033 due to automation, affecting a wide range of industries.*

42. **The Singularity Is Nearer** (2023), Ray Kurzweil, *The pace of technological change is accelerating exponentially.*

43. **Too Smart** (2020), Jathan Sadowski, *Reclaiming control in the digital age requires recognizing the value of personal data and making informed choices about technology use.*

44. **Understanding Artificial Intelligence** (2021), Nicolas Sabouret, *AI algorithms are step-by-step approaches to solving tasks, but they have limitations due to the complexity of problems and computational constraints.*

45. **What To Do When Machines Do Everything** (2017), Malcolm Frank, Paul Roehrig and Ben Pring, *To turn your company's data into something meaningful, you need a good business analyst who can transform reams of data into insights that can be used to take action and make profits.*

46. **Why Machines Learn** (2024), Anil Ananthaswamy, *The math behind machine learning might be the same as what makes up our own intelligence.*

APPENDIX: TRAINING TRANSFORMERS AND ATTENTION

Neural Networks And Deep Learning

Neural networks are at the forefront of modern artificial intelligence, emulating the way the human brain processes and interprets information. These sophisticated systems consist of layers of interconnected artificial "neurons," enabling them to excel at pattern recognition, problem-solving, and making predictions. By exploring their structure and functionality, we can better understand how neural networks transform raw data into actionable insights.

At their core, neural networks are built around the concept of layered processing. These layers are categorized into three main types:

1. Input Layer: The entry point for raw data. For example, in an image recognition task, this layer might process the pixel data from a photograph.

2. Hidden Layers: The intermediate layers where most of the computation happens. Each neuron in a hidden layer processes inputs from the previous

> layer, applies mathematical operations, and passes the results forward. By combining simple features, these layers identify intricate patterns and relationships within the data.
>
> 3. Output Layer: The final layer delivers the network's predictions or classifications. For instance, it might decide whether an image contains a cat or a dog or recognize a handwritten digit.

The neurons within these layers form dense connections, passing information forward to process and refine data. Neurons act as decision-makers, evaluating inputs and determining whether to "fire" signals to subsequent layers. This decision-making process relies on activation functions, such as the sigmoid function, which scales values between 0 and 1 to simplify computation. More advanced functions like ReLU (Rectified Linear Unit) provide flexibility tailored to specific tasks, enhancing the network's performance.

The layered structure of neural networks is key to their effectiveness. Each layer tackles part of the problem, breaking it into smaller, manageable components. For example, in a handwritten digit recognition task, early layers might identify loops and lines, while deeper layers combine these features to form the complete number. This hierarchical approach mirrors human perception, where simple elements are assembled into coherent concepts.

Neural networks improve their performance through a process called training, which fine-tunes the connections (or weights) between neurons. Training starts with a dataset of input-output pairs. The network makes initial predictions, compares them to the correct answers, and calculates errors. These errors guide adjustments to the weights, gradually refining the network's accuracy.

A well-trained neural network is not only adept at recognizing patterns in its training data but also skilled at generalization

—applying its knowledge to new, unseen data. For instance, a network trained to recognize handwritten digits should still perform well even when the numbers are slightly distorted or written in unfamiliar styles.

This ability to generalize makes neural networks invaluable across various fields. In image recognition, they detect objects in photos. In natural language processing, they enable machines to understand and generate human language. In finance, they analyse historical data to predict market trends. Neural networks excel wherever large datasets require transformation into actionable insights.

The power of neural networks lies in their ability to simplify complex tasks through layered abstraction. By mimicking human cognition, they break down problems into smaller, solvable steps, allowing them to identify patterns invisible to traditional algorithms. This innovative architecture has made neural networks indispensable tools in the rapidly evolving landscape of artificial intelligence.

The Training Process

Training a neural network involves a cyclical, iterative process aimed at improving its predictive accuracy. Backpropagation, short for "backward propagation of errors," is a cornerstone algorithm in training neural networks. The key steps in this process include:

- Forward Pass: Input data moves layer by layer through the network, with each layer processing the information and passing it to the next. At the output layer, the network produces a prediction.
- Compute Cost: The cost function evaluates the difference between predictions and actual outcomes, quantifying the error.
- Backward Pass: Errors—calculated by comparing

> predictions to actual outcomes—are propagated backward through the network. During this phase, gradients are computed for each parameter, revealing how changes will influence the cost function.
> - Update Parameters: Weights and biases are iteratively refined based on the calculated gradients.

This sequence repeats over many iterations, fine-tuning the network's parameters and improving its performance.

Backpropagation is fundamentally an algorithm for computing gradients—values that indicate how sensitive the network's prediction error is to changes in specific parameters, such as weights and biases. These gradients guide adjustments, allowing the network to systematically reduce its prediction errors over successive training iterations.

The cost function acts as a roadmap, showing how far the network's predictions are from the desired outputs. A high cost reflects significant errors, while a low cost indicates better accuracy.

Gradient descent works by systematically navigating the "error landscape" to find the optimal parameters that minimize this cost.

The process involves two main steps: calculating gradients and updating parameters. Gradients represent the slope of the cost function concerning each weight and bias. Gradients are calculated using partial derivatives derived from the chain rule of calculus. They indicate the direction and magnitude of parameter adjustments needed to reduce the error. Using these gradients, weights and biases are updated incrementally, moving them in the direction that reduces the cost function. This iterative refinement steadily guides the network closer to the optimal configuration.

Although backpropagation involves numerous calculations, it is a manageable step-by-step process, from the end (output) back to the beginning (input). Starting with the output layer, the error is computed between the predicted and actual outputs. Then the gradients are calculated for the output weights and biases. By partial differentiating using the chain rule, it is determined how much each parameter in the output of the previous layer contributes to the error. This process is repeated and propagates backward. The gradient calculation process is repeated for each preceding layer, updating parameters iteratively.

The cost function landscape can be visualized as a multi-dimensional terrain of peaks and valleys. The goal of gradient descent is to locate the global minimum, the point where the cost is lowest. However, challenges arise as the algorithm may sometimes settle in local minima, smaller valleys that are not the lowest possible point. Modern techniques, such as adaptive learning rates and careful initialization, help neural networks approximate the global minimum effectively.

Neural networks operate in parameter spaces with thousands or even millions of dimensions, making direct visualization impossible. Despite this complexity, gradient descent remains effective. Its iterative approach allows it to navigate these vast, abstract spaces efficiently, systematically reducing errors at each step.

The effectiveness of gradient descent lies in its simplicity and adaptability. By identifying the direction the gradients indicate whether to increase or decrease a parameter to reduce error. And by determining the magnitude the gradients also guide how large each adjustment should be.

These small, deliberate updates ensure consistent progress, making gradient descent an indispensable tool in training neural networks. Its ability to handle high-dimensional complexity enables it to optimize models across a wide range of tasks, from image recognition to natural language processing.

Large Language Models

Large Language Models (LLMs) like GPT have revolutionized the way machines understand and generate human language. These advanced systems, which function as sophisticated word predictors, are capable of producing remarkably coherent and contextually accurate text.

At their core, LLMs are mathematical functions designed to predict the next word in a sequence based on probabilities. For example, if given the phrase "The cat sat on the," an LLM would analyse context to determine that "mat" is a likely next word. By repeating this process, LLMs construct full sentences, paragraphs, or even entire articles that sound natural and meaningful.

This predictive approach enables LLMs to engage in conversations, complete sentences, and generate creative text that aligns with human expectations of language structure and flow.

The process of text generation hinges on probabilities. LLMs analyze input text and assign likelihoods to potential next words based on context. They then select the most probable options, ensuring that outputs are logical and coherent. For instance, in answering a question, the model uses the input's context to prioritize relevant information and avoid nonsensical or off-topic responses.

The seamless flow of LLM-generated text is achieved through this iterative prediction, guided by patterns the model has learned during training.

Training is a cornerstone of LLM performance. These models are exposed to vast datasets containing billions of words, including books, articles, and internet content. The scale of this data is staggering. This breadth of exposure allows LLMs to understand diverse language styles, terminologies, and cultural nuances, making them versatile tools across various domains.

Training LLMs is an immensely resource-intensive process. It involves adjusting billions of parameters within the model, each representing a connection or relationship between different pieces of information. This fine-tuning requires computational operations numbering in the trillions, performed in mere weeks using advanced hardware. The result is a highly refined system capable of generating accurate and context-aware text based on the patterns embedded in its parameters.

LLMs have found applications in a wide range of fields, demonstrating their utility and versatility. Some key use cases include:

- Chatbots: Enhancing customer service and personal assistance through natural, conversational interactions.
- Content Creation: Generating articles, reports, and creative writing with minimal human intervention.
- Translation: Providing context-aware translations that preserve meaning and nuance.
- Education: Assisting in learning by explaining concepts, generating practice questions, or summarizing information.

Their ability to understand and generate language has made LLMs indispensable in industries ranging from healthcare to entertainment.

Despite their impressive capabilities, LLMs face several limitations. While they excel at generating fluent text, LLMs may produce less likely or contextually odd responses, especially when confronted with ambiguous input. Training and deploying LLMs require enormous computational power, posing challenges for scalability and accessibility. The reliance on vast datasets introduces risks of bias or misinformation, as the model's outputs reflect patterns present in the training data.

Addressing these challenges is crucial to ensuring that LLMs remain reliable and responsible tools for future applications.

Understanding Transformers In LLMs

Transformers are a revolutionary type of neural network that have transformed the landscape of artificial intelligence, powering some of today's most advanced tools, including GPT models, image generators, and text-to-speech systems. Originally introduced by Google in 2017, transformers excel at processing sequential data, such as language, making them a cornerstone of modern AI advancements. Unlike traditional neural networks, transformers are uniquely equipped to handle sequential data effectively.

Transformers represent words as high-dimensional vectors called embeddings. These embeddings capture nuanced meanings by mapping words into a mathematical space where similar concepts are closer together. In GPT-3, embeddings use a staggering 12,288 dimensions, enabling the model to understand subtle relationships and context with incredible precision.

Transformers consist of multiple layers that process data iteratively, refining their understanding at each stage. Probabilistic functions like softmax are employed to calculate the likelihood of each word in a sequence, ensuring accurate token predictions.

The backbone of LLMs is the transformer architecture, a groundbreaking framework that introduced "attention mechanisms." Unlike earlier models that processed text sequentially, transformers allow LLMs to consider all parts of the input text simultaneously, enabling them to capture context more effectively. For example, in the sentence "The cat sat on the mat because it was tired," the model uses attention mechanisms to link "it" to "the cat," ensuring clarity and accuracy in interpretation. This dynamic evaluation ensures that transformers generate contextually appropriate responses.

The attention mechanisms enables LLM's to selectively focus on the most relevant parts of input data, regardless of its position in a sequence. This ability is critical for tasks like language processing, where the meaning of a word often depends on its context within a sentence.

Attention In Transformers In LLMs

Attention mechanisms enable LLMs to focus on the most relevant parts of the input text, dynamically refining their understanding as they process information. This capability is critical for producing fluent, coherent, and contextually appropriate responses. By prioritizing certain words or phrases over others, attention mechanisms allow the model to resolve ambiguities, handle complex sentences, and maintain a consistent narrative across long passages of text.

The attention mechanism is a transformative innovation in artificial intelligence, serving as the cornerstone of transformers and enabling large language models (LLMs) to process and generate text with remarkable fluency and contextual awareness. Introduced in the landmark 2017 paper "Attention is All You Need", this mechanism has revolutionized how AI interprets language by allowing models to focus on the most relevant parts of input text, regardless of their position within a sequence.

Transformers process language by breaking down input text into smaller units called tokens. Tokens can be individual words, subwords, or even single characters. Each token is then transformed into a high-dimensional vector representation, or embedding, which captures its semantic meaning.

These embeddings reside in a high-dimensional space, where the direction of each vector encodes specific attributes of meaning, such as gender, tense, or topic. For example, tokens related to "king" and "queen" might share similar spatial relationships, reflecting their semantic similarity but differing in their gender dimension.

At the heart of the attention mechanism lies the query, key, and value framework, which enables transformers to evaluate the relationships between tokens dynamically. The Query is a vector that seeks information relevant to a specific token. The Key is a vector that encodes potential matches for queries. And finally, the Value is a vector representing the contextual information associated with each token.

The interaction between these vectors determines how much focus the model places on each token in relation to others. For instance, in the sentence "The cat sat on the mat because it was tired," the query from "it" might prioritize the key of "cat," enabling the model to infer the correct antecedent.

The model calculates attention scores by comparing queries and keys. These scores measure the relevance of each token to others in the sequence. Next, the scores are converted into probabilities using a softmax function, ensuring they sum to 1. Higher probabilities indicate greater relevance. Finally, these values are weighted by these probabilities and aggregated to update the embeddings, enriching each token with contextual information. This process ensures that tokens are not interpreted in isolation but are influenced by their surrounding context, creating nuanced and coherent representations of meaning.

One of the most powerful aspects of transformers is their use of multi-head attention, where multiple attention mechanisms operate in parallel. Each attention head focuses on different aspects of meaning or context, such as syntactic structure or thematic relationships.

For example, in analysing the sentence "She bought a book about quantum physics," one head might focus on the relationship between "She" and "bought," while another examines the connection between "book" and "quantum physics." This parallel processing allows transformers to capture a broader range of patterns and relationships within the text.

While the attention mechanism is conceptually elegant, its real-world application can be complex. The attention weights generated by transformers are often intricate and difficult to interpret. Each attention head learns unique patterns from the training data, and their combined outputs form a sophisticated network of contextual dependencies.

Despite these challenges, the attention mechanism remains the key driver behind the impressive capabilities of LLMs. By dynamically focusing on relevant parts of the input, transformers achieve an unparalleled ability to process and generate coherent text.

The value matrix plays a critical role in refining the embeddings by integrating context-specific information. For instance, if the input sequence includes "I left my keys on the table," the value matrix ensures that "keys" retains its association with "table" in the output embeddings, enabling accurate comprehension and generation. This continuous adjustment of embeddings ensures that the model incorporates the most relevant background details, enhancing its predictions and contextual understanding.

The primary objective of transformers is to predict the next token in a sequence with the highest possible accuracy. Attention mechanisms allow the model to analyse both nearby and distant relationships within the text, ensuring that its predictions are contextually appropriate and semantically rich.

So Where Is The Information Stored?

Large Language Models (LLMs) like GPT are powerful tools capable of recalling a vast array of facts, from historical events to pop culture references. But how do they store and retrieve this information? The underlying mechanisms involve intricate neural network architectures, particularly the role of multi-layer perceptrons (MLPs), which work in conjunction with attention mechanisms.

At their core, LLMs store facts within their parameters, a process that arises during training. These models are exposed to vast datasets containing billions of words and diverse types of content. Over time, they learn to associate patterns in the data, effectively "memorizing" relationships between concepts. For example, an LLM can connect "Michael Jordan" with "basketball" because these terms frequently appear together in relevant contexts during training.

This process does not involve explicitly programming the model to "know" specific facts. Instead, the knowledge emerges naturally as the model optimizes its ability to predict the next word in a sequence.

Transformers, the foundational architecture of LLMs, consist of two primary components. The attention mechanisms distribute contextual information, ensuring that relevant relationships between tokens are emphasized. Where the Multi-Layer Perceptrons (MLPs) handle deeper computations, encoding complex patterns and relationships.

Recent research, including studies by DeepMind, has shed light on the role of MLPs in storing and processing factual information. MLPs are a significant component of transformer architectures, consisting of layers that perform straightforward matrix multiplications to refine the model's understanding of input data.

MLPs act as the repositories for deeper computations, processing relationships between input tokens and embedding these connections within the model's parameters. For instance, MLPs might encode the relationship that links "Albert Einstein" to "physics" or "Paris" to "France."

DeepMind's findings suggest that certain layers within the MLPs are particularly adept at retaining factual knowledge, indicating that specific areas of the network are specialized for this purpose.

Together, these components enable the model to process input efficiently. While attention mechanisms dynamically adjust focus based on context, MLPs store and retrieve facts to inform the model's predictions.

Consider the example of associating "Michael Jordan" with "basketball." When the model encounters the input "Michael Jordan is known for," the attention mechanism identifies relevant context within the input, while the MLPs retrieve stored associations to predict "basketball" as the next word. This process highlights how the interplay between attention and MLPs allows LLMs to generate accurate and context-aware responses.

While the mathematical operations within MLPs, such as matrix multiplications, are straightforward, interpreting how specific facts are stored and represented is more challenging. Each layer of the MLP refines the model's understanding, but the precise mechanisms through which it encodes detailed factual knowledge remain an active area of research.

Despite these complexities, insights from studies like those conducted by DeepMind are helping researchers optimize LLMs for better fact retention and retrieval.

The ability of LLMs to store and retrieve facts is a testament to their capacity to build on prior knowledge. The training process enables models to generalize from patterns in the data, allowing them to make connections even in novel contexts. This capability is central to their versatility across tasks, from answering trivia questions to generating detailed explanations.

Conclusion

Large Language Models (LLMs) mark a groundbreaking advancement in artificial intelligence, combining vast training datasets, transformer architectures, and attention mechanisms to generate text with exceptional fluency and coherence. Their ability to predict words, interpret context, and produce human-like responses has revolutionized industries and enhanced daily interactions with technology.

Transformers, the backbone of these models, have redefined language processing through the innovative use of attention mechanisms, high-dimensional embeddings, and multi-layer architectures. This approach enables machines to dynamically adapt to complex linguistic patterns, powering applications like chatbots, virtual assistants, and creative content generation. By leveraging the interplay of queries, keys, and values in multi-head attention, transformers achieve unparalleled accuracy and contextual understanding.

Central to LLMs' success is their ability to store and retrieve facts, a function attributed to multi-layer perceptrons (MLPs) within the transformer framework. These neural structures embed relationships between concepts into model parameters, allowing for the seamless recall of contextually relevant information. Whether connecting "Michael Jordan" to basketball or explaining intricate scientific ideas, LLMs showcase the transformative potential of AI.

For further information please check out Grant Sanderson on YouTube with his channel 3Blue1Brown. He has made marvellous graphical representations of the mathematical backbone of LLMs. The examples in this appendix are taken from his series.

WE'D LOVE TO HEAR
FROM YOU!

Thank you for purchasing *AI - Augmented Intelligence*! Your support means the world to me, and I hope the book has inspired new ideas and insights on the transformative power of AI in our lives.

I'd be grateful if you could take a moment to share your thoughts. By scanning the QR code, you can quickly provide feedback and your email address.

Here's what's in it for you:
Stay Updated: Receive exclusive updates on future projects and upcoming books.
Free Digital Editions: Enjoy free digital copies of any future editions of this book.
 Privacy Guaranteed: Your email address will never be sold or shared — your trust is my priority.

Your feedback helps shape future editions and ensures that *AI - Augmented Intelligence* continues to add value to readers like you.

Click or scan now, and let's keep the conversation going!

ABOUT THE AUTHOR

Anthony Van Den Hondel

 Anthony is a seasoned expert in concrete maintenance with over 30 years of experience in damage assessment, consultancy, and the design of advanced systems for structural preservation, particularly cathodic protection of reinforced concrete. In the last decade his work has extended to integrating AI-driven tools and methodologies to enhance diagnostics and optimize maintenance strategies in infrastructure projects. Known for his innovative approach, Anthony combines technical expertise with forward-thinking solutions, demonstrated in projects he has worked on.

Beyond his professional achievements, Anthony is passionate about leveraging AI and productivity systems, to improve workflows and decision-making processes. He lives, works and teaches in Rotterdam, The Netherlands.

AI — AUGMENTED INTELLIGENCE

"AI is no longer a distant future — it is our present reality, reshaping the way we work, think, and interact."

What does it mean to live in a world shaped by artificial intelligence? In **AI — Augmented Intelligence**, the author provides a fresh perspective on how this transformative technology impacts our lives, industries, and societies. This book explores not only the groundbreaking advancements of AI but also the ethical challenges and opportunities it presents.

Packed with insights from over two decades of experience in expert systems and rule engines, this book serves as your guide to understanding AI's true potential. It examines its capacity to enhance — not replace — human intelligence, offering practical tools to navigate the societal, ethical, and personal implications of living in an AI-powered world.

From dispelling common myths to illuminating AI's role in creativity, decision-making, and productivity, **AI — Augmented Intelligence** delivers an accessible yet profound look into the technology that is shaping our shared future.

For professionals, enthusiasts, and curious readers alike, this is a must-read exploration of the technology revolutionizing our time.

www.ingramcontent.com/pod-product-compliance
Lightning Source LLC
Chambersburg PA
CBHW061505120726
48001CB00004B/1220